Jennie Erdal worked as an editor and translator for many years. *Ghosting* is the first book to be published under her own name. She lives in St Andrews.

2014

Merry Christmas,
Nell.

Love, Luke
x x x x

GHOSTING

A DOUBLE LIFE

★

Jennie Erdal

CANONGATE

Edinburgh · New York · Melbourne

First published in Great Britain in 2004 by Canongate Books Ltd,
14 High Street, Edinburgh, EH1 1TE

This edition published by Canongate Books in 2005

10 9 8 7 6 5 4 3 2 1

British Library Cataloguing-in-Publication Data
A catalogue record for this book is available on
request from the British Library

ISBN 1 84195 637 6

Book design by James Hutcheson
Typeset in Bembo by Palimpsest Book Production Limited,
Polmont, Stirlingshire
Printed and bound in Great Britain by Clays Ltd, St Ives plc

www.canongate.net

For N-H
without whom

Many people have helped me, and I am most grateful to all of them. In particular I would like to thank Alistair Moffat who first encouraged me to write this book, Jamie Byng for believing in it, Jenny Brown for her positive spirit and unflagging support, Mairi Sutherland for her sensitive editing skills. And Tiger who inspired this story and allowed it to be told.

Jennie Erdal

This is the way light fell on the picture for me; for others it will have fallen differently.

My Darling

A love letter, so they say, is a window on the soul. After all these years the glass may have dimmed a little but the fire in my soul still burns as brightly as the moment I first looked upon you.

Socrates said that if you get a good wife you will become happy; if you get a bad one, you will become a philosopher. The Delphic Oracle pronounced Socrates the wisest man alive, but personal happiness eluded him. I am a luckier man than Socrates.

On this day, your birthday, I write to mark the love that has bound us together in our long marriage, whose mysterious elements are a constant source of wonder. When I think of you there is no single name for what I feel, more a constant singing in my heart.

Without love we are nothing; life consists in the giving and getting of it. For what would we know of love if no one had loved us first? How and where would we begin? In time our children leave us and love elsewhere, in a different way from the way we have loved them. Different, but related. With God's help, this is how life continues, its delicate patterns interconnected by the filaments of love. And eventually, as Larkin understood, what will survive of us is love.

With deep tenderness

A love letter. The love of a man for a woman. What does it tell us? That a man is writing to his wife, that he loves her and feels loved by her, that they have been together a long time and that the love has endured. And what of the man himself? Evidently he is something of a romantic, he is not afraid to express his feelings, he believes in God, and he reads poetry.

What else can we tell from the letter? There is a tendency towards aphorism, and the style is slightly high-flown, perhaps a little gallant and old-fashioned. And like all love letters, it is highly personal, the most intimate form of communication any of us makes, more permanent than a phone call, more romantic than e mail. In reading it we feel we are encroaching on something private. It is, as the writer of the letter says, a window on the soul. We have glimpsed into his heart.

Or have we? What if this letter were not written by a man at all? But rather *for* a man, and *by* a woman. Whose heart would it then be?

For nearly fifteen years I wrote hundreds of letters, ranging from perfunctory thank-you notes and expressions of condolence to extensive correspondence with the great and the good – politicians, newspaper editors, bishops, members of the House of Lords. The procedure I followed with a more intimate letter was to type it onto my laptop, double spaced in large font, and print it out. My employer – the sender of the letter – would then copy it painstakingly onto embossed notepaper using a Mont Blanc pen and blotting paper, signing it with a flourish at the bottom.

All the letters were written on behalf of one man, an extraordinarily complex and charismatic character who made his mark in London's literary set. There was no dictation, no taking of shorthand, just the lightest of intimations, often accompanied by facial contortions and gestures, which, over the years, I came to understand as one might a private language or a cipher. The tone of the letter, whether angry, ingratiating, reflective or passionate, would generally be arrived at by a kind of osmosis.

In reality, the love letter on the opening page was created specially for this memoir. But not out of thin air. In order to protect private information, the real letter was replaced by another, imaginatively drawn from similar material penned over time, and distilled until exemplary in style and content.

The letters mattered greatly to the man who put his name to them, for they often expressed what he was not capable of articulating on his own. They opened doors and gave him an eloquent sophistication, which he coveted but did not naturally possess. The pleasure he derived from sending the letters was evident in the way he often read them aloud before adding his signature. He savoured each sentence, pausing over every nuance, weighing up the effect of this or that word. Occasionally he was visibly moved by what they contained, and his voice would break as he recited them back to me. He loved imagining the letters being received, being read and re-read. Some would be slept on, so he hoped, perhaps even dreamt of. When he was pleased, I too was pleased. We worked well together, and on the whole I was a willing partner, interested in the job and fascinated by the psychological processes involved on both sides. Over the years I learned a great deal about ego, vanity, the desire to belong, the lengths a man will go to in affecting to be something other than he is. And the lengths a woman will go to in colluding with the pretence.

Aside from the correspondence, there were many newspaper articles, a weekly column, speeches, the occasional poem and about a dozen books, amongst them two novels. The books generated lots of reviews and profiles of the man whose name appeared on the cover. A number of literati entered into correspondence with the 'author', unaware that the replies came from a hired hand. We make a great team, the author often said. And we did.

Ghost-writing is not new. It might almost qualify as the oldest profession if prostitution had not laid prior claim. And there is more than a random connection between the two: they both operate in rather murky worlds, a fee is agreed in advance and given 'for services rendered', and those who admit to being involved, either as client or service-provider, can expect negative reactions – anything from mild shock and disapproval to outright revulsion. A professor at my old university, a distinguished classicist with feminist leanings, was appalled when she heard what I did for a living and pronounced me 'no better than a common whore'. This – the whiff of whoredom – is perhaps the main reason why most people opt for absolute discretion.

There is usually also an uneasy alliance between the person paying the money and the person earning the money or 'working'. It comes from the awkward interdependence of the dealings – both parties benefit, but both usually struggle to retain self-respect. This can be achieved in a variety of ways: sometimes by adopting a simple, business-like attitude to the proceedings, sometimes through mutual contempt, sometimes through affected indifference to the nature of the transaction, sometimes simply by choosing to deny it to oneself or to lead parallel lives.

$\sim$

In the natural world there are many degrees of interaction and mutual dependence between different species. These range from symbiosis, which we generally regard as good and beautiful, to parasitism, which we tend to view as bad and ugly. In life as in nature, some feed and others are fed upon. But what can appear to be a parasitic invasion can sometimes result in harmony and felicity. What could be more beautiful than an orchid? Yet the orchid depends on a fungus for the germination and growth of its seedlings. For the partnership to succeed, a true symbiotic balance must be achieved and maintained. Otherwise both will wither and die. The relationship between host and parasite is fragile, easily disturbed; but in true symbiosis the association is intimate and both partners profit.

As in nature, so in life. What follows is a memoir drawn from several stages of a life, but containing at its heart the story of an unusual relationship, part symbiotic, part parasitic. It concerns two people from very different backgrounds: a man and a woman, who, for different reasons, in various ways and over a period of twenty years, came to live off one other, and in a sense to inhabit each other's minds. The story involves deception and self-deception on both sides, a blurring of truth and reality, some bizarre happenings, secrets and lies. Yet it also contains generosity, goodwill, absurdity, laughter, tenderness and a good measure of love.

Part One
A Meeting

So strange and exotic is he that he could be a rare tropical bird that you might never come face to face with, even in a lifetime spent in the rain forest. The plumage is a wonder to behold: a large sapphire in the lapel of a bold striped suit, a vivid silk tie so bright that it dazzles, and when he flaps his wings the lining of his jacket glints and glistens like a prism. He sees that I am startled and he smiles. He takes my hand in his and lays it on the silk lining. *You want to touch? Go on, touch! It's best Chinese silk. I have only the best.*

It is a lot to take in all at once. Under his suit he wears one pink sock, one green, two gold watches on his right arm, a platinum watch on his left, and on his fingers a collection of jewels: rubies, emeralds, diamonds. This is the jungle bird in human form – flamboyant, exaggerated, ornate – a creature whose baroque splendour surely has to be part of the male mating display. And yet the brightness of the eyes and the set of the smile give him an amused look that suggests a degree of self-parody. A touch of the court jester perhaps? Only perhaps, for nothing is yet sure. The head is large, in keeping with the frame, and the ears look as if they might have been an exuberant afterthought. The hair, dark and wiry, seems to be a separate entity, a thing apart. It perches on top like an eagle's nest.

1

It is a Saturday morning in 1981 and I have travelled from my home in Scotland to an address in Mayfair. A uniformed porter opens the door of my taxi and ushers me inside. He asks me to take a seat while he telephones to announce my arrival. He presses a button to call the lift and, with a touch of his cap, sends me on my way. As the lift doors open, the bird of paradise is already standing there in all his finery. I had little idea of what to expect, but the reality is a good deal odder than anything I might have imagined. A psychedelic experience without the need of drugs.

His demeanour conveys generosity and impeccable courtesy. His eyes sparkle like precious stones. His hands are large and beautiful, and they feel so soft that they seem quite new and unused. But his handshake is not the limp, wishy-washy how-do-you-do of an Englishman; it is a firm and cordial clasp, like a lingering embrace. His voice is velvet and beguilingly accented, and it is speaking now in short unfinished bursts, gentle, apologetic, cajoling, pampering. *Come . . . come . . . please . . . only one minute . . . be so kind . . . because the telephone . . . it happens always.* His body is never still but moves to the rhythm and cadences of his speech pattern. He does a low salaam and beckons me to follow, like a Bedouin prince inviting an honoured guest to his tent. *Please . . . sit . . . two minutes . . . then I'm back . . . you're very kind.* He glides off leaving behind eastern scents – musk, saffron, sandalwood.

The walls of the tent are festooned with rugs, and on the floor there are more rugs with small exquisitely carved tables and dark-wood chests on top. More Marrakesh than Mayfair, it seems to me, though I am not familiar with either. The decoration is rich but not oppressive, the lines are clean and disciplined. There is no evidence of normal day-to-day living, none of the randomness of ordinary clutter. And no photographs, just a picture of a tiger in the corner by the door. On one of the chests — it could be rosewood inlaid with mother-of-pearl — there is a careful arrangement of antique ivory bracelets. Someone has gone to a lot of trouble to achieve the desired effect. He glides back in. *Sorry . . . sorry . . . can you come now . . . we will go quickly . . . the chauffeur is downstairs.* He hurries off down the long corridor, leaving behind a vapour trail of blandishments. I follow him, eyes down, counting the kelims as I go. It feels like an absurd passage in a dream.

Out on the pavement, the chauffeur is standing beside a silver Rolls Royce, holding the door open for us to get into the back seat. I have never been in a Rolls Royce before, but find myself behaving as if it is a common occurrence. I have no idea why I am pretending. It certainly does not occur to me to be myself. I give a nod to the chauffeur, decidedly *de haut en bas*, and sink into the plush leather like Lady Muck.

We are on our way to Oxford, the dazzling publisher and I, to visit a woman as old as the century. It has the feel of an adventure, the beginning of something.

～

Anything counting as a significant happening usually involves the chance occurrence of a number of events. Each event means nothing in isolation, or so it seems at the time, but taken together and viewed from the ringside seat that is given to us by hindsight, each turns out to have played a part in what Raymond Chandler liked to call the Start of Something Big.

The particular events that led to my journey from London to Oxford in the back of a Rolls Royce that Saturday morning in 1981 were something of a rag-bag. Here is a selection from the rag-bag:

- the study of Russian language and literature
- an exhibition at an art gallery in St Andrews
- the birth of babies (three)
- the undertaking of a translation
- visits to Oxford to look at paintings
- a commission from a London publishing house
- a Russian artist's visit to Palestine in 1924.

The longer version of events is that in the early seventies I spent four years at university reading Russian and philosophy. My undergraduate thesis was a study of the poet and novelist Boris Pasternak. When the University of St Andrews opened a new art gallery with an exhibition of the works of Leonid Pasternak, father of Boris, I was asked to write a profile of the artist for the exhibition catalogue. The research for this involved reading Pasternak's memoirs in Russian and consulting with the artist's two daughters, Josephine and Lydia. After the exhibition they encouraged me to translate their father's memoirs but, since I had two small children and a third on the way, it seemed an impossible undertaking. When the third child was born it was even more impossible, but by then I knew that if I was going to be a fit mother I needed also to do something that was not mothering. Translation seemed to offer a solution.

In any case the memoirs were interesting and colourful, painting a vivid picture of Russian artistic life in the late nineteenth and early twentieth centuries. They begin with a kind of miracle which hooked me and pulled me in – the story of how the artist nearly died of convulsions in 1862 when he was only a few months old. The family lived in simple rooms in the corner of a large sprawling coaching-inn on the outskirts of Odessa by the Black Sea. There were stables and a dung yard where children played amongst the poultry and pigs, and the lodgings were filled with Tartar tradesmen, coachmen and assorted merchants. They would arrive in huge tarantasses straight out of Gogol. The air was heavy with noise and liquor. Suddenly, above the din, a mother started screaming that her baby was dying. Everyone crowded round to watch helplessly as the infant convulsed and turned blue. Only one man, a Jewish tailor and sage of the local shtetl, knew what to do. He raised a huge earthenware jug above the baby's head and smashed it on the dirt floor. The baby, startled out of his fit, turned pink. 'Now you must change the child's name,' the tailor said to the mother, 'so that the Devil can't find him again.' And so Isaac Pasternak, as he was then called, became Leonid, and he went on to live and work through one of the greatest periods of Russian culture.

Leonid Pasternak knew and painted Einstein, Rimsky-Korsakov, Rubinstein, Scriabin, Rachmaninov, Prokofiev, Rilke, Chaliapin and many other eminent figures. But perhaps the main fascination of the memoirs lies in his friendship with Tolstoy who invited him to illustrate *Resurrection* as he was writing it. Pasternak visited Tolstoy's home at Yasnaya Polyana many times and completed a number of portraits and studies, the last on 20 November 1910, when a telegram summoned him to draw the great man on his deathbed.

At the end of 1980 the translation of the Tolstoy chapter was complete and I sent it off to a London publisher – the exotic jungle bird who now sat beside me in the back of the Rolls

Royce. Within a week or two the book was commissioned and, to the delight of the artist's family, it was to include about a hundred reproductions from his work and an introduction by his daughter Josephine. She lived in Oxford, having moved there with her parents in 1938. At that time her father was a successful artist exhibiting in Germany, but the rise of Nazism meant that all Soviet citizens were being expelled. The family decided to move to Oxford, where Lydia, the other daughter, was already settled. Leonid and his wife Rosa hoped to return to Russia one day, but it was not to be. They both died in Oxford, Rosa a week before the start of the war, and Leonid in 1945, a few months before it ended. Josephine wrote in her introduction that when her mother died it was as if harmony had abandoned the world, and when her father died it seemed that truth had left it.

I made several visits to Josephine during the course of the translation, checking out details of her father's life and helping to choose which pictures would go into the book. She was over-joyed that her father's memoirs were at last to be published. She had spent many years trying to promote his work – writing articles, giving interviews and, together with her sister Lydia, arranging exhibitions in Oxford's Ashmolean Museum, and also London and Edinburgh. Both daughters felt their father had been unfairly overshadowed by their brother Boris, and they were determined to do everything they could to even things out. Boris, they were keen to point out, was first known in Russia as 'the son of the great artist', and it was only in the west and after the publication of *Dr Zhivago* that people started to refer to Leonid as 'the father of Boris'. It was a travesty, they believed, and David Lean's contemptible film of *Zhivago* had only made matters worse. They were both impassioned on this subject.

The house in Oxford's Park Town where Leonid had spent his last years was chaotic and ramshackle, but wonderfully so. There were pictures everywhere – on the walls, stacked in corners or crammed in large wooden crates that had been carried from country to country, surviving war and revolution. There were landscapes, portraits, still lifes, tender, intimate studies of his wife and children done in every medium – oils, chalks, charcoal, watercolours, pastels. It was a vast inheritance and evidently a formidable task for Josephine and Lydia to sort through. As they got older, the problem of how best to proceed became more urgent. Their dream was one day to establish a Pasternak museum as a permanent memorial to their father and to prevent his work being dissipated and lost.

In their attempts over the years to get the pictures more widely known there had been some bruising experiences. For example, they had given a treasured charcoal sketch of Boris to the Tate Gallery only to find that it was hung for a while next to the ladies' toilets before disappearing permanently into the stacks. They also gave a major work, a life-size portrait of the artist's four children, to the Tretyakov Gallery in Moscow, but it was never even hung. On another occasion, in the mid-seventies, they lost some of the best work to a London dealer. And so, by the time I met them a few years later, they were absolutely resolute on one matter: no more pictures would be sold. Which was awkward, because the purchase of paintings was the whole *raison d'être* of our trip to Oxford that day.

～

Fate had ordained Leonid Pasternak to travel to the Holy Land in 1924. He had been commissioned by a Parisian art journal to produce a series of paintings of the people and the land-scape. He also did a variety of drawings and sketches – figures with long flowing robes and turbaned heads, donkeys with huge loads, street scenes in Jerusalem, caravans in the desert, the Tomb of Rachel, a Palestinian city wall in dark chocolate brown with a gunpowder gate.

In an office in London some sixty years later, the publisher of Pasternak's memoirs held transparencies of these pictures up to the light and wept.

'I must buy them,' he said when he telephoned me out of the blue to ask where he could see the originals.

'They're not for sale,' I said, explaining the background and the firm resolve of the Pasternak sisters.

'You don't understand,' he said. 'I *have* to have them. It's imperative. They remind me of my childhood, my homeland. It's all gone now, all destroyed. *I have to have those pictures.*'

After some discussion we made an arrangement to go together to Oxford, where he would meet Josephine Pasternak and offer to buy the paintings of Palestine.

'But she won't sell,' I said emphatically.

'She'll sell to me,' he said, and put down the phone.

And she did sell, which was astonishing. The Josephine I had come to know was determined and high-minded. She embodied a rich cross-cultural mix – a kind of enlightened Puritanism and intense aestheticism. She had studied philosophy in Berlin and had written on Aristotle. And though her European intel-lectual rigour was tempered by a soulfulness recognisably

8

Russian in origin, she was erudite, firm of purpose, strong-minded and disarmingly candid.

But in the presence of the publisher's fine plumage and splendid colours, this sensible woman became girlish and coquettish. The exotic bird, confident of his charm, prepared for his courtly dance, sticking out his glorious chest and flapping his wings, all the while cooing and wooing, warbling and trilling. He eulogised the artist, he emoted over the lost land of Palestine, he flattered and fawned, buttered and oiled. It was a spectacular show, fascinating to watch. After a feeble fight Josephine Pasternak succumbed to the seductive display. She sold him the paintings.

On the way back to London, there was jubilation.

'You see, I told you I would do it,' he puffed.

'Yes, you did,' I said.

'What an amazing woman she is,' he said. '*Formidable.*'

'Yes, she is,' I said.

'Pasternak – I like the name. Is it Russian?'

'Yes, it means "parsnip".'

'Parsnip? *Parsnip?* You're pulling my leg!'

'No.'

'What a shame. Such a nice woman and she's called parsnip.'

During the journey I heard a lot about other successes – business deals, theatrical productions, film ventures, publishing *coups*. The list was mesmerising and seemingly without end. He talked quickly, with alarming enthusiasm, an unEnglish fanaticism, hardly pausing to breathe, the words tumbling over one another. There was a passion and an urgency in everything he said, and occasionally the suggestion of an intimacy, as if he were sharing a terrible family secret. He constantly touched my arm as he talked, sometimes cuffing it with the back of his hand or patting it gently, sometimes clutching it suddenly as if to prevent a fall, mostly holding it for a few seconds in his strong grip. His voice ranged over two octaves at least, the pitch in perfect equilibrium with the level of emotion. It was another breathtaking performance.

And now it was my turn to be seduced. During the journey I had said very little – there was no need – but as we neared London he started asking about my life and what had led to my translating Pasternak's memoirs. He listened intently and then surprised me by saying that he had always wanted to publish foreign language books and that I must come to work in his publishing company and manage the Russian list. There had to be a catch. If you have three children under five it is possible to believe that you will never work again, that you will never read anything other than bedtime stories. And yet here I was being offered an interesting, brain-alive job, working from home in my own time, as much as I could manage to fit in with the children. There was no catch, at least none I could see. The salary would be £5000 plus expenses – 'All my girls start on £5000 a year, isn't it?' – and I was to begin straight-away. I was to travel from Scotland to attend editorial meet-ings, work for a day or two a month in the London offices, and the rest of the time I could be at home and keep in touch by telephone. It seemed too good to be true. We shook hands on it in the back of the Roller.

He then told the chauffeur to take a detour to his offices where he would show me round.

'You are going to enjoy working for me. I have a good feeling about it. My motto is when we work, we work, and when we play, we play. That way everybody is happy, isn't it?'

As we climbed the stairs to the top of the building I pondered his interesting use of the 'isn't it?' tag. There are terrible complications in the English language when it comes to inviting someone to agree with you or to confirm what you've just said. Most languages make do with a one-size-fits-all solution along the lines of *n'est-ce pas?* or *¿no verdad?* or *nicht wahr?* But in English there is no single phrase that can be used on all occasions to mean 'isn't that so?' And so the unsuspecting are ensnared by opting for a simple *isn't it?* When actually what is needed is an *aren't they?* or a *didn't she?* or a *can you?* It hardly seems fair.

We arrived in a spacious penthouse overlooking the heart of Soho. The first thing I noticed were the pictures on the walls – not the gentle landscapes of the Holy Land I might have expected, but an assortment of naked or semi-naked women and several large cats clawing their way out of gilt-edged frames. But the centrepiece, mounted on the wall behind the leather-topped desk, was not a painting at all: it was a huge tiger skin and head. Apart from the fact that it was dead, it seemed very alive, its bold orange and black stripes setting the wall ablaze.

'You like it?' he asked, motioning me to sit down opposite him at the desk. 'I call him Kaiser. You know what is Kaiser?' And then, as if it explained everything, he added, 'My father fought on the side of the Germans in the First World War.'

'Where did you get it?' I asked, keen to show an interest.

He smiled. It was evidently the right question. With obvious pride and joy, he told me it had been shot after escaping from a German zoo. But originally it had come from South China – the very best tigers lived there and only about thirty of them were left in the wild. Every part of the tiger could be used – skin, claws, liver, bones and blood could all be made into potions and drunk to make you live longer. Even the whiskers could cure toothache. He had had to pay a lot of money for it – 'It cost a *fortune!*' – but it was worth every penny. And he launched into a passionate discourse on the tiger's qualities – its nobility, its power, its courage, its strength, its mysterious aura. The tiger was admired and feared at the same time, he said, its claws were sharper than a razor blade, and it could cover ten yards in a single leap. He described its method of hunting, how it waited patiently and in solitude to catch its prey, biting the throat of animals twice its size.

'I identify with the tiger,' he said, without a hint of abashment. 'The tiger eats everything, but *nothing* eats him. He will even eat a crocodile if he wants to! He is King of the Mountain, King of the Forest, King of the World.'

He drew himself up, regally, in his chair. The tiger's head was just above the talking head, its eyes shining brightly, curiously round and manlike. For just a second, in that little corner where fantasy and reality collide, the two heads merged and became one.

'What would you like me to call you?' I asked as we shook hands on parting.

'You can call me what you like,' he said. 'I shall call you Beloved – all the girls who work for me are Beloved – but you can call me whatever you want.'

'In that case,' I said, 'I shall call you Tiger.'

'I like it,' he said, and kissed my hand.

Part Two
Back to the Beginning

When people talk about their childhood, everything tends to be lumped together, glossed over, captured in the one word 'happy', or the other 'unhappy'. I'm not sure I believe either word. For a start, happiness is a rare blue moon sort of thing. The most anyone gets is a sense of harmony with the world, contentment perhaps, but even that is quite rare. As for unhappiness, well, that is quite hard to sustain through all the new dawns and fresh hopes. Besides, you can get over most wounds inflicted in the early years. Even if they remain as little pinpricks on the surface of your skin, they serve the purpose of 'placing' you in the world, giving you an argument with it. Psychologists have told us that bad things are passed down the line – cruelty, ignorance, secrets and lies. The persecuted become persecutors, the abused become abusers. Yes, but the chain can always be broken, provided the last link wants it enough.

All narratives are suspect, unreliable. The stories we tell to make sense of our lives are essentially made up. We tell these stories to protect ourselves from the existential nightmare scenario – the idea that our lives have no pattern, are going nowhere. We grapple with the notion that ordinary life is absurd, contingent, accidental, full of chance. The concept of randomness is hard to bear, so the mind scampers around to impose a structure on random bits of experience. A humming-bird takes to the air and the tide of human history is altered.

To understand the world is a basic human longing, powerful and urgent. The idea that there is rarely any point to anything is not to be borne. So the child in this story looked back and tried to understand. Here is some of what was understood: that not everything in the literal world can be made sense of, that you sometimes have to leave it behind and enter the poetic world where making sense is optional; that things are often not what they seem; that language is precarious, that sometimes there is not a name for what you feel; that you take love where you find it; that even when everything is concealed you can end up being open to the world.

In the small Fife town where I grew up, no one went abroad much. The minister at our church, the Reverend Musk, claimed to have a son called Chad who was a missionary in Africa. Africa was about as abroad as it was possible to be. Each Sunday, after a sermon about God's mercy and just damnation, we prayed for Chad, insincerely in my case. We had never met Chad Musk, never even seen photographs of him, and with a name like that it was impossible to believe in his existence. The Scots are famed for being explorers, but the pioneering instinct seemed to have passed us by. Mining was the thing in our town. Underground, not overground.

Travel, insofar as anyone did it, seemed to narrow the mind further. The place looked in on itself, suspicious of anyone or anything that didn't belong. The town's only famous daughter was Jennie Lee and, in our household at any rate, she too was regarded with mistrust. Too radical, too fervent, too much an iconoclast. And to make matters worse she had gone to England and married a Welshman, a fellow socialist who had had the gall to oppose Churchill during the war. 'It just goes to show,' said my mother, as she so often did, but quite what it went to show or how or why was never made clear.

Being a child is a job like any other. Some children are good at it, others never quite master it. You understand quite early on that the job consists mainly in trying to please adults, but though I tried to please adults quite a lot, they hardly ever seemed pleased with me. As a child I was vaguely aware of disappointing my parents without ever intending to or understanding quite how it happened. The atmosphere at home was thick with ill-defined threats and admonishments. *You'll get what's coming to you, you're in for your just deserts, you won't know what's hit you.* What on earth did it all mean? *Just deserts* were unfathomable; on the other hand wasn't it obvious that I would get something if it was indeed coming my way, and why would I not *know* what had hit me? It was all very mysterious. Sometimes my father threatened to knock someone *into the middle of next week*, which, despite not being able to imagine what that might involve, I especially dreaded, even though he usually made a point of adding, as if by way of polite afterthought, *if you're not careful*. I was never absolutely sure about what being careful might entail, or how it might be achieved. Nothing was adequately explained. Questions were hardly ever permitted. It felt dangerous sometimes even to think about asking why.

15

Nowadays children have to be engaged in creative play; they have to be stimulated and nurtured so that they can achieve their full potential. Babies have to be given educational toys in order to increase brain activity, toddlers have to have their cognitive skills sharpened up by special diets and flash cards. But in the fifties and early sixties, provided you didn't bother your parents too much, it was perfectly acceptable to be aimless and unmotivated.

Our front door was painted red and it was opened with a flourish every morning by my mother. The earlier it was opened, the better she appeared to feel. There would be a hint of triumph in her swagger along our hallway. It was not clear to me why opening the door, or more precisely opening the door bright and early with such verve, could in itself lead to a sense of wellbeing. But I remember feeling glad that she was glad. When the sun shone, a curtain was drawn across the shiny tiled vestibule to stop the red paint blistering. Red was my mother's favourite colour – red doors, red garden gate, red carpets, red Formica in the kitchen. I pretended to like red too. Other houses had lobbies where our vestibule was. I wasn't allowed to say *lobby* because lobby was common. I had to remember to say *vestibyhool*. I sometimes practised whispering it to myself again and again. I could make it sound like bullets flying through the air.

Our house was large and smelled of damp and old potatoes. The smell came from the cellar. It seeped through the floorboards and hung in the cold air. Most of the houses in the streets round where we lived did not have cellars. I secretly envied my friends their lack of cellars, and many other things besides. The other houses were in the scheme, which was evidently not a good place to be. There was talk of coal being kept in the bath, furniture being bought on the never-never. According to my mother, the people from the housing scheme had no *finesse*. Was a finesse like a cellar, I wondered? I decided quite early on that our finesse was probably part of our large bathroom, a place which gave rise to particular perplexity on account of its being strictly out of bounds to members of the family except on Sunday evenings.

The bathroom was my mother's pride and joy. My best friend's house had a lavvy, but we had a bathroom. It was a long narrow room with a very high ceiling and no heating. The red bath mat and towels were neatly folded over a towel rack made of wood and painted red. All the mats and towels had a huge embroidered C denoting our family name, though none of the family was ever permitted to use them. My mother said they were just for show – a potent concept in our family. In addition to the thick red carpet there were two woven rugs, both red, one at the door, the other curved round the toilet bowl. The toilet bowl had a red seat and lid. The lid was kept closed at all times. Like the lounge, and just as cold, the bath-room was reserved for the use of chance visitors. It was there-fore also a source of great anxiety to my mother since it had to be kept clean at all times in case someone needed to use it.

In reality, hardly anyone visited us by chance. But in my mother's world, uncertainty was pernicious and had to be guarded against at all times. Only on Sunday evenings, there-fore, when it was absolutely certain that no one would call, were we allowed a bath. This was quite a ritual and one attended by my mother's thin-lipped umbrage. She approached it in the spirit appropriate to arranging a hanging – it was something that had to be done but there was no joy to be had in it. As if to set an example, she herself never had a bath. In much the same way as she believed that washing machines didn't wash – at least not *properly* – and electric mixers didn't mix, so she believed that having a bath didn't get you properly clean.

My brother and I always had the first bath since our father's dirtiness was deemed to be greater than the combined grime of two children. And during our bath the stove in the kitchen could be stoked to provide a top-up of hot water for our father. In winter the air temperature in the bathroom was so cold that getting out of the water required huge mental discipline followed by a mad dash to the kitchen where our pyjamas were warming on a rail by the stove. By then my father would be stripped down to his underpants, ready for his dash in the opposite direction. Waiting for our father to arrive back in the kitchen, goose-pimpled and raging at the world, was a time filled with fear and anticipation, at once sweet and sharp. He would burst through the kitchen door, bent like a question mark, an improbable survivor of some natural disaster, his face seeming to contain all the agony of mankind. The scene that followed, it now seems to me, was something out of the theatre of the absurd: there was an apparent absence of purpose, a lack of harmony with the surroundings, a sadness to the point of anguish, but also a kind of laconic comedy. While my father ranted and raved, fighting all the while with his towel, taming it into submission in an effort to get warm and dry, my mother performed an emotional *pas-de-deux*, alternately pleading and reproaching, her mouth tight and hard, waiting for him to be calm so that she could undertake the radical cleaning of the bathroom.

18

For the next part of the drama, however, there was absolute quiet. The scene was sombre but curiously edifying, a kind of Victorian death-bed moment. My father, now dry, would go to a corner of the kitchen, turn his back on us, drop his towel and bend down to step into his pyjamas. This was the moment worth waiting for, the fascination and appallingness of it undiminished by its weekly repetition. For there, hanging down between my father's legs, was a sort of pouch, loose and macerated like an oven-ready bird and, to make matters worse, there was another bit, peeping out from the base of the pouch, a pink dangly thing. When my father raised first one leg, then the other, to enter his pyjamas, the pink dangly thing moved as if it had a life independent of my father's bare body. No one ever said anything. The wrinkled arrangement between his legs was clearly some unspeakable deformity, which my father to his eternal shame had to endure. I felt sorry for him, and sometimes when he was angry with me I made allowances for him because of his misfortune.

Mostly he was not angry with me, however, and much of the time we got on well. I helped him in the garden, and he praised me when I did things exactly right. Everyone else's father was a coalminer but mine was a market gardener. Before I was born, he had been a building contractor, but he never spoke of that time. My mother mentioned it sometimes, but only during the worst rows when she would use it as a taunt. He had had his own business with two lorries, but there had been a fire in the garage and no insurance. Some of the burnt out garage still stood like a rebuke in what had been the builders' yard and inside its shell there were the charred remains of the lorries with the words EDWARD CRAWFORD BUILDER just legible on the sides.

My father taught me many things: how to sow brassicas, how to remove side-shoots from tomato plants without damaging the main stem, how to prick out bedding plants using a wooden template and a dibble, how to write *Mesembryanthemum* so neatly that it fitted onto a wooden label measuring only two and a half inches. The common name for *Mesembryanthemum* is *Livingstone Daisy*, which has exactly the same number of letters and sounds much better, but because the two words had to be separated by a space it was impossible to fit them onto the label. I also learned from my father how to drown baby mice in a rain barrel, crush a clipshear between my thumbnails, and assist in the skinning of a rabbit.

My father believed that skinning a rabbit was a dying art and he took trouble to pass on his skill to me in scrupulous detail. First he would place the rabbit upside down between his knees and make a cut with his army knife at the hind feet, moving from one thigh to the other in a perfect arc. My job was to hold the feet – 'Steady as a rock now' – while my father pulled the skin off the legs, gently at first, then tugging firmly to separate it from the whole body, like removing a tight vest from a baby. If all went well the flesh would be perfectly pink and unblemished – there would be no knife mark or blood-stain. I loved the shared intimacy of skinning a rabbit. It made me feel we knew things that other people didn't.

Before long, however, skinned rabbits became part of the impenetrable mystery that was the world. One Saturday morning when I was about ten years old, I was sent off shopping – doing the messages we called it. I normally took the bus up the hill to the shops and walked back. As I waited for the bus a man wandered up and stood a few yards away on the other side of the bus stop. My parents had warned me about talking to strangers but this man was smartly dressed in a suit and wore a soft hat, so I could tell that he didn't come from the housing scheme. From time to time he looked over in my direction and gave me a friendly smile. Then, just as I noticed the bus coming in the distance, he delved into a gap at the top of his trousers and produced a skinned rabbit. Amazing. He was grinning now, and so was I, then just before the bus pulled up he quickly pushed the rabbit back into his trousers again. But for some reason he didn't get on the bus and just waved it on.

I could hardly wait to get home to tell my parents. I thought they would be delighted and interested, as I had been, but instead they went white with an inexplicable anger and started firing furious questions at me. *Who was the man? What did he look like? Had I seen him before? Had he touched me?* I could not remember seeing them so angry. When two policemen arrived and asked me even more questions, I started to cry. One of the policemen wanted to know if the man had made me hold the rabbit and if he had hurt me with it — such a stupid idea that I wept even more. How could you hurt anyone with a rabbit, especially a dead one which was skinned every bit as well as my father could have done? The man was *a bad man*, they said, *he should be locked up*. But what did they know? I wished I had kept quiet. From now on I would be careful not to tell my parents anything they didn't need to hear.

~

It is often said that children are accepting of everything because they know no different, or they have nothing to compare it with. Where did this untruth originate? Just because you have no life beyond the one you know, it doesn't stop you thinking that there might be a different kind of life possible. Children hop and skip rather than walk, not just because they have an abundance of energy, but also because they have a sense of possibility, of marvel. This is in the nature of being a child. Of course, the child is generally seen as 'belonging' to its parents, being the repository of parental beliefs and attitudes, an offshoot in the literal sense and others. This is undoubtedly true, but only up to a point. Only up to a point. The child is also its own person.

At the same time, most children do their best to meet the puzzling requirements placed upon them by adults, and I was no exception. I spent a great deal of time listening at doors and looking through keyholes, trying to find out how not to disappoint, how to be loved. There was a lot to remember, what to say, what to do, what not to say, what not to do. *Why?* I sometimes asked, or more often, *why not?* The answer invariably invoked the rules.

Learning the rules was a misery without parallel in adult life. There were no evident principles at work; something was just as likely to be against the rules as not. The rules governing the use of language were especially puzzling. Language can often give the impression of order and harmony, but in our house it could be a chaotic and discordant thing. Looking back – though I think I also knew it at the time – my parents seemed inordinately confident in the way they spoke and the words they used. They both had fresh and crisp Scottish voices, my father's slightly gritty like sand in ice cream. My memory tells me that for a while at least I shared their confidence. But

I soon learned that it was risky to import words I had heard elsewhere, in the playground or in the houses of my friends, for example. Or even to repeat things I'd heard my teachers say. That could lead to accusations of sounding like Lady Muck or putting on my pan loaf. Far safer simply to follow my parents' lead, repeating and imitating the structures and shapes of their sentences. If ever I strayed from the clear road-markings into the central reservation of *bad* words or, worse, *dirty* words, there was a terrible price to pay. It must always be *bottom*, never *bum*, I always had to say *bust*, never *bosom*, *pants*, never *knickers*. Dirty words, according to my mother, could *inflame* men, something that had to be avoided at all costs. Whenever my friends used the wrong words I would feel agitated on their behalf in spite of, perhaps even because of, their insouciance. I was afraid my father might knock them into the middle of next week.

Gradually I became aware of the power of language, not just in the sense of having energy and vitality and strength, but also as a means of exerting control and authority. It was clear that there were right ways of speaking, and just as clear that there were wrong ways, which could explode in your face as randomly as any land mine.

My mother had an impressive range of voices, a sliding scale of airs and graces and altered vowels. There was her telephone voice, her doctor's surgery voice and, poshest of all, a diningroom voice which accompanied the gammon and pineapple we served twice a year to the minister and his wife and the church elder who did not have a wife but who delivered tiny envelopes once a month to our house. The point of the envelopes, which had CHURCH OF SCOTLAND on them in bold letters and the name of our parish beneath THE REVEREND FREDERICK MUSK BD in slightly smaller print, was to allow church members to make a discreet donation and drop it into the collection plate at the Sunday service. Our envelope always contained a ten shilling note so that it would float lightly, but conspicuously, into the collection plate while other envelopes containing mere coins landed with a thud and a jangle.

My father had left school aged fourteen to become a brickie, a builder's labourer. My mother stayed on at school for an extra year and evidently showed great academic promise until she was forced to leave to look after her mother who was dying of cancer, and to manage the household, which included her grandparents. My father lacked formal education, but my mother had begun it and aspired to more, and for the rest of her life she felt the bitterness of having been denied it. She appreciated school and had a taste for learning, sometimes speaking wistfully of French and Latin lessons, which she loved above all and wished she could have continued. At some point before I was born, she must have understood that she was never going to be the woman she might have been, the person she desperately wanted to be before circumstances had conspired against her. Only when I was much older did I understand that she had been crushed by this, weighed down by the thought of how different her life could have been. This surely was the real well-spring of her disappointment. At the time, however, and in the thick of it, I never wondered about its causes; I was conscious only of its effects.

Besides, I actually felt quite at home with disappointment, my mother's in herself and the more general kind that pervaded our family life. At least you knew where you were with disappointment; whereas with its opposite number, cheerfulness, anything could happen. Evidence of good spirits in my mother called for the greatest circumspection. They could easily come about as a result of others' misfortune, particularly if it involved our Catholic neighbours; or worse, it could mean she had uncovered some dreadful wrongdoing – my father's or mine – and was waiting for her moment to pounce. My mother's cheerfulness was never a laughing matter.

In 1962 when I was eleven years old, three things happened more or less at the same time. First, a small plaque, measuring about three inches by two, suddenly appeared on the wall by our front door just above the doorbell. Second, a succession of complete strangers began to call at the door, and after being welcomed in polished tones, they were taken upstairs by my mother to her bedroom. And third, there was a spring in my mother's step. What could it all mean? Naturally, I asked what was going on, but that got me nowhere.

The plaque at the front door had my mother's full name on it and written beneath in italics were the words *SPIRELLA AGENT*.

'What's an agent?' I asked my father as we weeded the bed of dahlias together.

'Don't go bothering me with your silly questions,' he said, 'and watch what you're doing with that hoe.'

I weighed up the risk of asking another.

'What's a Spirella then?'

My father jabbed his hoe bad-temperedly into the earth.

'Now, that's enough! Don't get me started! There are some things that don't concern you, and that's one of them.'

I had learned how to use a dictionary at school so I looked up *Spirella*. It wasn't there. But I found *agent* quite easily, and it turned out there were two meanings: (i) a person who acts for another in business, politics etc. and (ii) a spy. Since it was self-evident that my mother had nothing to do with business or politics, that left only one possibility. My mother was a spy. *My mother was a spy.*

It was a crystalline moment. Everything fell into place – the nameplate at the front door, the strangers calling, always alone, and being led upstairs for confidential discussions. I was never allowed to meet them but I peered at them through a crack in the door at the end of our hallway and could follow them with one eye up the first three steps before the staircase curved round on itself. After that I could hear the footfalls overhead coming through the ceiling from my mother's bedroom. The strangers were always women – evidently female spies stuck together. And there was the smart brown leather suitcase with hard corners which my mother had suddenly acquired and which she took to the bedroom whenever another agent called. The case was very heavy – I could only just lift it – and I longed to know what it contained. Of course, I tried to find out, more than once, but it was always kept locked. On the back cover of the book my father had borrowed from the barber's, I read: *The Spangled Mob hire undercover agent James Bond to smuggle diamonds into America . . .* Could the case contain diamonds, I wondered? Diamonds would almost certainly account for the weight of the thing. Was my mother a criminal as well as a spy?

It was always possible to tell the days when my mother

expected a visitor. She made thorough preparations, and I would watch her carefully to try to discover her secret. First she would strip down to her underwear to wash at the kitchen sink – face, neck and under her arms. Then, with one deft movement, she would remove her pants and sit in a red plastic basin on the kitchen floor where she washed what she called her in-between bits, before drying herself and dressing in her smart red skirt and matching twin set. Next she would pluck the stray hairs from her eyebrows before carefully applying makeup – putting on her war paint, my father called it. When she was completely ready she would sit down, brushing away imaginary bits of fluff from her cardigan, watching the kitchen clock till the doorbell rang. There was a sort of excitement in her manner, a slight dampness on her upper lip, an air of pre-occupation too. She hardly noticed me at all at these times.

From time to time when my mother was hanging out washing I would creep into her bedroom to look for clues. But I had no idea what I was looking for. In any case, everything seemed just the same – the red candlewick bedspread, the two soft armchairs with embroidered antimacassars, the dressing table with a three-piece vanity set, something else that was strictly just for show. It became clear to me that one way or another I would have to find out what was in the suitcase. Nothing else would do.

My opportunity came one day when my mother was seeing off one of the visitors at the front door. She was a large woman, and I remembered she had been shown to the bedroom once before. She had the jowls of a basset hound and her elegant clothes struggled bravely to contain all the flesh. From the crack in the door at the end of the hallway I could tell that she and my mother were embarking on a lengthy chat. It was now or never. I opened the hall door a few inches, lay down flat on my front like a commando and pulled myself by my elbows along the hallway till I reached the safety of the stairs. The blood was thumping in my head. I scampered up on all fours to the first landing and my mother's bedroom. The door was ajar. The large woman's scent lingered in the air. I felt a thudding in my bust.

There is a Spanish proverb to the effect that the shock that does not kill you makes you. I cannot claim that what I saw that day 'made' me, but at the time the shock seemed to threaten my whole being and I felt lucky to survive it. Certainly nothing had prepared me for it. Most of us can identify those moments in life when you trip on the frayed edge of the carpet. It's been curled up for years waiting to catch you, and you've somehow always known that one day it would, but everything has held together wonderfully till that moment when you trip and, as you fall, you can see all the structures of your life coming apart, and you think, if I could just go back to that moment before I took the tumble. Only there's no going back.

What I saw in my mother's bedroom was much worse than a cache of diamonds, more terrible even than guns. Spread out on the candlewick bedspread was a huge poster-size photograph of near-naked women. The women all had a look of astonishment, as if they had been captured without warning. They were evidently prisoners, confined in some strange constraining garments. The caption on the poster read: *You'll like the way you feel – they'll like the way you look*, and the writing under the photographs was in a strange language I didn't understand: heavy duty girdles, long line brassières, thigh controllers, spiral steel stays, reinforced gussets. Beside the poster there was a measuring tape, a pencil and a large printed pad with lots of columns and figures and diagrams. The suitcase lay open on the floor, disgorging its hideous contents – whalebones, metal suspenders, steel clamps, as well as several long narrow boxes containing the unthinkable garments from the photographs. Each had a label with one of the inflaming words I wasn't allowed to use: SPIRELLA WEAR MUST BE TRIED ON OVER THE CLIENT'S INTERLOCK KNICKERS.

I felt faintly hysterical. I was scrabbling about in that tiny space between illusion and reality. But in that tiny space two things became clear: that the large lady with the acres of flesh had taken all her clothes off in our house; and that my mother had participated in this outrage. All the evidence pointed to the fact that she had even measured the woman's bits. And I knew too, with the certainty that passes all understanding, that there had to be another world possible, something different beyond, a way of life that was not this one.

Part Three
A Different Life

Arriving in Tiger's publishing house for the first time was like turning up in someone else's dream. It seemed a very long way down the rabbit hole. There were no familiar points of reference, no compass bearings. It felt high-voltage and slightly dangerous. The first thing to notice was that there were abnormally high levels of emotion – lots of spirited laughter, shrieking and embracing. The atmosphere seemed to teeter on the edge of hysteria, and it was hard to work out the sounds. Were they angry, or were they just loud? None of it made sense to begin with. It did not seem to accord with any place of work, real or imagined. I suppose I had the mistaken idea that only clever serious people worked with books, and that they probably operated in a quiet, meticulous and, well, bookish, manner. I had pictured earnest men of letters, old-fashioned gentlemen, slightly tweedy and with pale skin that was seldom exposed to natural light.

In fact, the building sizzled with youthful vigour, in the shape of stunning, sophisticated young women. They had patrician accents, exceptional poise and uncommonly long legs. Their skin was not pale but healthy and bronzed. And there wasn't a man in sight. Indeed the mythical Martian, if he had happened to drop in, could not have imagined that women had ever been oppressed, or that their role had once been secondary and passive. Here in this office, in 1981, women ruled. Yet there were no bluestockings, only silk stockings.

The premises were in a run-down part of Soho and extended in a ramshackle way over two buildings, separated by an Italian restaurant and a hairdresser's salon. A faint odour, a mixture of garlic and hair lotion, hung in the air. The offices covered four floors, with staircases slightly aslant and walls off-centre. The furnishings were quite shabby and a layer of black London dust rested on the surfaces. Everywhere there were piles of books and high-rise manuscripts. And, curiously for a publishing house, there were clothes everywhere, suspended in door-ways and draped from light fittings, as if the premises might actually be shared with a dressmaker. Boas and belts hung on the backs of chairs, and on several doors there were coat-hangers bearing evening gowns and stylish camisole jackets. In the loo, I found underwear, tights and nail varnish.

Tiger's girls, as he called them, were well-born and highly bred. They included a Heathcot-Amery, a Bonham-Carter, a Sackville-West and a Vane-Tempest-Stewart. There was still a lot of class about in those days. A de Chamberet, a Ferdinando and a von Stumm added an exotic touch. Nearly everyone, it turned out, was the daughter of an aristocratic or similarly prominent family. 'Famous Englishmen write to me about their daughters,' Tiger had told me when we first met. 'What else can I do?' he said, 'I have to find a job for them.' And he shrugged his shoulders in a gesture of resigned benevolence, as if not to employ them might be considered a perfidious act, a crime against the ruling classes.

Tiger had a conglomerate of companies connected with publishing, fashion, films and theatre. He had been dubbed 'a cultural tycoon' by *The Times* newspaper and he lived up to his dubbing assiduously. The ethos in the empire was not one of profit and loss, but of name and fame. In the latter, so it became clear, he was greatly assisted by these daughters of famous men, for they were scarcely ever out of the gossip columns and they always knew somebody who knew somebody. Even when they were not at work they were still working – at dinner parties, first nights, charity events, gallery openings, fashion shoots and hunt balls. Their most important work, as Tiger himself affirmed, was done out of office hours, for they ensured that news of his latest exploits was trawled through London's most fashionable hotspots. The smart outfits hanging from the office doors began to make sense.

I was introduced to Cosima, Selina, Lucinda, Davina, Samantha and two Sophias. There seemed to be a conspicuous homogeneity of Christian names. Surely there ought to be a collective noun for this phenomenon, I thought, this concentration of cognates. An assonance perhaps? An artillery? I then met Andrea (a Baroness) and Sabrina (an heiress) and, in due course, Alethea, Rebecca, Nigella, Eliza, Candida, Mariella, Zelfa, Georgia, Henrietta and Arabella. It was a lot to take in, the sort of list I would have been made to learn by rote at school, like books of the bible or irregular Latin verbs. When walking around London, I sometimes recited the names to myself, trying to fix them in my head, marvelling at the sound patterns they made. After a while I found it was possible to turn them into the wonderful metrical patterns of English poetry – for example, you could get a perfect trochaic tetrameter if you started with:

Arabella, Henrietta
Cosima, Lucinda, Georgia

as in the *Song of Hiawatha*:

By the shore of Gitche Gumee
By the shining Big-Sea-Water.

And by playing around with the stressed syllables you could achieve the more dramatic metre of *The Charge of the Light Brigade*:

Half a league half a league (Candida, Cosima)
Half a league onward. (Sélina, Georgia)

Names of course are not neutral; they are charged with meaning. And when there is more than a random occurrence of the same denomination it can seem as if they have a special aura. Davina and Sabrina were not just names, but seemed to contain the mystical properties of Davinahood and Sabrinaness. There was, too, a look that went with these abstract nouns – perhaps it came from generations of selective marriage and careful breeding. Each person was beautiful in her own particular way but there was also a generic beauty. It had something to do with bone structure and posture and ease of movement. You could tell that the bloodlines had been kept pure.

'Do you like my girls?' Tiger asked not long after I had started my new job. He was wearing crocodile skin shoes and odd socks in purple and yellow. 'They are amazing, isn't it?' We were sitting in a much smarter building a few streets away, in his penthouse office with the tiger skin on the wall above his head. Without waiting for an answer, he continued, 'And here is my *most* amazing girl!' At this he grabbed hold of Henrietta, his personal assistant, and tugged her hair. 'She looks so soft,' he said, 'but underneath she's a tigress. Only I can tame her!' And as if to make the point, he squeezed her tight and smacked her bottom. Henrietta did not seem to mind.

In truth everyone loved to please him, and he loved to be pleased. It was fascinating to watch, and it had the feel of a phenomenon, something bordering on the fantastic. There was a cult of personality in place, and the worshippers came from all over to demonstrate the strength of their veneration. The air thickened with encomia as they vied for a mark of favour, a preferment for a friend, a sister, a beautiful daughter. When he uttered the simple words, 'I will see what I can do,' he gave hope to the worshipful and was hailed as a saviour. It was evidently an honour to have an audience with Tiger, a latter-day opportunity to pay homage at the imperial court. And it *was* an empire of sorts – not quite Versailles perhaps, but with rules and routines that were in some respects just as precise, and just as remote from ordinary living.

At the palace there was a retinue of attendants – valets, scribes, equerries, foot messengers, maidservants, not to mention a chamberlain figure, who had the difficult job of balancing the books. Things had to be done in a particular way and at a particular time, and the various ceremonies were attended by the modern equivalent of curtsies and bows. The emperor's exactitude came over as an amazing thing, a glorification of reverent observance. At the touch of a button, a maid on stiletto heels delivered an apple cut into eight segments and carefully arranged on a silver plate. A different signal summoned a beautiful vision bearing a tiny gold-encrusted cup containing black coffee to which, under her master's gaze, she added two drops of rose water in the manner of a holy rite.

Life at court was ordered in such a way as to delight the emperor. Mastery of detail was ranked highly, and if ever the detail was mismanaged a heavy price was exacted. Even the minutiae of the court were accorded great importance: the way an envelope was sealed, the positioning of the blotting paper on the leather desk, the hanging of an overcoat in the cloakroom – each task was managed with painstaking care. Everything was codified into a precise system on which the smooth running of the empire depended.

The emperor's personal grooming was also a matter for the most careful attention. Each morning before arriving at work he went first to the barber and then to the hygienist. In those days I was a bit unsure of what a hygienist might do – it is one of those words that sounds so very clean that it might actually be dirty. As far as I knew we didn't have hygienists in Scotland, but so frequently and cheerfully did Tiger say, 'I have just come from my hygienist' that I was fairly certain there could be nothing shameful involved. Eventually I asked one of the girls in pearls, who said matter-of-factly, 'Oh, it's teeth. He goes to get his teeth cleaned.'

The barber was an even more important figure in Tiger's life, a man of near magical powers. Throughout the eighties Tiger had one of the most spectacular cover-ups in the country. He was not yet ready to accept that he was bald on top – that would take another dozen years or so – and the concealment of this fact must have presented a serious challenge. But the challenge was well met: the hair, crinkly and wiry like a pot-scourer, was persuaded to travel from a line just above his ear to be pomaded into place over the crown. It was a substantial thatch, by no means the few lean strands that are combed over many a male pate. People in ancient times used to believe that good and bad spirits entered the body through the hair on one's head. But Tiger's canopy was thick enough to prevent any spiritual traffic, good or bad. In fact it looked as if it could be its own bio-sphere, capable of supporting diverse organisms. In fresh winds, it became separated from its base and hovered independently, like a flying saucer preparing to land. In addition to having his hair fixed every day, Tiger had a shave there three times a week. He had complete faith in his barber. 'He is wonderful,' he would purr. 'I adore him. You know, he heats the shaving cream and wraps my face in a warm towel.' Whenever he spoke of his barber, a beatific smile crept onto his lips. 'He looks after me so nicely. I feel soothed by him.' Long ago the barber was regarded as the most important man in the tribe – medicine man and priest rolled into one. Some of this belief lived on in Tiger.

It was with Napoleonic thoroughness that Tiger controlled every aspect of the day-to-day running of his empire. He maintained absolute authority in a number of ways: by keeping the court guessing about his next move, by never showing his hand completely to anyone, and by possessing a medieval *savoir-faire*. There were at least two Tigers: one was the exotic, flamboyant, quixotic, lovable character, defined by his generosity, compassion and energy; the other was a vainglorious dictator. The latter was generally in the shadow of the former, but both versions were real.

His natural inclination was towards lavish extravagance, and he encouraged immoderation in others. 'How much will it cost?' he often asked when a member of staff went to see him about something, usually to do with publicity or marketing. 'Two thousand pounds! Is that *all*? Then *do* it, darling! What are you waiting for?' But every so often there would be a crack-down, and he would rail against expenses claims, overuse of the telephone, fringe benefits and sundry perks. '*What*! Take an author to Bertorelli's? You must be *mad*! Where am I supposed to get the money to pay for these bloody authors and their bloody lunches?' Storms broke and storms blew over, leaving always a little wreckage behind, but nothing so devastating as to bring about any radical change.

Naturally, the empire offered excellent conditions for the propagation of envy, resentment and all manner of psychological warfare. Tiger himself loved to stir up jealousies among the girls – it amused him, he said, his eyes quick with mischief. Gossip and rumour were just as good as the truth, and more interesting. When someone was summoned to the palace, for example, all eyes and tongues were turned on the chosen one. Tiger knew this and exulted in it, invariably enquiring into the repercussions of some intrigue he himself had set in motion. People could be playthings, their feelings a rich man's sport. 'Was she upset?' he would ask gleefully. 'Did she weep?' On being told that, yes, she was, and yes, she did, he was eager still for more. 'You are *sure*? You saw her tears?' There was no harm intended; it was simply an entertainment for him.

It was regarded as an honour to be asked by him to do something, however trivial, and a noticeable *frisson* would percolate through the Soho offices whenever a call was received from on high. There was a particular deportment that marked the imperial guard, a sort of latter-day flattery and lickspittling, a way of behaviour I soon learned to adopt, in spite of its being utterly against my grain. What he said was deemed to be oracular, and he had only to mention that he wanted such-and-such for the thing, whatever it was, to be pursued and hunted down with Holy Grail zeal. 'Find me an orchid, darling!' he would command, his voice full of life-or-death urgency. 'I *need* an orchid – the best in town.'

Whenever he became agitated about something – a regular occurrence – it was noticeable that everyone competed to placate him. If children have tantrums, parents are generally advised to keep calm and ignore them. But Tiger's tantrums were both heeded and indulged; girls hosed him down with one gush after another as they rushed to pick up his toys and put them back in the pram. They swished their hair back and forth like curtains and drenched him with love till he calmed down. He wallowed in all this. Indeed there seemed to be a degree of self-awareness about the tantrums. 'I got *hysterical*,' he would often say when recalling some incident that had upset him, his voice rising an octave or two in the recollection. And to a sober bystander his behaviour did come over as a kind of hysteria, the sort that in days gone by would have earned a woman a slap on the face and a threat to remove her womb.

In Tiger's publishing house there were many passions. People often seemed to be in a bad mood, or at least pretended to be – I was never entirely sure about what was real and what was affected. What confused me was the amount of embracing that coexisted with the girls' rages – a fascinating sequence of aggressing and caressing. There was also a degree of unsisterly cruelty as they jostled for position and tried to curry favour with Tiger. I say 'they', for it was clear that I did not belong in this world. I was looked upon, with some justification, as one of Tiger's whims: I lived in Scotland after all, and I turned up only for editorial meetings, staying for just a few days at any one time. Even then it was clear that I was just passing through this foreign land – I was in it, but not of it. Besides, I didn't know anyone. Not even anyone who knew anyone.

It was a strange place for me to dip into and out of, and its sheer otherness never lost its impact. At home in Scotland, there were two small children and a baby, the centre of my universe. But in the London office I never mentioned the fact that I was a mother. I was at pains to fit in, and I sensed that talk about children would not be wise. I therefore pretended to be someone else, someone I was not.

There were two others who didn't belong, at least not in the social élite, but they were both men and usually worked in a separate building. One occupied the role of chamberlain, treasurer of the household, a trusted aide-de-camp and a magician with figures. He was a cultured man, shy and sensitive, as different in character from Tiger as it was possible to be. The other was a member of the Old Guard who had access at all times to the throne. His distinctive Cockney voice was peppered with glottal stops and unaspirated aitches, and he always referred to Tiger as The Chairman, which had the ring of His Worshipful Highness or His Sublime Majesty, being charged with the same reverence. In days of old he would have been the chief courtier. As it was, he served as Tiger's eyes and ears, his spy-master, and though he behaved as if he were one of the gang, his loyalty to the throne was absolute. If ever anyone complained that Tiger was being unreasonable, he would listen for a while, drawing heavily on a cigarette, and then solemnly recite: 'Look 'ere, 'e's The Chairman and wha' 'e says goes.'

Loyalty was in fact prized above all else. Loyalty meant, among other things, plenty of fawning at the feast and not questioning any policy decision. Some members of staff were inefficient and occasionally unprincipled but, provided they were loyal, their jobs were usually safe. Tiger himself would sometimes say 'I know she fiddles her expenses, but she's very loyal'; or perhaps, 'She drives me mad – she's always talking on the telephone, but on the other hand she's very loyal.' In fact, he tolerated all manner of wild, anarchic behaviour; indeed he seemed to relish it. Tales of wayward conduct amused him and he would often exclaim, in squeals of delight, 'My girls are delinquents! They are hooligans!' Once during a party at an exclusive club on Pall Mall, one of Tiger's girls, something of a free spirit, was caught urinating in a wash-basin in the gents. Despite a grovelling apology to the club, a lifetime ban was imposed on the publishing house and its staff. Tiger was mortified, or affected to be. For weeks on end he would say to everyone he met, 'CAN – YOU – IMAGINE?' He gave the same stress to all three words and thumped them out in turn on the table. 'Peeing in the basin! She's a *complete* liability. She will *ruin* us!' But after a perfunctory rant against her character, he always finished by saying, 'But, you know, I love her! She's so loyal!' Unsurprisingly, it was disloyalty – a potent and protean concept – that was the unforgivable sin.

After a while I discovered that the girls came and went with striking regularity. When I travelled to London to attend monthly editorial meetings, I would find that Cosima had been replaced by Nigella, or Sophia by Candida. There were new arrivals as well as bare survivals. And even occasional revivals, since it was not unknown for a girl to be recalled from the wilderness into which she had been so precipitately cast. Tiger alone had the power to pardon the condemned; no amount of special pleading by anyone else on behalf of the offender had any effect.

In due course Lucinda left to marry an Earl and Sabrina was put in charge of a book club. She claimed never to have read a book – she even confessed this to the press – but it didn't seem to matter. It was enough that she had been the girlfriend of a member of the royal family. It was clear that Tiger's appointments policy was full of purpose and intent, and I soon began to notice interesting patterns in the hiring, and also in the firing, a rare but always dramatic occurrence. On these occasions, reason was set aside while emotion did its dirty work. No one understood the specific trigger, but the reaction was extreme. Knives would be sharpened, and over the next day or two the girl in question, often quite oblivious of the offence she was alleged to have committed, would be branded and traduced. Tiger put energy into umbrage; his pique was majestic. And when his pique finally peaked, the most faithful member of the Old Guard would be called upon to do the necessary. Tiger himself was unable to face it.

Every so often he got a gleam in his eye, and we knew that he had fallen in love. Again. It was always a *coup de foudre* followed by complete infatuation. It had the energy of a natural phenomenon – a typhoon maybe, or a freak storm. Single orchids would be sent to the chosen one and French perfume would arrive by special courier. At these times Tiger behaved like a little puppy, rolling over on his back, paws in the air, simpering and slavering, hoping that his tummy might be tickled. Just like the rest of us, this mighty potentate could be made ridiculous by love. The girl so beloved would be designated *La Favorita* – a recognised position at the imperial court – and a job would usually be found for her in public relations. In the days that followed she would dine at the best restaurants and occupy a box at the Royal Opera House. Previous holders of the position would drop down in the pecking order, and for a while there would be furious spitting and pouting. Being *La Favorita*, however, was generally a short-lived affair. Though the after-tremors could be felt for some time, Tiger fell in and out of love quickly and decisively.

Now and then I sat at my desk on the top floor of the publishing house and listened to the complex sounds coming from the rest of the building. Telephones rang, kettles boiled, hairdryers wheezed. And some people didn't just talk, they squawked. They spoke, as it were, in italics, so that perfectly ordinary sentences were brought into prominent relief. Something as simple as 'What are you doing?' was invariably 'What *are* you *doing*?' – which gave normal dialogue a theatrical quality. They also spoke in shrill absolutes, so that someone was a *total darling* or a *complete noodle*. They said *grotty* and *golly*, they complained of a *frightful pong,* and they were never just angry, but always *absolutely livid*. The way they expressed themselves seemed every bit as significant as what they were speaking about; in some strange sense it was indistinguishable from it.

Of course, a lot of time was spent on the telephone, which was used just as much for making social arrangements as for conducting business. The collective sounds of Tiger's girls on the phone to their friends were not so very different from the whooping at a children's party. It seemed that if you were out of the top drawer you did a lot of shrieking. At closer range it was possible to make out the words, the discussion of menus and venues, of the night before and the night to come. And always of what was worn and what to wear. But the language was alien, brimming with chumminess, and there seemed to be no way in for those not born to it. You can come to imitate the way someone speaks, but you cannot take the substance as your own. Theirs wasn't a private language exactly, more a system of communication that naturally excluded. The vowels were particularly distinctive, springing from a place way down the larynx and travelling up fine, swan-like necks before emerging in beautifully modulated tone patterns. The Scots have short, stunted vowels, cut off in their prime, strangled humanely before they get too long and above themselves. They sprout from pinched throats and squat necks. Of course, this is to speak generally, for there are longer shorts in Kirkwall, say, than in Kirkcaldy. Even so, vowels can never be underestimated – they are basic in forming, and sometimes impeding, social contracts. Mercifully, human beings need very little to be able to understand each other's way of speaking – just a few sounds strung together in a sentence or two are usually enough to get the gist. But there is so much to distinguish one kind of speech from another, to separate us one from the other. There's nothing quite like language for coming between us.

~

I had been puzzled by language from an early age. When I was five years old my mother told me I was to have elocution lessons.

'What's elocution?' I asked, but all she would say was that it was to help me *get on*.

'Get on what?'

'Just get on,' she said, squelching the possibility of more questions.

I asked my friends if they knew what it was, but none of them did. My brother's friends were three years older, and one of them claimed to know. 'It's whaur they learn ye tae speak proper,' he said in his broad Fife accent, and he gave a sort of snigger. I could not imagine such a place.

The lessons were to be on Tuesdays after school. They would take place in Dunfermline, an eight-mile bus journey away. While I was having the lesson, my mother would do some shopping. 'Elocution costs a lot,' she said, 'so make sure you listen and learn.' When the day arrived, I was excited about going on the blue double-decker bus and even risked asking if we could sit upstairs, though I knew it wouldn't be allowed. Every few hundred yards the bus stopped to let on women with large string-bags bulging with groceries. It was raining outside, which made the air inside heavy. It smelled of wet wool and raw mince. I soon began to feel unwell. I watched the condensation trickling down the windowpanes, zig-zagging whenever the bus lurched. It was difficult to breathe, and for some reason I had to keep swallowing. When the vomit darted up from my tummy like a lizard, the bus conductor pressed the bell three times to make the driver stop. Everyone stared, and out on the pavement my mother told me she was black affronted, which I knew was one of the worst things a mother could be on account of her children.

Miss Menzies, my elocution teacher, was stiff and corseted.

She had a breathy, hot-potato voice and told me her name was pronounced Ming-is. I must never make the mistake of pronouncing it Men-zeez, she said – only people who didn't know any better did that. I thought at first that her legs were bandaged on account of her thick stockings and swollen ankles. Poor Miss Ming-is, I thought. But it didn't last.

On the wall there was a chart with a diagram of half a human body, the top half. On either side of the chest there were two red shapes that looked like huge mutton chops. According to the chart, these were lungs, and they were surrounded by a mass of tubes and pouches, all connected to one another. Miss Menzies took a long wooden pointer and picked out the parts I was to learn: ribcage, thorax, diaphragm, and something called the bronchial tree. She said the names while tapping with the pointer, and I was to repeat them after her. This was not at all what I had thought elocution might be. 'Never forget,' Miss Menzies warned, '*sound* conquers *sight*.' As she said this, she pointed first to her mouth, then to her eyes, but what she meant by it I had no idea. The diaphragm looked like the round top of a hill, and there was a sort of volcano underneath. This was to show, said Miss Menzies, how the breath was drawn into the lungs. She said that everything was capable of expanding and contracting, even the thorax – a truly alarming piece of information. Then there was the larynx, a hollow passage that led to the lungs, and the pharynx – a black cave behind the pink wiggly bit dangling at the back of the throat.

'Before being able to speak properly,' said Miss Menzies in very clear tones, 'you have to learn to breathe properly.' I was five years old and had been breathing for all that time, but

45

evidently I had been doing it wrong. 'We have to breathe deeply, so that we can finish the sentence before taking another breath,' she said, though she didn't explain why we couldn't just take another breath. I wondered what the reason could be. We did lots of breathing exercises together, during which we stood facing one another at either end of a small rug. But even something as simple as standing had to be learned from the beginning again. My back had to be straight, my hands – not clenched – by my sides, and my feet positioned like the hands of a clock reading ten past twelve. It was a lot to remember, and that was even before I had started the proper breathing.

For the next bit, the breathing bit, Miss Menzies bellowed the instructions: 'FILL your lungs! CHEST in! ABDOMEN out! HO-O-O-LD – one, two, three – and let GO-O-O-OH – four, five, six.' Miss Menzies' chest was enormous, and her abdomen bulged despite the corset. When she showed me how to breathe properly she became like a rolling cargo ship.

After that we tackled vowel sounds, the long vowels, the short vowels, the -oo- sound and the -igh- sound, as in *moon* and *soon* and *night* and *light*. We held each vowel for fifteen seconds on only one breath. It sounded like a strange kind of singing. We practised short nonsense sentences that I couldn't imagine ever saying to any of my friends – 'My, oh my, how bright is the night.' There were also things called *diphthongs*, which Miss Menzies said were vowels that moved, since they started out as one vowel and became another halfway through. Like *few* and *loud*.

As the weeks passed I discovered just how hard it was to speak properly. Apart from all the vowels and the diphthongs there was something called RISP – Rhythm, Intonation, Stress and Pronunciation. According to Miss Menzies, all four were vital for elocution, and without them you could not project your voice except by shouting – something you must never do. The hardest thing to learn was pronunciation: the way a word was meant to sound. Words like *paw* and *poor* and *pour* all sounded the same when Miss Menzies said them. I much preferred the way we said them at home – that way you could tell them apart. It seemed funny to pronounce *he sawed* and *he soared* in exactly the same way; how would you know what was meant if you just heard it? It could surely lead to all sorts of trouble.

To practise my RISP I was given little printed poems that had to be pasted into a notebook with hard covers and learned off by heart. I liked pasting them neatly into the book, but I thought the poems were silly. My very first poem, which was to help with my -ee- and -oo- sounds, went as follows:

> I'm going to sweep the dirt away
> I'm going to sweep the dirt away
> I'm going to sweep the dirt away
> Whoosh! Whoosh! Whoosh!
> If you come in with muddy feet
> I'll sweep you out into the street
> Whoosh! Whoosh! Whoosh!

I hated reciting it. It made me feel babyish and stupid, and Miss Menzies said she wanted much more *oomph* in my *whooshes*, which only made matters worse. And when I practised it at home, my brother sniggered in the background. It was a ridiculous poem. But it has stayed with me, painfully, all my life.

Besides poems, I had to memorise and recite tongue-twisters like 'The Leith police dismisseth us', and 'She sifted seven thick stalked thistles through a strong thick sieve.'

Miss Menzies marked the RISP of my recitation every week and wrote a few lines in spidery letters that were hard to read. She also gave marks for what she called 'deportment and carriage', which had to do with my shoulders and feet. She never smiled, but sometimes she stuck a star in my book to show I had done well. A gold star was best, followed by silver and green. To please my mother, and because the lessons cost a lot, I tried very hard to get gold stars. There were competitions too, held once a year at the Assembly Rooms in Edinburgh, in front of a row of judges at a long table. I always felt terrified on these occasions and had to steel myself for the ordeal of walking onto the stage. Before the recitation I had to remember to arrange my hands and feet correctly, not to mention my head, which Miss Menzies said had to be tilted upwards slightly. When I started the poem, I always heard my voice ringing inside me, as if something had plugged my ears and was forcing everything inwards.

Elocution was a thing apart. It was something that happened on Tuesday afternoons in Dunfermline, and it did not get mixed up with the other days. At school I knew better than to speak in my poetry voice – everyone would have laughed – and I didn't even think much about the position of my diaphragm, as Miss Menzies had told me I must. At home, too, the way we spoke was not at all the way Miss Menzies taught and my mother bought – except if the minister or the doctor or the church elder came to our house, when there would always be a marked change towards the genteel. This involved frequent use of words like 'sufficient' and 'require' and 'partake', as in '*Have you had sufficient to eat?*' or '*Will you partake of another scone?*' or '*Will you be requiring to visit the bathroom?*' I knew that I too was expected to play my part on these occasions. Sometimes, for example, I would be asked by my mother to run an errand or get some coal for the fire, after which she would make a point of asking, very precisely: 'Have you *accomplished* it?' Since a one-word answer would have let the side down, I had learned to give the reply that was expected of me: 'Yes, I have accomplished it' – though it always sounded terribly put-on. On the days when there was no need to behave differently, however, there were hardly any vital vowels or dangling diphthongs or high-flown words. And although my mother could readily change her voice, my father didn't seem to bother much, certainly not with the length of his vowels. I suspected he was not in favour of elocution lessons. When I asked him why my brother did not have to have them, he said with a grunt that it wasn't anything a boy needed to learn. I thought then how unlucky it was to have been born a girl.

In our house it was usually easy to work out what was good and what was bad. Some things were regarded as good in themselves: for example, eating slowly, Formica, curly hair, secrecy, patterned carpets, straight legs, Scotch broth, bananas, going to the toilet before leaving the house, not crying whatever the circumstances – the goodness of these things was not open to challenge. Thus a child with curly hair who liked bananas and never cried was praised to the skies. By the same token, eating fast, straight hair, plain carpets, and so on were bad things and, where possible, not allowed. If it was not possible to ban them, they were simply frowned upon. All this was clear-cut and easy to follow. However, in the way we spoke and the words we used, it was much harder to know good from bad, right from wrong. The rules seemed not to be fixed. Working out what was allowed, or when it might not be, was something of a leap in the dark.

The person who came most often to our house was Uncle Bill. He wasn't a real uncle, but he was my parents' oldest friend and had been best man at their wedding. He was a lovable, cheerful man and was always telling jokes, though he also talked a lot about death. Someone had usually just died and – this amazed me – he always knew who it was and how it had happened. We would all listen intently as he reported the grimly fascinating details: a man discovered dead in his bath, a woman lying frozen by her own coal bunker, a newly married couple run over on a Belisha crossing. The summing-up took one of two forms: people were either cut off in their prime – this was described as 'a blinkin' tragedy'; or else they had had what was called a good innings – in which case it was usually 'a bloomin' mercy'. I didn't know any dead people, and I used to wonder what it must feel like to know so many. The main thing to notice, however, was that when Uncle Bill visited, something happened to the way we spoke.

It is difficult to describe exactly what it was that happened, but it had to do with the shape of the sentences and the words that were in them – they seemed to be just the right words in the right place. The sound of my parents chatting with Uncle Bill was a joy – they used words like *scunner* and *glaekit* and *puggled* and *wabbit* linked together by lots of *dinnaes* and *winnaes* and *cannaes*. Uncle Bill led the way, and my parents seemed to take their cue from him. In my recollection they seemed happier at these times than at any other, laughing a lot, sharing together, not holding back or being secretive. They still argued with each other, but it wasn't serious in the way normal arguments were when Uncle Bill wasn't there. And even when they disagreed, there was still a warm feeling, as if something tight had loosened. They were relaxed in the rhythms, at ease with the words – as if they were real *owners* of this language, not just borrowers. And not pretenders either, for their conversation was real and full of rich meaning. It couldn't have been more different from elocution lessons, with all that *whooshing* the stupid dirt away. I loved joining in, and my parents seemed pleased with me when I did. It was like drinking hot cocoa. Everything felt safe when Uncle Bill was there.

When he went away, however, the mood would suddenly shift back to something less certain, less safe. Of course, I wanted it to carry on, and I would try to hold onto the magic that had bound us together only minutes before. I would repeat some of the things Uncle Bill had said, using his words and expressions, following the rhythms, trying to get my parents to respond, to be the way they had been. But everything had already fractured to bits, and there was danger everywhere. 'Don't talk like that!' my mother would say, 'You know that's no way to speak!' I felt crushed by this, by the unfairness of it all, so much so that I would appeal to my father. But all he would say was 'That's enough now.' He said it quite gently but firmly, in a way that made any kind of protest impossible. Sometimes it felt hot behind my eyes and I would have to breathe in the way that I knew would stop the tears coming.

That scene, repeated many times, is still sharp in my mind – I can see it as if I'm watching a sequence in a film. Yet it may not have been that way at all, and as I write it I am conscious of how differently my parents might have described it. Would there in fact have been anything for them to describe? Were they even aware of what I felt? Did they feel it too? I think not. Memory is not always to be trusted – it can make things so much worse or better than they were. But there is such a lot that is forgotten, so much that doesn't make it past the hippocampus and simply disappears into oblivion; with the result that the parts we do remember cry out to have sense made of them.

What sense do I make now of the confusion surrounding the way we spoke and the words we used? Judging by the rigidity of their rules, and the strictness with which they imposed them, my parents appeared to me to be certain about everything. I now think that I was mistaken. The sheer fluidity of their position on language was surely a sign that they were feeling their way in the dark just as much as the rest of us. Both my parents were fiercely proud of being Scottish: they felt *ipso facto* supreme in the pecking order of nations. They were fond of reciting the names of Scots inventors – a list to make you proud, they said. Without the Scots and their inventions, so they claimed, the world would be *nothing* – no trains, no telephone, no roads, no television. And if it hadn't been for James Watt and his steam engine we'd still be getting around on donkeys. In fact, when you think of it, we'd scarcely be alive at all without all that penicillin and anaesthetic, not to mention the antibiotics. It was a subject they returned to again and again, affirming and reaffirming the peerlessness of their country.

My country too. They also honoured Scots traditions – haggis on Burns night, black bun at New Year – and spoke with swollen hearts of the unparalleled beauty of the Scottish landscape. When they saw pictures of far-flung countries on television, they would scoff: 'Huh! Not a patch on Bonnie Scotland!' It mattered not at all that the place where we lived was mostly unbeautiful, that we were surrounded by bings – our name for slag-heaps – and that the topographical features they praised were wholly absent – no mountains, no glens, no coastline. They were devoted to Scottishness, especially what is perceived by the outside world as Scottishness – whisky, bagpipes, kilts and Balmorality. We even had a family plaque on our front door displaying our clan tartan and coat of arms.

But when it came to language, that other potent symbol of national identity, my parents' attitude, particularly that of my mother, was equivocal. With its colourful dialect words and distinctive accent the Scots tongue was – still is – a vigorous, vital and varied thing. And it was something my parents clearly took pleasure in. But in common with parents the world over, they wanted the best for their children. They wanted them to *get on*. And it can't have escaped them that the status of the Scots language in wider society was low. If you spoke in the way it felt natural to speak, the way you heard spoken all around you, you were marked in the eyes of the world beyond. It was daylight snobbery, but that's the way it was. My mother was fiercely aspiring, and my father, perhaps in the interests of peace, went along with her. English was the thing; hence the elocution lessons and all that pitiful vowel management.

Neurologists tell us that there is part of the brain specific to verbs, another specific to nouns. In my own brain, I have come to believe there must be a part directed towards vowels; and what a muddled, messed-up part it is. Alas, some things learned in childhood are difficult to unlearn, however much you might try. Thus, I have never been, am not now, confident of the way I speak. I hardly ever use the vernacular – 'the guid Scots words' that brightened my childhood – except self-consciously or mockingly; everything is slightly adjusted, depending on where I am, and those I am with. This irony is not lost on me. My mother and Miss Ming-is have prevailed.

Like its proprietor, the publishing house was *sui generis*, and it had a reputation quite disproportionate to its size. It was known to be radical and risk-taking – unafraid of the odd lawsuit, real or threatened. And although commercial viability was rapidly becoming the most important factor in the rest of the publishing world, it was not yet a feature of this independent house. Tiger took chances with books and seemed to act mostly on impulse. He would meet people at a party and sign them up on the spot. Sudden ideas were converted into improbable publishing ventures, and books were invented that ought never to have existed. He acted speedily and never flinched from taking a decision. He loved controversy, courted it indeed, and any whiff of scandal merely strengthened his resolve to publish. 'Let them sue! Let them sue!' he would say, rubbing his soft hands together. 'But I am a fighter, and I fight to win!' Tiger basked in this image, and we basked in it too. By association, we felt as if we were also fighters, that we too would win, and although at editorial meetings there was hardly ever a discernible rational plan, the atmosphere was highly charged and there was a lot of heady talk about noble ideals. There was, too, a good deal of frivolity, but the frivolity was curiously serious, and much of the time we behaved as if we might be engaged in decisions of supreme importance.

There wasn't an obvious hierarchy, but there seemed to be an appetite for titles and an abundance of directors. There were editorial directors, marketing directors, publicity directors and public relations directors. According to my business card I was a commissioning editor. But whom was I going to commission, and what was I going to edit?

Nothing much was explained, though a lot could be picked up from looking and listening, and from reading trade publications. Much of the time, however, I had a vertiginous sense of bafflement about what I was meant to be doing. And people were suspicious of the New Girl, partly because of the atmosphere of mistrust in the sultan's seraglio, where New Girls might easily elbow out those who were not quite in mint condition. I wanted to tell them that they had nothing to worry about: that I was no threat, that I just wanted a job to stop my brain softening, that I had no need of orchids or perfume, that I didn't want to disturb their domain. Yet I said none of this.

Instead I studied Judith Butcher's *Copy-Editing* and stumbled upon a fascinating new world full of rules and regulations, all set out with biblical authority: where to put the spaces when showing degrees of temperature, how to convert footnotes to endnotes, what to do with trade names, and which typeface to use for classical Greek. It amazed me that someone had made decisions about all of these things and had set a clear

standard. Copy-editing, so I discovered, is a complicated business – an intricate system of textual symbols and marginal
marks contained within a rigid structure of spelling, grammar
and punctuation. It seems to be part science, part art, and it
even has a strange and wonderful language of its own: widows
and wrap-rounds, bleeds and blocks and blurbs, serifs and slugs
and stets. It is oddly alluring.

After a few months I had managed to learn quite a lot from
the Butcher bible, and in due course typescripts began to arrive
on my desk with a note asking me to 'cast an eye' over them,
as if they might be part of a window display. But the work
was detailed and precise and it could not be rushed. Copy-
editing felt like leaving the world for a while, and the exact-
ness of it was strangely restful. It was also obsessive. I would
scour each page for split infinitives and hanging participles; or
pounce on a widow and gleefully rearrange the spacing to
remove all trace of it. Before long I began to see inordinate
beauty in marginal squiggles or the hieroglyphs of textual marks,
and though neatness and orderliness had never been my
strengths, I soon found that I was keeping my pencil, ruler and
eraser in a little wooden box on my desk and guarding them
fiercely from casual thievery. I straightened and patted the pages
of each typescript into even blocks, and if ever anyone asked
to borrow my pencil-sharpener I had to stop myself from
screaming. During the working day I was neurotically perfec-
tionist about everything, and at night I dreamed of tiny wooden
compartments containing my children's milk teeth, toenail
clippings and chickenpox scabs.

Further estrangement from normal life was averted by a visit
to the Frankfurt Book Fair in October 1981. I had been in

touch with agents representing writers from the Soviet Union (as it then was), and we had arranged to meet at Frankfurt and talk about English language rights. I began to see the possibility of setting up an interesting list of Russian books in translation. I was determined to seize this opportunity – if only to justify my existence at work.

The journey to Frankfurt gave me my first taste of travelling with Tiger. We met outside his house in Mayfair where the chauffeur was waiting, this time in a shiny black Bentley, to drive us to Heathrow. Tiger was wearing a long overcoat of wild mink, which he removed before getting into the car. 'Do you like it?' he asked, stroking himself with both hands. 'It's by Fabienne of Mayfair – my wife gave it to me as a Christmas present.' Underneath he wore a Hermès jacket in red and blue suede, and shoes made from red lizard skin. 'For Frankfurt I always like to dress casual,' he explained.

Like fine wine, and cats in baskets, he did not travel well. Every stage of the journey – driving to Heathrow, queuing up at the check-in desk, boarding the plane – was attended by a high degree of angst. Would the traffic make us late? Would the plane leave on time? Would there be a screaming infant in the row behind? On the way to the airport he made countless calls from his car phone, announcing his imminent departure and giving out contact details, apparently to anyone he could think of. In the 1980s the advertisers of the first generation of mobile phones targeted the business traveller, promising that effective use could be made of time spent travelling – 'dead time', they called it. Working his way through the list of numbers in his Filofax, Tiger made this dead time zing. 'I shall be in the air for just over one hour. My plane lands in

Frankfurt at 14.45 local time, but you can reach me . . .', he boomed down the phone again and again. I doubted whether any of this was strictly necessary, but it had the desired effect of aggrandising the trip and creating a sense of urgency.

In the business of communication Tiger was ahead of his time. He acquired one of the earliest versions of the mobile phone, upgrading it as soon as a new model came on the market, and he seemed to understand before anyone else that it was an index of the future. 'Look at it!' he would say, cradling it fondly in his hands. 'Isn't it amazing? Isn't it beautiful? Can you believe how neat it is?' He drooled over the design and knew instinctively that the size, the fascia, the foldability – all these things would come to be very important. In fact, he was also one of the earliest examples of the useless but self-validating *I'm on the train* culture. As we trundled down the motorway, he yelled into the mouthpiece a running commentary on weather conditions, traffic congestion, exact location, proximity to Terminal One, and so on. And in the back seat I experienced the first stirrings of those feelings now common among travellers whose basic entitlement to peace and quiet is being violated. I had no idea then that within twenty years a billion people would be jabbering into mobiles.

Once we were on the aeroplane Tiger's anxiety levels increased, though it was striking that he didn't have the concerns people traditionally have before take-off: will the plane actually get off the ground? Does the captain know what he's doing? Should I have written a letter to my children? Instead he fretted about whether there was enough bread on board so that he could have extra with his lunch, and whether his state-of-the-art mobile phone would work in Germany. In between he kept checking his three watches, certain that we were going to be late in leaving, all the while scowling at his fellow passengers as if they had no right to be there. He worried dreadfully about the possibility of contagion, and he listed the ghastly diseases he could catch, fearing it might already be too late. He hated it when people coughed or blew their noses into handkerchiefs. He was also acutely sensitive to smell, and the moment everyone was seated he puckered his nostrils and probed the air for anything malodorous. 'Oh, my God, the smell!' he said to me, screwing up his face and glaring at the man across the aisle. 'It's appalling! Can't you *smell* him?' He pushed the call-button to summon the stewardess. I felt sure he was going to complain about body odours, but instead he asked for a glass of water. 'I have to keep drinking,' he explained to me. 'My wee-wee is yellow.' Moments later, he pressed the call-button again and said to the same stewardess: 'Excuse me, I am a London publisher. I need to see the *Financial Times* for reasons of business. Would you be so kind as to bring it to me?' – a sentence that seemed to have been plucked from a phrase book for travellers abroad: *'Can you help me, please? I am an English tourist. My car has run out of petrol. Would you be so good as to direct me to the nearest petrol station?'*

Matters improved when the in-flight meal arrived, and there were squeals of joy and relief each time the stewardess appeared with a basket of bread rolls. I marvelled at the constant expenditure of emotion – how could he keep it up? When we arrived at Frankfurt airport, however, things took a turn for the worse. Ignoring the familiar injunction to passengers to remain seated 'until the plane comes to a complete halt', Tiger leapt to his feet, collected his bag from the overhead locker and perched himself on the arm of his seat, straining forward like a horse at the starting-gate. 'Quick! We have to get ready!' he whispered. 'Otherwise we will get caught.'

The next trial took place at the baggage carousel. Tiger pushed his way through the crowd so that we could stand right by the mouth of the machine where the bags are disgorged. His expression was dark, his mouth set hard against the unfairness of life. Happily, his case was among the first to come through, but mine took longer. After a minute or two, he asked me what colour it was. 'Black,' I said, full of regret, since all the cases tumbling out looked black, or blackish, or nearly-black, or semi-black, and Tiger asked me unremittingly about every one of them, 'Is it *this* one? Is it *this* one?', his agitation increasing each time it wasn't. 'Then it must be lost,' he said, 'or stolen – they steal them, you know, these bloody crooks on the lorry, sons-of-bitches, it's always happening, you'll never see it again.' By the time my bag turned up, quite safe, I was exhausted by all the emotion.

Nothing can prepare you for the sheer scale of the Frankfurt Book Fair: a row of huge hangars connected by bus lanes, escalators and moving walkways, and inside each hangar a whole city constructed of books. Each city is divided into American-style blocks, with numbers and letters for the interlocking streets. The effect is spectacularly commercial, and the imperative, as in any cattle market, is to sell. 'Frankfurt is a *must*,' Tiger had told me. 'If we don't go to Frankfurt, people think we are either dead or bankrupt. We have to be *seen*.'

I walked through the urban grid reading off the names of distinguished publishing houses that up till then I had read only on the spines of books. This was 1981, before the major mergers and takeovers, when independent companies were still much in evidence: Hamish Hamilton, Jonathan Cape, Michael Joseph, Chatto & Windus, The Bodley Head – names glorious in the pre-conglomerate age. The stands were colonised by diverse species – men in cream suits with spotted bow-ties and long hair, ageing aesthetes alongside city slicker types, women dressed like out-of-work actors, or else wearing sensible skirts and stout shoes. Was it really possible that all these people were here to stave off rumours of death or bankruptcy?

People spoke of 'Frankfurt fever', and evidently with good reason. For in this vast place, filled with neon and noise, rumours abounded: secret deals, manuscripts being read under secure guard, big books, big bucks, big buzz. There were life-sized cardboard effigies advertising popular characters from children's books, and high above, floating in the rafters, there were huge coloured balloons. Gossip was spread like dung on fields, and the dung-beetles – in the form of publishers, agents, scouts – wallowed in their element, hatching, feeding, regurgitating. In the bars that were dotted around the halls, people talked over beer and sausages of The Next Hot Thing. Figures were plucked from the air and were doubled, even trebled, before they had a chance to be written down.

As I wandered along the aisles between the bodice rippers and the diet manuals, the art books and the bibles, the foreign language texts and city guides, there was no doubting that publishing had become big business. This was unquestionably a massive trading centre. It was hard to imagine that writers themselves had changed much – theirs would always be a solitary activity undertaken away from the big lights – but those in the publishing business had learned how to sell the writers, how to package their books, make them pop up, change colour, talk, smell and grab the reader in every way possible. In Hall Five I saw a middle-aged woman sitting in a large cardboard carton with the words POET IN A BOX inscribed round the top. She was writing verses in ink with a tulip-shaped pen – a silent protest against the hypermarket.

The days at the Book Fair were tiring and headache-inducing. There was the constant hubbub of large numbers of people talking and moving around, and the air in the huge halls was heavy and smoke-filled. By contrast, the evenings were spent in the cool air of Wiesbaden, a beautiful spa town about twenty miles west of Frankfurt with over two dozen natural hot springs. The first impression on entering the town from the autobahn was one of opulence combined with gracious living. It is one of the oldest towns along the Rhine and, unlike the rest of Germany, most of its buildings came through the Second World War unscathed, including a Russian Byzantine chapel with five golden domes and a splendid theatre built in neo-baroque style for Emperor Wilhelm II.

Tiger had booked his usual accommodation – the presidential suite in a luxury hotel in Kaiser Friedrich Platz. 'Wait till you see it,' he said to me. 'It's where they put all the presidents – they keep it for me every year.' The four or five other members of staff, who had travelled ahead to Frankfurt to set up our stand, stayed in a smaller hotel nearby, but I was given a room in the grand hotel so that – this was how it was explained to me – Tiger would not have to eat by himself or travel alone, two things he detested. Besides, I spoke German and he wanted me on hand for any interpreting that was needed. A sign above the desk stated that our hotel was one of the world's best. The whole building had the feel of a grand stately home, with all the rooms lavishly furnished and decorated. It was built on top of one of the springs, which fed into a huge swimming pool surrounded by glass. On arrival Tiger was fêted like a demigod. The *maître d'* welcomed him back effusively and was at pains to show that he had remembered all his special requirements – continental breakfast at 7 a.m., a board under the bed, and so on. When I asked Tiger why he chose to stay in Wiesbaden and not in Frankfurt where the Book Fair was, he was aghast. It was clear that I had made a *faux pas*. 'Do we want skyscrapers?' he asked, throwing his hands in the air, 'Do we want concrete? Do we want the filth of the city? Of course we don't! We want to be comfortable. We want to live in *style*. Isn't it?' There was certainly style aplenty in Wiesbaden, with its wide tree-lined avenues, elegant arcades, jewellery shops and select boutiques.

In the evenings we all had dinner together. Although everything was new to me, a routine had clearly been established over the years. On the first evening, for example, we all met up in the hotel bar and went on to dine in the in-house gourmet restaurant. The next few evenings were spent at different restaurants a short stroll away. Tiger was in his element on these occasions, taking full charge and clearly relishing the role of host. He had all those French qualities that there are no words for in English: panache, éclat, *élan*, *savoir-vivre*. He attracted a good deal of attention, not least because he was dressed to kill – a spangle of silks and cashmeres, rubies and diamonds. To study the menu he took from his top pocket a pair of collapsible spectacles. They were made, so he said, from Inca gold. 'Aren't they cute?' he smiled, unfolding them from a tiny pouch. 'They were made for me by Asprey's. Exclusive for me. Look, they even have diamond hinges!'

Tiger communicated with his whole body, waving his arms around, slapping his thighs, smiting his brow, clapping his hands together. It was all so very physical. Those sitting on either side of him got a regular thwack on their upper arms whenever he was trying to make a particular point. He needed a lot of space to function even at a basic level, but when he was ordering from the menu or telling a story, it was a kind of circus act, a cross between juggling and slapstick. What did our fellow diners make of it all? Next to him, so I thought, the rest of us must have seemed like a dull group from a faded photograph, though we probably all felt a little vicarious *folie de grandeur*. Once the food arrived, he ate very fast and exhorted us to do the same. 'Go on! Eat! Eat!' he said, as if at any moment our plates might be whipped away. He had a talent for talking exuberantly at the same time as eating, with no spaces between one word and the next. He was full of indiscretions and innuendo, and he spoke in great tidal waves that gathered and swelled and filled and quickened before crashing on the rocky shores of sense and syntax. Once he got going, the English language did not know what had hit it. Subject and predicate were in a kind of happy free-fall, with the component parts, unable to agree, fighting it out and coming near to killing one another.

The Book Fair opened at nine o'clock in the morning, but Tiger didn't want to spend the whole day there. The others travelled early to Frankfurt by car, but we usually took a taxi later in the day. There were some fine antique shops in Wiesbaden, and Tiger loved looking round for whatever he was collecting at the time. He was ecstatic when he found something for his collection and, though it was in his nature to haggle, once he had set his heart on something he had to have it no matter what it cost. I loved his freedom and flair with money. My mother, who came from a long line of Presbyterians, always found it difficult to part with money, and when she did it seemed to make her miserable. It was culpable to be profligate, and she felt guilty if she spent money on herself. Tiger had no such hang-ups.

He did have other hang-ups, however. For example, he was very particular about planning the days, announcing in advance what we would do and when. Each event or activity was given an allotted span, timed to the nearest five minutes. 'In fifteen minutes,' he would say, looking at his watches, 'we shall walk in the park.' And just in case I got the idea that it might be an open-ended walk, the sort you might prolong if the sun was shining and the birds were singing, he would add, 'We will walk for twenty-five minutes exactly, then we will return to the hotel.' During the walk, he would check his watches compulsively, apparently unable to relax into the moment, always having an eye to the next thing. 'In ten minutes we will turn round . . . in five minutes we will be at the hotel . . . in twenty minutes we will take some tea,' and so on. *Carpe futuram.* Sometimes we sat around in the hotel lobby waiting for the next event – usually lunch – but not in the relaxed, easy-going way of hotel guests who are happy to watch the world go by while they wait. No, the waiting itself was the heart of the matter; it assumed an existential significance and threatened his peace of mind. He would become furious with himself – how could he have failed to arrange our programme properly? How could he have slipped up so badly? Now there was this terrible wait. At these times he was in a state of, as it were, dispersion, unable to engage with the world, the people around him, the newspapers on the table, anything at all; for he was already looking away, agonised by the intermediate. He was unmoored, nonplussed by this brief enforced standstill in a restless existence. His impatience was baneful, making it impossible to do anything other than join him in it. Together, we willed it to be midday when the restaurant opened its doors.

The moment we sat down in the restaurant his spirits lifted. The white linen, the beautiful wine glasses, the prospect of lunch – everything was suddenly well with the world. 'Isn't this amazing?' he said, as a beautiful waitress brought a platter piled high with a dozen different breads. 'You know, bread is my favourite thing. I love it!' It was engaging to be in the presence of such naked pleasure. Once the bread had started to take effect he summoned the *sommelier* and went through the wine list with him. When, after some discussion, a bottle was finally chosen, he rubbed his hands together in anticipation. 'Just wait till you taste it! It will be like nectar for the gods!' Tiger knew a lot about wine, and he enjoyed sharing what he knew. 'White wines are never actually white,' he would sometimes say, holding his glass up to the light. 'They can be yellow or amber or green or golden – the more colour, the more flavour there is. But watch out if a wine is brown – it's almost certainly bad. Worse than piss.' He also delighted in the elaborate rituals attached to the serving of wine, and though haste was important in every other corner of his life, he was respectfully unhurried in the presence of a Château d'Yquem. When the waiter poured the first trickle for tasting, Tiger had a long look at it to begin with, turning the glass round by its stem, then took a quick whiff followed by a second deeper whiff, and only when he had exhaled completely did he put the glass to his lips and take a sip. 'Ah, the taste, the fragrance, the sensation,' he whispered, slipping into the language of love, the gratification of desire. Everything was purified and rendered new. It was hard to believe that this happy man could have been morose in the hotel lobby only minutes before. A fine wine can change the world.

On the last day of the Book Fair, my colleague from the Old Guard, the one who dropped his aitches, sidled up to Tiger and announced: 'The eagle 'as landed.' Tiger gave a nod and said, 'Understood.' When the Old Guard left, I risked asking Tiger what this meant, but he wouldn't tell me. He said that I would find out that evening and added, mysteriously, 'We have a tradition at Frankfurt.' During dinner there was an air of expectancy, and afterwards we went back to Tiger's hotel suite. He put a DO NOT DISTURB sign outside the door, drew back the curtains, opened all the windows and arranged the chairs in a circle. I prepared mentally for some black magic ritual. I earnestly hoped it would be brief and untroubling. A few moments later, however, once we were seated, two spliffs were solemnly removed from a box, lit and passed round. No one said a word. We puffed in turn, in stoned silence.

By the end of the Book Fair I had made several contacts with literary agents, some in the UK, others in Europe. As soon as I got back I set about buying books in Russian and giving them out to professional translators. It felt like a real job now. A year later, towards the end of 1982, I got an unexpected break.

~

At 8.30 a.m. on 10 November 1982, Leonid Brezhnev, First Secretary of the Communist Party, died of a heart attack. In keeping with Soviet tradition, however, his death was kept secret for over twenty-four hours. The first sign that something was amiss came on the evening of 10 November when television schedules were suspended and sombre music was played instead. This gave rise to speculation that Andrei Kirilenko, a prominent member of the politburo, was gravely ill, or even – as *The Times* suggested in its headline the following day – dead. Rumours about Kirilenko's terminal illness had been circulating for some time, but they were actually part of a disinformation process orchestrated by Andropov, then head of the KGB. In fact, Kirilenko was alive and well; he was simply in the process of becoming invisible.

The gap between Brezhnev's death and the official announcement gave me my first (and only) publishing coup. As so often in these cases, timing played a crucial part in the sequence of events. A few weeks before, towards the end of October, I had been asked by one of my colleagues, a formidable 'young woman with connections' (YWWC), if I would read a manuscript in Russian – something rather special and hush-hush, she said – for one of the editorial directors at Collins publishers. The book had come highly recommended by the literary agent but the publisher urgently needed a reader's report to help him decide. The report had therefore to be done quickly – in a matter of days – but Collins would offer a decent reader's fee as an incentive. The YWWC said all this *sotto voce*, in the manner of someone plotting, or at least someone entering into the spirit of someone else's plotting. I was intrigued and agreed to have a look at it.

Since I was travelling back to Scotland that very day, the YWWC arranged for the manuscript to be sent over by motor-bike courier – even this was a bit of a thrill. Inside the fat package there was a covering letter on headed notepaper with tantalising references to the confidential nature of the arrangement I was entering into. The manuscript, entitled *Red Square*, was 'shit-hot', so it said, and I was to speak to nobody about its contents. I was to report within three days to the publishing director summarising the plot and giving a view on its commercial potential. In addition I was to say how it compared with *Gorky Park*, the recent thriller by Martin Cruz Smith, also published by Collins.

With the manuscript tucked tight under my arm, I arrived at King's Cross station, feeling the *frisson* of conspiracy and subterfuge. I looked around, half-expecting to be mugged or pierced by a poison-tipped umbrella. On the train I found a seat with a table, laid out the huge typescript, about seven hundred pages, and started reading.

The book began with a telegram appointing a special investigator at the Chief Public Prosecutor's Office to look into the circumstances surrounding the death of the First Deputy Chairman of the KGB, a man by the name of General Tsvigun. A classic beginning in the detective novel mode, except that Tsvigun was not a fictional character, but the actual former

First Deputy Chairman of the KGB and also the brother-in-law of Leonid Brezhnev. Earlier in the year, *Pravda* had reported Tsvigun's death as the result of a 'prolonged illness'. According to Kremlin-watchers, however, this was an implausible explanation since his health had been good. In *Red Square* the special investigator conducts an inquiry into whether Tsvigun had committed suicide – the version of events favoured by Andropov, head of the KGB – or whether in fact he had been murdered.

By the time the train arrived in York I had established that the book before me was a compelling blend of fact and fiction, a kind of *réalité à clef*. It relied heavily on reportage and our natural fascination with corruption in high places. The joint authors, Topol and Neznansky, presented much of the material through official documents, telegrams and internal memos, all precisely dated and timed. The unfolding story therefore had an authentic ring, helped no doubt by the fact that one of the authors had worked in the Prosecutor's office and later practised as a lawyer in the Moscow City Collegium. By Newcastle I was hooked, and by Berwick-on-Tweed I was wishing that the agent had offered it to me for consideration instead of to the man at Collins. By Edinburgh, there had been two murders and several death threats. Inverkeithing, Kirkcaldy, Ladybank and Cupar were swallowed up in a rush of espionage, sex and corruption.

Over the weekend I wrote a reader's report of *Red Square* recommending it unreservedly for publication. I said it compared well with *Gorky Park*, and because there was a blend of known facts and events it had the added advantage of sounding more true-to-life. I posted the report and sent the manuscript under separate cover to Collins in London. A few days later, on 10

November, I had a telephone call at home from a literary agent whom I had met in Frankfurt the previous month and from whom I had bought a couple of Russian books. She said that she was ringing to offer me 'something special' and that she would send it to me provided she could have a quick answer on it. When she said the book was a thriller and that it was very hush-hush, I had a sense of something familiar.

'What's it called?' I asked.

'*Red Square.*'

'No need to post it then – I've read it.'

'But you can't have done,' she said. 'I've only shown it to one other publisher. Apart from that it's been kept completely under wraps.'

I explained the situation and told her that I had written a favourable report for Collins. She said they had declined to make a firm offer and, as far as she was concerned, the deadline had passed. She would be happy to do business with me if I wanted to make a 'reasonable offer', but she couldn't give me much time. Although it was late afternoon and I was busy with the children, I said I would get back to her that day. Tiger never left the office before 6 p.m. I telephoned him immediately. 'Buy it!' he whooped. 'Make her an offer.' His enthusiasm was sometimes quite wonderful. If an idea appealed to him, he never minded spending money. He was also able to make his mind up immediately, an unusual quality in a publisher, and once he had done so he didn't waver or go back on his decision. Within an hour, the deal was concluded and the English language rights had been secured for £4000. At around six o'clock the agent and I shook hands on it over the telephone.

The next morning it was announced to the world that

Brezhnev was dead. Very dead. Indeed, when I was negotiating to buy *Red Square*, Brezhnev was already laid out for burial. If this had been known at the time, the price would have been many times what we paid for it. In an instant the book had become extraordinarily topical: it dealt with an attempted coup on the Kremlin, spearheaded by Andropov for his own political gain; and with Brezhnev now dead, Andropov was poised to take over as leader. Suddenly this book was dynamite.

Tiger was delighted. He immediately issued a press release saying that we hoped to publish early in the New Year.

'How soon can we do it?' he asked me.

'I've no idea. But 150,000 words – that's a huge undertaking.'

'Nothing is impossible,' he said.

'I'll see what I can do,' I promised. It was the sort of thing builders say when they know it's hopeless but don't want to lose the contract for the new roof.

'It has to be January, not February,' he said. And then, as if imparting a state secret, he lowered his voice. 'Beloved,' he said, 'February is too late. It *has* to be January. Otherwise we're dead.'

Tiger said 'otherwise we're dead' a lot, which rather lessened its intended impact. In the present case, however, time was obviously crucial. We had to take advantage of the huge surge of public interest in the Soviet Union. But the length of the book was too much for one translator to handle in the time available. It would have to be a collaborative effort.

After a few phone calls I had managed to get three old friends from the Russian world on board. Part of the agreement was that their identity would be protected – they did not want to be named as translators of the book. It was important to them to be able to travel to the Soviet Union, and this sort of work might have put their visas at risk. They were academics, all of them excellent linguists, and quite keen to earn some extra money. It helped a lot that Tiger had made a large budget available for the translation.

For the second time the manuscript made its way up to Scotland, this time on an aeroplane. The first thing to do was to make three more copies so that the translators could read it as soon as possible. I had already decided that I would not simply divide the book into thirds – that way the breaks would surely be obvious. I thought it would be better if everyone did a stint from the beginning, the middle and the end. My job would be to iron out the stylistic creases and cracks, to homogenise the whole translation.

Meanwhile a scurrilous story appeared in *Private Eye* alleging that Tiger had outbid Collins for the book when they had believed 'they had the deal sewn up'. I was named as the villain of the piece and, though I was elevated to the rank of professor and described as 'a noted Russian expert', I had evidently 'duped' Collins into allowing me to read the manuscript 'for a substantial fee'. Tiger reached for his lawyer and threatened to sue. He delighted in being litigious, seemed energised by it. Faced with my sworn affidavit and Tiger's threat of a lawsuit, *Private Eye* published a retraction, which included the information that my substantial fee had been £65, minus the cost of the postage.

To make the January deadline, we were told we would have to have everything at the printers by 1 December. That gave us only eighteen days. It would take two days for the team to read the manuscript before the translation could even get underway. That left sixteen days, just over two weeks. It seemed impossible.

But somehow we managed it. Eighteen days of furious cottage industry, midnight oil, loss of sleep, black coffee and increased phone bills. There isn't much daylight in Scotland in late November, so we became like creatures of the night, toiling away in the dark. Every three or four days, we met at my house, usually in the evening after the children were in bed. We all had young children and working partners, so looking after children often had to be fitted around the translating work. During these meetings we made a list of questions for the authors, usually about slang from the brothel or prison, which none of us felt confident about. The authors were both recent immigrants to the USA, so I made long transatlantic phone calls, often in the middle of the night, to try to sort out the problems. The authors also faxed additional pages to remove anachronisms and take account of the latest political events. The whole translation also had to be typed up since the translators all wrote in longhand – it was before the days of personal computers. It was a formidable task, frenetically executed, and we could certainly have done with more time. But we got away with it. *Red Square* was delivered to the printers on 1 December and the first 10,000 copies were ready by 23 December. The book was published in January 1983 and the story it told made the *One O'Clock News*. A week later I was interviewed by David Frost on the launch day of the breakfast television programme *TV-am* – after adverts for washing powder and before Madhur Jaffrey talking about Indian cooking. The paperback rights were sold to Corgi for £25,000, and Kyril Fitzlyon, the distinguished translator of Tolstoy and Chekhov, wrote in his review that the translation was 'superb to the point of invisibility'.

Part Four
Moving Sideways

In the dead of night, alarms went off at the palace. The police rushed to the scene but by the time they arrived the burglars had fled. Tiger, summoned from his residence in Mayfair, was distraught. He didn't care about stolen office equipment and other standard swag. The only thing that mattered was that Kaiser, his beloved tiger pelt, had gone. It was an incalculable loss. New Scotland Yard took on the case, but when they failed to get a quick result, Tiger took matters into his own hands.

'I am going to infiltrate the underworld,' he declared.

Over the next day or two, notices appeared in the classified columns of the *Evening Standard* appealing for information about Kaiser's whereabouts and offering a reward for his safe return. Meanwhile Tiger sat by a special phone connected to a tape recorder, waiting for news from the hostage taker, living and breathing every moment of the drama. He made hundreds of calls on another line, his voice alternating between hushed conspiratorial tones and, when it came to the police whom he thought incompetent, full-scale roaring. 'My tiger is *irreplaceable*. I *need* to get it back! Don't you *understand*?' Like onlookers at a road accident, his entire retinue stood by, entranced by the ghastliness of it all. It was hard not to conclude that at some basic level Tiger enjoyed the excitement – he thrived on sensationalism, and the case of the kidnapped tiger skin had all the necessary elements. It also gave him a chance to take control. His plan was to outwit the police and tackle single-handed the shady world of gangsters and goons. It was pure theatre. In between phone calls he talked about the mindset of the criminal, telling Gothic tales of villainy and violence among the scarfaces, their wickedness redeemed only by a strict code of honour. It was this last point that convinced him that his 'baby' would be returned safe.

'I know these people,' he said. 'They will slit your throat, but they have tender hearts.'

He was right. The tender hearts soon got in touch and a plan was hatched. One of Tiger's girls – he always called her La Diva on account of her sultry looks and passionate tempera-ment – was to walk up and down Bond Street wearing a scarf in distinctive colours. Contact would be made, provided there was no police presence and she brought with her £1000 in used notes.

'She will carry the money in her knickers,' announced Tiger, masterminding the operation.

After parading in Bond Street for about ten minutes, La Diva was whisked off in a fast car and driven to King's Cross station where, in exchange for the £1000, she was given a key to a left-luggage locker in which she found Kaiser safe and well. Tiger and Kaiser were reunited, and both smiled for the cameras. 'I have paid a king's ransom for a king,' he told reporters.

~

Over the next year or two, the Russian list made good progress. The success of *Red Square* helped subsidise a number of less obviously marketable writers, mainly dissidents who risked reprisals at home by publishing their books abroad. Others, such as Kornilov, Kuznetsov and Voznesenskaya, had been expelled from the Soviet Union and now lived in exile in Germany. Many Soviet writers were drawn to Munich, the home of Radio Liberty (which broadcast to countries behind the Iron Curtain), and they were usually represented by literary agencies in Western Europe, mainly in France, Germany and the UK.

Perhaps the most famous exiled writer at the time was Georgii Vladimov. He had an international reputation as both a novelist and a champion of human rights, and in 1969 he had written a book called *Three Minutes' Silence*, first published in a censored version in the Soviet journal *Novy Mir*. It was set on board a trawler and provided a devastating critique, both explicit and symbolic, of Soviet society. Previous attempts to translate it into English had failed because of the almost insuperable difficulties of conveying the richly textured language of the sea together with the trawlermen's slang. Michael Glenny was arguably the finest translator of Russian literature in the whole of Europe – he had already captured Bulgakov, Solzhenitsyn and Nabokov brilliantly – and I was thrilled when he agreed to take on the Vladimov. Michael Glenny had a musical ear and he loved words. Their sounds and rhythms together with the power they contained were all elements that he excelled at bringing into English. *Three Minutes' Silence* was a formidable undertaking but he was equal to it, and the English translation came out in 1985. Just five years later, at the age of sixty-two, Michael died suddenly in Moscow after a heart attack. He was there to work on the archives of writers who had perished in the camps and he had arranged to receive documents from the KGB, the organisation most feared and detested by all dissident writers. This was an irony that Michael above all would have appreciated.

Another interesting writer on our list was Julia Voznesenskaya. She had founded the first independent women's group in her country, and as a result she had been sent to a Siberian labour camp. At home she was known as a poet, but after her expulsion she became the voice of those she had to leave behind. *Letters of Love* was an anthology of letters from women political prisoners to their husbands and children, written on whatever scraps of paper were available in the camps and smuggled out to their destinations. We also published *The Women's Decameron*, her account of ten women quarantined in a Leningrad maternity hospital, detailing the hardship and grim reality of their lives.

Naturally enough, most of these émigré writers wrote harrowing tales reflecting their own experience, and after a while the weight of all this misery was quite oppressive. Just by looking at the titles on the list I could feel the load of human suffering. In 1984, however, I was offered a book that was beguilingly different from the others. It was a haunting, magical tale of a young boy's first love and the discovery of something mysterious that threatened both him and those closest to him. It followed the cycle of the seasons and was set on the shores of Lake Baikal, the deepest lake in the world and so beautiful that Chekhov called it 'the pearl of Siberia'. Threatened by terrible industrial pollution, it was the perfect metaphor for the tension between old and new values in Soviet Russia. The book's author, Leonid Borodin, was first arrested in 1967 for being a Christian. In 1969 he had gone on hunger strike along with Yuli Daniel and Aleksandr Ginzburg at the infamous Camp 17, one of the strictest camps in the whole country, reserved for those who were feared for their ability to influence other prisoners. In spite of all this, Borodin continued to believe in the incorruptibility of the Russian soul – for him even the prison guards were not by nature bad men. This gracious faith shaped his novel and gave it a dreamlike quality. When I finished reading it, I decided not to give it out for translation but to work on it myself. In Russian the book was called *God Chuda I Pechali*, which became in English *The Year of Miracle and Grief*, a title that in some measure was to foreshadow the next part of my own life.

~

On a Monday morning in November 1985, I drove to Edinburgh airport to meet my husband. He was returning from Australia where he had spent two months on an academic fellowship. It was a clear day, the sun was low in the sky, and as I drove through Fife towards Auchtermuchty the curve of the Lomond Hills was a huge green dragon on the horizon.

On the way, I had dropped the children off at their primary school. They were madly excited at the prospect of their father coming home. Jonathan, aged seven, had been promised a boomerang and couldn't stop talking about it. His sisters, five and nine years old, chose bright yellow ribbons for their hair to mark the special day. Two months is a long stretch in the lives of young children, and at the start they had found it impossible to imagine the size of so many days and weeks lumped together. To help them get the idea, I acquired a huge roll of paper from a local mill, cut two pieces measuring ten feet by six, stuck them together for extra strength, and bound the edges with strong masking tape. With the help of a long ruler, felt tip pens and six small hands, the sheet was divided into sixty squares, each square representing one day and marked with the date and the day of the week. The children all liked the idea of filling the squares with 'something for Daddy' – a poem, a picture, an account of something that happened at school, a message or a short letter that he could read when he got back. I said it could be a sort of diary, a record of what they had been doing or what they had been thinking about when he was away. In a way it would be like speaking to him. I told them they didn't need to do something every day, just when they wanted to.

The huge paper sheet was pinned up in the kitchen. It stretched from floor to ceiling and took up nearly the whole wall. I explained to the children that for the first few weeks they would have to stand on a stepladder to fill in the squares, but as time went by they would be able to reach without the ladder, just by standing. When they could sit or kneel on the floor to fill in the squares, it would nearly be time for their dad to come back. The wall chart looked intimidating at first, very white and empty, but soon it began to fill up. And as the weeks passed it was transformed into a wonderful specimen of modern graffiti art. There were complex compositions in bold leaning letters or soft curly script, thoughtfully decorated with polka dots or crosshatching; and every so often, great surrealist splashes. Emily, the eldest, filled some squares with more abstract pieces that reminded me of the paintings of Mark Rothko – indeterminate shapes in muted, tender colours.

I arrived early at Edinburgh airport and sat down to watch the comings and goings. You are allowed to sit and stare at an airport without being judged a snoop, without feeling that you have to look away. You can even feel a kind of closeness with complete strangers. It's interesting to try to spot the different types of journey – you can easily tell the short business trip from the six months abroad, for example – and after a while you become expert at it. With young lovers, the length of separation is more difficult to judge; they kiss and embrace at the edge of a volcano, thinking themselves free and outside the rules, not yet doubting their ability to stay true. Young people can still bear the weight of love.

Observing men and women meeting and parting can tug at the heart, but you often see the best of people at this time, the moments when they are saying goodbye to one another, or else waiting for someone to arrive. Their faces tell a particular story – you see the precarious happiness in their eyes. The emigrations are unmistakable: there are usually elderly relatives in attendance, not knowing quite how to fill the last moments, trying to hold onto something before it slips away. The women touch their hair, the men hitch up their trousers. There are lost continents in these partings.

After an hour or so, the information screen said the plane had landed, and I made my way to the arrivals gate. The prospect of seeing my husband again made me light-hearted and light-headed. It was long before the days of electronic chatter, and telephoning Australia was still quite expensive. It had been a long time, without much contact, and we weren't very good at being apart. Up till then we had been separated for only a day or two at a time. Over the weeks we had written long, loving, missing-you letters – I have them still – in which we had vowed never again to be apart for so long.

Which was only one of the reasons why it was unthinkable, inconceivable, *incomprehensible* that just a few minutes after he arrived – at the edge of the luggage carousel, during the ding-dong chimes of information announcements, with passengers grabbing their bags, and an airport cleaner sweeping around us, and people watching as I myself had watched only minutes before – he declared that we were to be apart for ever. When he walked through the doors towards me he had looked uncertain, exhausted and, before our first mad hug, I thought – I think I even said – you're home now, the long journey's over, everything's fine. But it wasn't fine: he had met someone else, he had fallen in love, he could not, *did not want to*, live without her; he had come back only because he had a return ticket and because his job was here; he was sorry, it was awful, but he would not be staying; he would be giving up his job and applying for work in Australia.

My husband had never learned to drive and St Andrews was fifty miles away. How did I get us back safely? I remember only two things about the journey home: a buzzing in my head, and every so often a sourness, bitter as bile, surging into my mouth, forcing me to gag and swallow. I was driving not under the influence of drugs or drink, either of which might land you in prison, but under the influence of something much worse, but for which there was no name, at least none I can think of, and no law against.

Over the next few days the marriage was dismantled, not

systematically or by process of natural atrophy, but randomly and with head-splitting cracks followed by great chunks of falling masonry. During lulls, the two of us, the talking wounded, slumped at the kitchen table. Just a few feet away the children's graffiti creation, thick with love, stood its ground – the writing on the wall.

He moved out on 13 November. The newspaper on the mat that day told of a volcano erupting in Colombia, burying 20,000 people from four villages in the foothills of the Andes. The sudden end of a marriage has no narrative integrity: it is the muddle following a natural disaster, or a violent derailment. It seems to take place in the murk, and the murk is lit only by moments of bittersweet poignancy. It feels like the death of love; and all that remains is the mourning of it.

Translation is perhaps a metaphor for what is a basic human need: conveying in words our experience of the world. Whether it's the birth of a baby, the sound of rainfall, the getting and losing of love – we search for ways of expressing these happenings in a language that can be understood by others. In that sense we are all translators.

Cervantes compared translation to looking at Flemish tapestries from the wrong side. I suppose he meant that, while it's possible to make out the general shape and colour of the pictures on the front, a lot is lost and obscured by all those dangling threads. Cervantes was right, but he has not given us a reason not to translate, because even the wrong side of the tapestry can be worth seeing.

For those who translate for a living, from one language into another, the difficulties are immense. Translation is so much more than mere words. Such a lot is bound up in any language – the way sentences are arranged, the order in which ideas unfold, the cultural nuances and so on – and each language has its own particular appearance, its own structure, its own texture and rhythm and flow. In the end, of course, it does come down to words, and the best translators have an abiding love affair with them.

It's noticeable that when reviewers praise a literary translation they generally call it 'smooth' or 'unobtrusive', often criticising passages that sound 'foreign'. It is an odd idea this, judging the translation of a work that started life in another country in another tongue according to its concealment of foreignness – as if it were the translator's job to turn Murakami or Dostoevsky into John Bull. The idea seems to have come about because we tend to assume that a text that doesn't read naturally in English must be a bad translation. Which isn't necessarily the case, partly because some literary texts can sound 'foreign' in their own language, and partly because a translation into what is generally known as 'good English prose' might easily have ignored or lost the integrity of the original work.

Ideally, of course, the translated work should be able to engage the reader in much the same way as the original, to replicate the author's vision and the particular spirit of the work. But this is a formidable task, and sometimes impossible, particularly in those languages that belong to different groups. In Japanese, for example, the sound of a word often imitates its meaning, but this apparently extends far beyond the plops and kerplunks and cock-a-doodle-doos that we have in English. In Japanese the whole of the natural world – the seasonal changes, the different kinds of rain and wind, the sun and the stars and the oceans – all of these are represented by sound. For instance *hyu-hyu* is a light wind, *pyu-pyu* blows a little stronger, and *byu-byu* is stronger still. The translator will be able to get round this with the help of breezes and gales, but the onomatopoeic element is lost. More strikingly still, the Japanese also use sound to express their emotional lives: they tremble *buru-buru,* they weep *shiku-shiku* they laugh *gera-gera*, and their hearts pound *doki-doki*. Every shade of feeling has a corresponding sound association, which even the best translator will struggle to render into English without some of the vividness vanishing.

In Russian the problems are different. Because it is a thoroughly inflected language – the endings of words changing in both conjugations and declensions – it has a particular elliptical quality that is absent in English. A single verb, for example, can be used to make a complete sentence: one word can tell you who is doing what, how many are doing it, whether they are male, female or neuter, when it was done, and even whether the activity was completed or whether it is still going on. Although it is possible to convey all this in English and keep the sense, it is not possible to match it or retain the ellipsis. Does any of this matter? To some extent it does, if only to make us aware that the architecture of any language goes much deeper than its inflections or other distinctive features. In some profound sense a grammar expresses the culture of its people, their way of thinking, their *soul* – whatever we mean by that. All of this is at stake in the translation process.

There are other even trickier problems. To take a famous example, the opening words of *War and Peace* in the original are: *'Eh bien, mon prince'* followed by long passages in French spoken by Russians as if it were their normal everyday language. The characters in question are aristocrats who converse with one another in French for reasons of fashion and snobbery – something the linking text (in Russian) makes clear. Ironically the discussion is about the possible invasion of Russia by Napoleon and *'toutes les atrocités de cet Antichrist'*. Since French was a foreign language for the Russian reader, it is arguable that every translation should keep those sentences in French. Yet none does. But even if the French were kept it wouldn't have the same connotations for an English readership. The problem becomes even more intractable when translating *War and Peace* into French.

To take another sort of difficulty: the first sentence of *Doctor Zhivago* in translation reads: *On they went singing 'Eternal Memory'*. This doesn't mean very much to an average English reader, but for Russians these opening words evoke the precise atmosphere that the author wants to create. 'Eternal Memory' is a funeral chant so well known to all Russians that they can probably hear its haunting tones in their heads. But the English reader has to carry on for a few more sentences before it becomes clear that the writer is describing a funeral procession to a graveyard. The American edition of the book translated 'Eternal Memory' as 'Eternal Rest', which is not only wrong but also inapt in a novel where memory is everything and a sense of repose is wholly absent. A few lines further on we are told that some onlookers joined the procession out of curiosity and, when one of them asks who is being buried, he is told 'Zhivago'. Again, the significance of the name is lost in English, *zhiv* meaning 'alive' in Russian and *ago* being the adjectival ending. The answer to the question 'Who is being buried?' is therefore 'The one who is living.' Pasternak was first and foremost a poet, and his novel is full of allusion and poetic resonance – huge challenges for a translator.

My own love affair with words took time to get going. As a young child I was always slightly afraid of words and the power they wielded, and it was only when I went to secondary school and started learning Latin and French that things changed. I felt a sense of liberation – though liberation from what exactly is not easy to say. Latin and French involved lots more words, which should have been off-putting, yet somehow the structures were clear and consistent, unlike at home where the rules seemed to lack harmony and cohesion. After a year or two, I added two more languages, German and Spanish, to my list of subjects. Soon my schoolbag bulged with foreign grammars and readers, and with a missionary zeal I took on Russian in my final two years with a view to studying it at university.

I don't think I had a special aptitude for languages; which makes my focus on them all the more puzzling. Looking back now, I feel sure there was something more complex and desperate afoot, a kind of quest to understand the world, whose secrets might conceivably be revealed through a heap of different-sounding words. This wasn't how it struck me then, but even at the time I felt a degree of compulsion about acquiring one language after another, as if carrying to extremes might lead to the vital clue. There was always a faint expectation – certainly a hope – that I was on the point of discovery, that all would become clear, and that the words spoken by other people in countries I had never been to might be the key.

My parents were naturally suspicious of all these foreign languages. 'You can get too much of a good thing,' said my mother with a shake of her head, and my father disapproved even more. He had served with the Eighth Army for the duration of the war and his hatred of Germans lasted his whole life. The very idea of learning their language was anathema to him. It turned out the Russians weren't much better.

'But you fought on the same side as the Russians,' I said.

'That's as may be, but they're a bunch of commies just the same.'

To be able to translate, it isn't enough to have learned a language, however well you have learned it. There must be a deep connection with the author, followed by a devoted faithfulness. It has to be an act of love, without betrayal. You must try never to overwhelm or compete with the author, but always strive to shape the original text in a form that connects with new readers who are strangers to the original. It is as if you are engaging in a very intense form of reading that involves much more than simply understanding the words on the page – you have to absorb them and live with them a little, after which you turn them into something new, unique but not original, creative but not inventive, a palimpsest of the first creation.

Translators have to do a kind of disappearing act, and I liked the invisibility. I also liked the solitude that goes with the job. But in the end I decided I wasn't good enough at it and couldn't become good enough. There was a slight feeling of loss each time I failed to translate in the most literal sense – *to carry over* into my own language. The nature of the task does of course entail losses, but for me there were simply too many.

~

To begin with I didn't believe it – a common reaction in those who suddenly step from one world to the next. It feels like a stage set and you'll leave presently to return to reality. Well-meaning friends looked me in the eye and said, he's gone, he's not coming back, but I couldn't accept it. I also didn't allow the children to accept it. Daddy isn't himself – he needs some time on his own, I told them, thinking I was protecting them; though now I know I prolonged their agony and mine. For a long time the pain kept fresh, forming and re-forming day after day into new blisters and boils. It took even longer for the sense of raw panic to die down. When at last it did, and I let the belief seep through, everything had to be faced all over again.

For the next few months I avoided the editorial meetings in London. The thought of being away from home for even a few days alarmed me, and leaving the children was unthinkable. But regular trips to London were part of the job, and the job was now more important than ever. Eventually I had to go. After the meeting I asked to see Tiger in private. He listened to what I had to say, and when I had finished he sighed, and then said, 'Well, it's his loss entirely.' Which was kind and well-meaning, though I was still stuck at the stage of thinking the loss was decidedly mine and the children's. He also told me not to worry, that my job was secure, and that everything would be all right. I was moved by his gentleness and compassion.

'Don't be sad,' he said when I left. 'The worst has happened and from now on it will get better.'

That evening he invited me to dinner with his family at Mr Chows in Knightsbridge – 'the best Chinese restaurant in the whole of London,' he said, 'where all the stars hang out.' Tiger didn't bother with menus but ordered a magnificent feast straight from Mr Chow himself. Throughout the meal his generosity and attentiveness were unabating – 'Are you comfortable? Have you got enough? Can I help you to something?' – as he filled everyone else's plate and ordered more whenever supplies ran low. Although an emotional man, he wasn't comfortable talking about feelings or painful events, but I could tell he was trying to cheer me up, and to this end he stuffed me with food and crushed me with kindness. By the time I left London to return to Scotland I felt pampered and consoled.

A day or two later Tiger telephoned me at home. 'I have been thinking about your situation,' he said, 'and how I can help you.' He then spoke in a great rush about his 'brilliant idea': a book on women that would be 'unprecedented' in the world of publishing, 'the biggest and best ever'. He was so excited that he was hard to understand. The words tumbled out in huge untamed gushes and, as I struggled to keep up, his sentences would suddenly turn tail on themselves. The gist of it was that he would interview fifty high-achieving, well-known personalities – politicians, film stars, aristocrats, actors and so on – record their thoughts on tape and publish the results. He spoke of his 'fabulous connections', how he was sure that he could get famous women to talk to him, and how he was the perfect person for such a book. 'I *love* women – I *glow* in their company!' My role would be to help devise the interview questions, to sort out the transcripts, collate the material into different sections and finally put the book together.

And to give it some weight, there would be a long introductory section on women throughout the centuries – this also would be my responsibility.

'It will take your mind off things,' he said. 'You will have to work harder than you've ever worked before. But it will make you some money. This book will be *sensational*. I guarantee it.'

A batch of twenty-five letters was immediately sent out with a brief description of the project. After paying tribute to the woman's achievements, the letter ended with the honeyed words: 'Your contribution to the book will be invaluable. It will also mean that I shall have the pleasure of meeting you.' This first mailshot resulted in twenty-five acceptances. 'Can you believe it?' Tiger laughed with delight. 'Not one of them said no!' Predictably, when the magic number of fifty was reached he couldn't bring himself to stop: he was having too good a time. The next target was one hundred, but even that was soon exceeded. Every time he flicked through a magazine or watched a television programme he would come across a woman he just *had to* interview. His enthusiasm for the undertaking was uncontainable, and it spilled over into every conversation. He described it as a drug and marvelled at his own addiction. 'I adore women!' he kept saying. 'I *admire* them.' Once he got to two hundred he would stop – 'I *have* to stop,' he said, 'and two hundred is such a nice number.' Whereupon he promptly decided that he couldn't confine himself to Britain – what about all those wonderful women in America and France and Italy?

Soon his days were measured out in boarding passes and hotel rooms and, as time went on and he became ever more womanstruck, he started talking about his interviews in terms of a mission, something he had been called to do. He told the newspapers: 'I'm writing about women because I love them. All my life I have loved them.' He could make this love sound like a unique experience, exquisite and ennobling, not granted to ordinary mortals. Women, flattered by his love, seemed to love him in return. Surprise was expressed in the gossip columns that nearly three hundred individuals, many of them sensible with balanced personalities, were prepared to talk about themselves in such a frank way. But those familiar with Tiger's style – a lethal combination of charm and chutzpah – were not in the least surprised. His voice was silkily persuasive, and by giving each woman his complete attention, he managed to wheedle and sweet-talk his way into her interior life. One journalist, bewitched into talking her head off, tried afterwards to work out what had happened to her. 'It sounds pathetic', she wrote, 'but he made me feel special, as if I were the only woman who mattered.'

Almost four hundred letters were sent out, and the refusal rate was less than ten per cent. One of the more interesting rebuffs – in view of subsequent revelations – came on House of Commons notepaper:

> Please forgive me if I do not greet your request for an interview with cries of delight. I must have done a dozen similar ones this year alone. I am not a radical or a feminist, have met no prejudice only encouragement, am happily married and love my job, and I'd much rather discuss the National Health Service or the state of the economy.
> Yours sincerely
> [signed] Edwina Currie

The diverse list included Marina Warner, Olivia de Havilland, Princess Yasmin Aga Khan, Janet Suzman, Soraya Khashoggi, Doris Lessing, Isabelle Huppert, Gloria Steinem. There were women with names that sounded both absurd and paradoxically grand: Marie-Hélène de la Howarderie, Christine Bogdanowicz-Bindert, Ariana Stassinopoulos Huffington. There were socialites, actors, designers, writers – even a rabbi and a couple of nuns. Most of the interviews took place in the palace dining-room where, after quails in chocolate sauce washed down by the grandest of *grands crus*, the tape recorder was switched on and the women given enough tape to hang themselves.

Each interview was recorded on a microtape, about the size of a matchbox, and immediately dispatched by special delivery to Scotland in the smallest jiffy-bag available on the market. The Royal Mail guaranteed delivery before noon, and nearly every day, around mid-morning, the postman would arrive in a van with a tiny package, sometimes several. Everything had to be signed for. After a while I could tell that the postman was desperate to know what the packages contained and why I got so many of them. When we reached around the two hundred mark, he asked me outright, saying that his colleagues in the sorting office had told him to find out. 'Oh, they're audio-tapes,' I said. 'For playing on a tape recorder.' I could tell he didn't believe me. He obviously thought it too dull for words and knew it would go down badly back in the sorting office.

True to form, Tiger was in a perpetual state of anxiety about the possibility of tapes getting lost in the post. The agreement was that I would telephone him as soon as a package arrived, but he was always too fretful to be able to wait for the call and would phone me repeatedly throughout the morning. 'Is there any news? Has it come yet?' On being told that no, there wasn't, and no, it hadn't, he worked himself up to full-scale-emergency pitch every time. 'Oh my God! It must have gone missing! Isn't it? This is a *disaster*! It's *irreplaceable*!' I never really understood this behaviour – it was such a waste of everyone's time and energy – and although anxiety was unquestionably part of his make-up, the constant high levels had a touch of artifice about them; they were more a way of imparting to others a proper degree of urgency and respect for the importance of the project.

'You really have to stop now,' I said when he reached two hundred and fifty. My side of the project was becoming unmanageable. The historical account of the treatment of women in literature and mythology was well advanced, but with all the extra interviews the workload was expanding while the deadline remained the same. Everything was geared to publishing in the autumn of 1987 in time for the Frankfurt Book Fair. 'Just a few more,' he said, affecting to be chastened. 'I *promise* I'll stop at three hundred.'

It turned into a book of biblical dimensions: 1200 pages in all, and weighing in at three and a half pounds. It was wrapped in a cover of dazzling blue – a photograph of lapis lazuli marquetry from the emperor's private collection – and on the back flap there was a picture of the author, tastefully *chiaroscuro*, by Koo Stark. Tiger had travelled over 35,000 miles, mainly in Europe and the USA, and collected over three million words on tape. This was reduced to 600,000, all in an upstairs room in a tiny village in the East Neuk of Fife. I was helped in this mammoth task by my good friend Norma, secretary in the university Russian department at the time, a completely reliable and cheerful woman, salt-of-the-earth and Old Labour through and through, and not in the least perturbed by celebrity or the orgy of confession that she typed up night after night. We worked for long stretches side by side, often all day and into the small hours. Every so often Norma lay down on the floor between the stacks of paper and fell instantly and deeply asleep. Absolutely nothing could wake her, but in ten minutes she would be conscious again and ready for work. It was like a party trick, and the children sometimes asked her to do it so that they could watch her comatose. They loved to pinch her flesh and check her vital signs, and since she was dead to the world it seemed harmless. As soon as she completed a transcript I edited it and marked up selected passages for inclusion in the various sections: Early Influences, Creativity, Motherhood, Relationships and Sexuality. After that it was a scissors and paste job, quite literally, cutting up cartloads of confidences and sticking them into the relevant sections. Even the children helped with this stage.

The party to launch the book was held at the beginning of October in the Victoria & Albert Museum. It was a grand and glitzy occasion awash with blue cocktails perfectly matching the book cover and seeming to phosphoresce under the lights. Tiger stood at the entrance beside a blue mountain of books, beaming seraphically as his girls floated around in long tight velvet dresses the colour of lapis. Each guest was greeted separately with a personalised effusion, and special guests – the stars of the book – were hugged and caressed and wrapped in love. 'You look beautiful tonight. Just *amazing*. I'm *so* happy you could come.' Paparazzi clicked their shutters, and reporters queued up for quotable quotes. 'It's like the Hite Report,' he told them. 'I have unearthed the secrets of women.' He was wearing a fine wool *gallabiya* trimmed with gold. 'Women are softer than men,' he said, embracing a soft young beauty in a Chanel jacket. 'Much nicer.' He praised women's qualities – their capacity to forgive, their vulnerability, their fortitude – and he rhapsodised on their bodies. 'So much mystique,' he purred. 'You know, even their sexual organs are on the inside.' There was a kind of innocence about all this, as if he had just happened on an eternal truth.

Before long he was being fêted as the man who had unlocked the mystery of half the human race for the good of the world. *The Times* serialised the book for a whole week, and the author embarked on a promotional tour, simpering and sashaying and emoting his way round the country. He gave countless interviews, all the while building momentum and making ever more magnificent claims for the undertaking: it was a work unlike any other, a noble enterprise representing the highest ideals of human achievement, throwing a unique light on the female sex at the end of the twentieth century; it would shatter preconceptions, it would shock and move and delight and alarm; it was a *necessary* book, vital for our quest into the social evolution of women, capable of filling the terrible void in our empty lives; it was a cause whose time had come.

One or two people were more doubtful. Mark Lawson, referring to the book as *Women Talking Dirty*, was perplexed by the compliance of Tiger's subjects, many of whom he described as 'reluctant to converse with their own mothers without an appointment'. And Germaine Greer described the enterprise as the nadir of vanity publishing. She said she was 'baffled' by Doris Lessing's participation. 'Normally she's totally unapproachable and I'm flabbergasted that she was taken in by the pitch that this book is an important work on the evolution of women.' But even Ms Greer admitted that Tiger would 'probably get away with it'. She put her finger on the reason in an article she wrote for the *Observer* magazine:

> [the author's] effrontery is balanced only by his charm. The day I went to interview him, I had a badly blistered mouth, four broken teeth and one leg hugely swollen and leaking from an insect bite. The dog-like gaze of the brown eyes gave no hint that I looked anything other than adorable.

The French edition, *Elles*, followed in due course. Photographs of Tiger alongside Béatrice Dalle, Isabelle Huppert and Emmanuelle Béart appeared in the French press under lurid headlines: ELLES DISENT TOUT – 300 FEMMES RENCONTRÉES ET ÉCOUTÉES PAR UN SEUL HOMME. The magazine *Marie-Claire* bought the serial rights, publishing pages of juicy excerpts under the banner: L'HOMME QUI, DANS LA VIE, A UNE PASSION, UNE SEULE: COMPRENDRE LES FEMMES. Tiger was in heaven.

The interview with Edith Cresson proved to be the most controversial. When she rose to become Prime Minister of France in 1991, Tiger sold the unabridged interview to the *Observer* newspaper. Her claims that Anglo-Saxon men were not interested in women, that they lacked the passion of their Gallic counterparts, and that one in four was gay – 'something you cannot imagine in the history of France' – created a new *froideur* in Anglo-French relations. It even gave rise to a question being tabled in the House of Commons. 'Mrs Cresson has sought to insult the virility of the British male,' protested Tony Marlow, a Tory MP and father of five children. All the newspapers covered the furore, and fired insults across the Channel. It was another triumph for the interviewer *extraordinaire*.

The *Women* book, as Tiger had predicted, did take my mind off things. And the £8500 bonus I received had helped to ease my financial situation. The immense workload, however, combined with lack of sleep, had taken its toll on my health. The months after publication were marked by one illness after another, and in the early summer of 1988 I was laid low for two weeks with a streptococcal infection.

At around the same time, my mother had fallen and broken her arm – not an obvious cause for alarm. But when I visited her with the children there was an uncharacteristic vagueness about her. In response to quite simple questions she looked vacant and uncomprehending, and she seemed scarcely to recognise her grandchildren. 'How long has she been like this?' I asked my father outside in the garden. But he was evasive, also defensive. 'There's nothing the matter with her,' he said. 'She's just tired.' When I got home I rang my mother's GP and told her the story. She hadn't noticed anything but promised to make a house call. Within twenty-four hours my mother was admitted to hospital. Tests showed that she had an abnormal parathyroid function, which in turn had released too much calcium into the blood and led to her confused state. By the time I visited her in hospital a day or two later she was completely deranged, hallucinating wildly and terribly distressed.

'No one must know about this,' said my father. 'We can't say to anyone.'

'But she's ill,' I said. 'It's not her fault.'

'I'm telling you – no one must know, and that's the end of the matter.'

The consultant said that it would be possible to operate, but only when she was well enough to cope with the operation – perhaps in a few weeks. She was put on an intravenous drip and her confusion gradually lessened, but not enough for my father to allow visitors from outside the family. Meanwhile, though I had recovered from the strep throat, a strange rash had begun to appear on my body – just arms and legs at first but definitely spreading. Since there was such a lot to think about – children, job, mother in hospital miles away – I more or less ignored it. There was also a new worry: the bank was threatening to repossess our house. Although I had kept up the mortgage payments, my ex-husband had borrowed against the house and it now looked as if the debt might be called in.

Before long, my whole body was inflamed and itching and pustulous. My GP arranged a speedy appointment with a skin specialist at the local hospital and, since the school holidays had started, the children came with me. When my name was called, I left them playing with Lego in the waiting room. As soon as the doctor saw me he asked if I had recently had strep-tococcal pharyngitis. It turned out that my rash was a text-book case of something called 'guttate psoriasis', a form of psoriasis that can be triggered by this virulent infection.

'Can you fix it?' I asked.

'Yes, but you'll have to stay in hospital for three to four weeks.'

I told him this was impossible – my mother was ill, the schools were out, and besides, I had a job.

'If you wait till the end of the school holidays the condition will only get worse, and then it will mean six to eight weeks in hospital.'

He said he would reserve a bed in his dermatology unit straightaway and suggested I let my husband make the necessary practical arrangements. To spare any embarrassment, I didn't enlighten him.

As soon as I came out of the consulting room, Emily asked me what was wrong. I had told the children there was no need to worry, but she didn't believe me and was on the lookout for anything ominous. I explained what the doctor had told me.

'You should go straightaway,' said Emily. 'I can look after the others.' She was all of eleven years old.

At home I phoned round friends but no one could take all three children, certainly not for several weeks. And the children wanted to stay together. In desperation I contacted my sister-in-law in Orkney and she heroically got on the next boat with her own two children and made the long journey to Fife to look after mine. I promised them they could come to Dundee every day to see me in hospital; there was already a rota of volunteer drivers. I then visited my mother – her hospital was miles away in the opposite direction – and told her it was perhaps best if I didn't see her for a while since I thought I had a cold coming on. Lastly I phoned Tiger to tell him the news – he wished me well and thanked God that it hadn't happened during the *Women* book. 'Can you IMAGINE?' he said. 'It would have been a TOTAL DISASTER!' I also told him about the threat of repossession.

'How much do you need?'

'Enough to buy out my husband and secure the house.'

'Don't worry – we will arrange a company loan. It's perfectly legal and it's interest free. You can pay it back out of your salary each month. Just concentrate on getting well.'

This was only one of several staggering acts of kindness during that time.

In hospital, treatment started immediately and I was plastered from head to toe in a thick gunge, like the wretched Marlow in Dennis Potter's *Singing Detective*. My fellow inmates fell into two groups: scaly and scabby or, like me, red and suppurating. I passed the time gawping ghoulishly at the festering bodies of other women – mercifully this was before the days of mixed wards – and comparing them with my own. But mostly I lay on my greasy bed, feeling unclean and remembering Sunday School readings about biblical plagues.

One evening, after I had been there for about a week, I was sitting with the other patients watching horrific pictures on the television news. An oil rig was ablaze in the North Sea – the Piper Alpha – and nearly two hundred lives had been lost. As we sat in silence, transfixed by the horror of it all, a nurse appeared and told me there was a telephone call for me. It was from the hospital in Kirkcaldy. My mother was dead.

The book on women marked the beginning of my time as amanuensis. It was a move sideways from translation and seemed to me to be on the same activity spectrum – catching the voice of the author and being a conduit for his creation. From the ranks in the imperial court I had risen unexpectedly to become Minister of the Pen. Tiger and I collaborated well together and it suited my circumstances perfectly to be able to carry out my duties from home. I felt lucky to have the job and didn't mind burning the midnight oil occasionally to meet deadlines.

Tiger had developed a taste for interviewing. He decided the next book would be a collection of in-depth interviews with prominent men – Harold Acton, Edmund White, Raymond Carr, Yehudi Menuhin, John Updike, Derek Hill, André Deutsch and about twenty others. 'Of course, it's *women* I love, but I want to show I can do men also.' In some ways men proved to be more troublesome than women. Lord Goodman had agreed to be interviewed, but only after vetting Tiger over a sumptuous breakfast and hearing about other distinguished celebrities who would be appearing in the anthology. Just before the book went to the printers, however, he wrote to Tiger withdrawing his permission for publication on the grounds that Richard Ingrams was to be in the same volume. 'It is inexcusable to have lured me with a number of respectable names, such as Lord Alexander and Lord Rees-Mogg,' he wrote, 'only to withhold the fact that Mr Ingrams was to be included in the book.' Evidently he had not forgiven the former editor of *Private Eye* for an alleged libel of him in the magazine. A placatory letter was sent to Lord Goodman reminding him of his avowed opposition to censorship and questioning the wisdom of bowing out in a pique. It worked, but his reply was designed to put Tiger in his place: 'In view of your pathetic plea, I am prepared, albeit reluctantly, to allow the interview to appear.' As an example of staggering pomposity, Goodman's letter is on a par with Mr Collins' epistle to Mr Bennet in *Pride and Prejudice*, about which Elizabeth Bennet asks her father, 'Can he be a sensible man, sir?' He answers, 'No, my dear, I think not . . . '

Read no history, said Disraeli, nothing but biography, and that's what I did to prepare for the interviews. Most of the interviewees had written autobiographies and I gorged on them. I loved formulating the questions, whether based on the research material or simply my own curiosity. We always prepared for an interview by going over the questions beforehand. I told Tiger what I had discovered about the person's life, explaining the reasoning behind some of the questions, and pointing out any sensitive or no-go areas. I always wanted more discussion time, but he was impatient to get it over with. These briefings became a form of jousting in which we both jabbed away, trying to get the edge on our opponent. 'Let me just *explain*,' I would say, but would be cut back immediately with a side wound. 'No, no! It's not necessary. I *understand*. You don't need to tell me.' Another lunge: 'But it's important – there's something you really should know.' Then the counter-lunge: 'It's OK. I know *everything* now. I'm very quick, you see.' And so it went on. I always had butterflies when I knew the interview was taking place, the sort of feeling you get when your children are sitting exams. I wanted him to do well and hoped he wouldn't fluff his lines. But I needn't have worried – he was always supremely confident. He gave the impression of having done his homework, and most people, flattered by his knowledge and interest, opened up to an astonishing degree.

Over time we both got better at it. 'We really are a fantastic team!' said Tiger. In the *Telegraph*, Bill Deedes compared his technique to that of a safebreaker, calling him 'a dab hand with the skeleton keys' and 'the smartest burglar in the business'. Tiger was ecstatic. 'He called me a *burglar*!' he trilled. Certainly he had the knack of inspiring trust, and the results were often remarkable. On the technical side, as it were, I learned how to shape and pace the interview, and also to insert into Tiger's text certain typographical aids to help things along. He had difficulty with words ending in *ism* or *asm* – they came out as *imsi* and *amsi* – so I was careful to avoid any socialism or idealism or spasms or fanaticism. Inevitably the questions sounded 'scripted', too scrupulously prepared, but the formula seemed to work. Once the question had been asked, Tiger was content to sit back and listen, something the subjects seemed to like and readers found refreshing.

Occasionally he fell on his face, usually when he bungled one of the questions, but generally he didn't know that he had and was therefore unaffected. It was I who cringed when I heard the tape. Once, in an interview with Julian Critchley, he misread 'John Buchan' and asked a question based on the writings of a certain John Buchanan. 'Buchanan?' said Critchley, taken aback. 'Buchanan,' repeated Tiger in a fancy-not-knowing-who-Buchanan-is tone. Another time, as I listened to the interview with Lord Amery, I remember curling up into foetal position and rocking back and forth. At an exquisitely moving point, Tiger is speaking about Lord Amery's brother who had been hanged for treason in 1945. He quotes the words of the famous hangman, Albert Pierrepoint, who said that, of all the people he had executed, John Amery had been the bravest by far.

'Did that make the pain all the harder to bear?' asks Tiger. A long pause.

'No, I think it was appropriate. He was an Amery.'

'He was a *what*?'

Another pause.

'He was an Amery.'

'*What* did you say he was?'

But the rough spots didn't greatly matter. What mattered was that Tiger had the talent for getting people to talk, and newspapers and magazines were keen to buy. There seemed to be no end to the number of people willing to put themselves through the Tiger treatment, and no one ever asked to censor the material or objected to anything that was published. Which was surprising in view of some of the eye-wateringly frank confessions.

The more interviews I edited, the more I noticed that even when the subjects didn't know the answer to the question being asked – had clearly never even considered it – they invariably felt obliged to give an account of themselves, and perhaps a more definite account than they genuinely felt. Someone who might have had no particular position on marriage and fidelity, for example, could actually sound as if his mind was made up. Tom Stoppard says somewhere that interviews should come marked with a warning: *This profile falls in the middle truth range.* By which he probably meant that the whole truth, the nothing-but that we swear to tell in the witness box, is a rare sort of beast. In interviews, perhaps even in most of our day-to-day dealings, we put forward versions of ourselves that are short of the whole truth.

The versions are interesting nonetheless. This is Enoch Powell describing how it felt to be a politician:

> It was rather like Luther in his reformation hymn: 'I hear the nightingale in the dark hedge, the dawn is coming . . .' That is to say, I sing in the hedge to my fellow countrymen in case the song I want to sing is a song which they also want to hear.

And here is Lady Soames, the only one of Churchill's children whose marriage survived, on the subject of infidelity:

> I'm always very sorry when I see that lack of fidelity has caused a marriage to crash to the ground. Fidelity seems to me to be a very important ingredient in marriage; it's part of the commitment. But equally I think it's in certain people not to be able to be faithful, and one must hope then that they are married to partners who can sustain that. For my own part I would have hoped not to know about it; and if I had, I would have hoped to keep it in proportion.

Tiger was drawn to people who had been involved in Hitler's Germany. He interviewed Diana Mosley at her house in France and corresponded with her for years afterwards. During the interview she managed to reduce the scourge of Nazism to fond, jaunty reminiscences about Hitler – 'He may have been cruel, but he wasn't mean.' She also said that the Jews behaved 'very badly' towards her husband, Oswald Mosley:

> In the end they practically made him into an anti-Semite. He never was one, it just wasn't in his nature, but he did think they were a perfect pest.

Tiger also travelled to Dublin to interview the writer Francis Stuart, who had spent the Second World War years in Berlin, from where he broadcast to Ireland on behalf of the Reich.

The basis of his hostility to the British was

> . . . their attitude of moral superiority. At one stage the
> Allied leaders, including Churchill, met in mid-Atlantic
> on a battleship and sang 'Onward Christian Soldiers'. That
> to me was so shocking.

Tiger was spellbound by him and afterwards searched for first editions of all his books. His keenest fascination, however, was reserved for the controversial film-maker, Leni Riefenstahl. After meeting her at the Frankfurt Book Fair in 1991, he bought the English language rights to her memoirs. 'She has such charisma,' he said. 'She hypnotised me.'

The German edition was over a thousand pages long, and had to be reduced by about a third to make it financially viable. Tiger asked me to work on the cuts and agree them with Leni Riefenstahl. At this stage a serious problem came to light. We had been told that there was an English translation – Riefenstahl herself had commissioned it – but it turned out to be deeply flawed, so full of clichés and mistakes and infelicities that it was virtually unpublishable. There was no budget to do a new translation, and the work would therefore have to be done in-house.

'How quickly can we do it?' Tiger asked me.

'I'm not sure.'

Since he wanted to publish the following year to coincide with Riefenstahl's ninetieth birthday, there wasn't a great deal of time. But it seemed too good an opportunity to pass up, and in any case I was getting used to tight deadlines. So 'we' did it.

In the autumn of 1991 we travelled to Leni Riefenstahl's

home in Pöcking, just south of Munich. It was a beautiful house on the shores of the Starnberger Lake, known locally as The House That Nuba Built – a reference to the royalties Leni Riefenstahl had received for her photographs of the Nuba in the Sudan. Horst Kettner, her long-time partner, invited us inside and served us coffee and cake. Horst had started as her cameraman in 1968 and remained at her side ever since. There was a whiff of excitement as we waited for Leni to join us. Upstairs we heard a door opening and a few moments later she made a dramatic entrance down the open staircase leading into the sitting-room, her high heels clicking on every step. The first impression was of a nimble, mobile woman who couldn't possibly be nearly ninety. She had yellow hair and painted fingernails and was wearing leopard skin leggings and a slinky sweater. She moved like a ballet dancer and welcomed us with a broad smile and both hands outstretched. Her manner was distinctly coquettish.

Before we got down to work she spoke in English about her reasons for writing her memoirs. She started off diffidently – 'I am not gifted for writing' – saying she knew the book wouldn't change things, and that because of her association with Hitler she would remain an untouchable. 'Nothing I say now will help.' She was quite hesitant in English, and before long she had slipped into German and embarked on an animated denial of the crimes of which she had stood accused for half a century. 'What's she saying? What's she *saying*?' Tiger couldn't bear to be left out. For quite a time she continued to dodge bullets that hadn't even been fired – she was interested in artistic excellence, not the glorification of the Reich, she had never promoted racism, she had never joined the Nazi party, she had no knowledge of the camps. 'I made films, that's all.

Films that won prizes.' She must have rehearsed these things so many times, yet she spoke with a terrific passion that seemed fresh and new, moving effortlessly between triumph and disaster, vainglory and self-pity. Horst began to look concerned. 'It's time to stop now,' he said.

I had imagined that she might be difficult to work with, but she wasn't at all. Despite her age she was still able to concentrate for hours at a time with only short breaks in between. I had already marked the suggested cuts in the text, and though each one had to be discussed at length she was generally in agreement. As we sat at the table, Horst hovered over her all the time. Was she all right? Did she want anything? Shouldn't she rest a bit now? He was completely devoted to her. He was only half her age, but this didn't seem to matter – they looked completely natural together.

At the end of our stay Leni took us downstairs to the basement to see her archive. It was a large, well-lit area, like a library stack-room, with rows of huge white cupboards behind sliding doors containing her cameras, editing equipment, slide collections and film reels. She was in her true element here. As she led us round the room her face was rapt, her eyes bright, her voice hushed. We were shown slides of Nuba tribesmen, slides of exotic fish from the Indian Ocean, slides of Japanese yakuza with tattoos all over their bodies. 'Look,' she said, 'even their penis is tattooed. They have suffered for their art.' Then she grinned. 'Like I.' Tiger loved this – 'Yes, the same like you!' he laughed.

As we examined different parts of the archive, Tiger kept saying 'Amazing! Amazing!' And indeed it was. Every part of her life had been recorded and labelled and catalogued, and it was all stored in box upon box, shelf upon shelf. The boxes were even colour coded: yellow for press cuttings, green for de-nazification documents, red for American correspondence, grey for German, white for personal letters and black for all the court cases – more than fifty of them. 'Amazing!' said Tiger, quite transported by the degree of organisation. He told her he had met his soul mate.

In September 1992, a few weeks after her ninetieth birthday, Leni and Horst came to London to mark the publication of her memoirs in English. I picked them up at Heathrow and took them to their suite in the Mayfair Hotel. She had agreed to do a number of interviews – against Horst's advice. He was cynical about journalists and very protective of her. 'They're all against her,' he said. 'They will destroy her.'

She got a mixed reception, and the questions were tough and often offensive. But she answered them sensitively and with dignity, especially on the subject of the responsibility of the artist. She insisted she was ignorant of atrocities and pleaded guilty only to irredeemable naïvety. By the end of the week she was exhausted, and during an interview at the BBC, on being asked yet again about the nature of her friendship with Hitler, and if they had been lovers, she broke down and wept. When we left the studio Horst was waiting outside, clearly furious about the grilling. He took her gently in his arms and held her till she recovered.

The launch party was held at the Museum of the Moving Image on the South Bank, an appropriate venue for someone who had changed the face of film-making. Earlier at the hotel she had laid out clothes on the bed and wanted me to help choose an outfit for the evening. '*Wie sehe ich aus?* – How do I look?' she asked when I went to pick her up later. She was wearing a silk dress in black and gold, a fur-trimmed jacket and sensational stilettos. 'Stunning!' I said. 'The most elegant ninety-year-old I've ever seen.' We had been laughing and I had meant it lightly, but she turned serious and told me that her longevity was a sort of curse: though she lived to be a hundred she would never be free of the burden of the past.[*]

'I'm too vain to wear my glasses,' she said, so she held onto my arm as we went up the steps to the entrance of the Museum of the Moving Image. 'Count out the steps for me – I want to hold my head high.' As she entered the crowded room under piercing lights, there was a hushed silence. Adulation was in the air. For one evening at least she was among friends, people who simply admired her artistic excellence and had come to pay tribute. Tiger, resplendent in a blue silk suit with gold lining, made a theatrical salaam before her and kissed her jewelled hand.

All round the walls there were giant screens playing *Olympia*, her film of the 1936 Berlin Olympics: breathtaking black and white shots of runners, pole-vaulters, and long exquisite sequences of divers flying through the air against a darkening sky, one image after another in slow motion like a tone poem. Artistic genius, or fascist celebration of the body beautiful? Whatever the truth – and we can never be absolutely certain – it is unlikely that she fully appreciated the significance of those moments in history in which she played such a prominent part. Perhaps she knew not what she was doing, only how to do it.

[*] Leni Riefenstahl died in her sleep on 10 September 2003, aged 101.

Part Five

La Belle France

Summer 1991. At Bordeaux airport we are greeted by the *gardien*. He has bad news. The goat has been killed.

'J'ai une mauvaise nouvelle. Éclair a tué la chèvre!'

Tiger reacts with horror, clutching his ears as if by doing so he could cancel what he had just heard.

'Ce n'est pas possible! Ce n'est pas possible!' he roars, and he goes into a sort of head banging routine, though in the immediate area outside the arrivals hall at Bordeaux airport there is very little in the way of suitable material to bang against, only the sultry French air. Tiger has a talent for making a bad situation terrible. The noises he makes are not quite human. In between the *pas possibles* he emits high-pitched mad-dog-barking-for-the-moon howls. He is hugging himself, his limbs taut, his head tilted oddly, his body revolving slowly on an axis of grief. He is wearing denim jeans and a loud shirt in colours not found in nature. I stand by feeling helpless and anthropological. Who would have thought the death of a goat could cause such anguish? It occurs to me that perhaps Tiger holds goats sacred the way Hindus do cows. At the very least it must have been a beloved pet to merit this scale of reaction. In which case, why on earth has this Éclair person killed the goat? And who is Éclair for that matter? Clearly a bit of a bastard.

He must have known how upset Tiger would be to have his precious pet killed for goat meat.

'Who is Éclair?' I ask after what seems like a decent length of time. Tiger is making repetitive movements like a caged animal. His distress makes him deaf to my question. I try the *gardien*.

'Qui est cet homme? Qui est cet Éclair?'

It turns out Éclair isn't a man at all, but a dog – one of three Dobermann guard dogs in fact, and Tiger's favourite. According to the *gardien,* Éclair is well-trained and normally of benign disposition, not overly aggressive. But recently he has embarked on a bit of a killing spree, first the laying hens, then the guinea-fowl, now the goat who was discovered in a pool of blood, his throat *déchirée*. For the avoidance of doubt the *gardien* makes a swift slitting gesture across his own throat. Éclair has even attacked one of the other guard dogs and – this aspect of things is evidently a particular affront to the *gardien* – it was Éclair's own brother, his own flesh and blood. *Sa propre chair!*

This was an inauspicious start to our first working trip to France together. Tiger's property in France had been portrayed as an idyll, a haven from life's stresses and strains. Now it appeared that the haven was overrun by mad killer dogs. There was no guarantee that this killing spree was at an end. Hens, guinea-fowl, his own brother, now a goat – he was obviously getting a taste for it. What – or perhaps *who* – would be next? The seeds of alarm were sown.

~

In the mid-eighties Tiger had responded to an advert in *Private Eye* offering the magazine's editorial retreat in the Dordogne for sale at a modest price. Apparently Lord Gnome needed to raise funds to settle a claim for damages. The property was described as 'unspoilt', which turned out to mean derelict and neglected, but Tiger bought it anyway, sight unseen. He set about restoring it at huge expense, and over the next five years or so, as more land was acquired, the modest retreat turned into two separate houses, a studio, a swimming pool, a man-made lake stocked with exotic fish, a vineyard and mixed woodlands, not to mention a whole landscaped hillside with *caves* tucked in underneath.

The journey time from Bordeaux airport to the heart of the Dordogne is a little over three hours by car, mostly on country roads with only a short stretch of motorway on the outskirts of Bordeaux. We made this same trip together several times over the years. Although Tiger himself couldn't drive, he took charge of every aspect of the journey. Mussolini made the trains run on time, and Tiger applied the same sort of efficiency initiative to our travel in France. Even before our plane touched down, everything had been planned with military precision. The *gardien* was to park the car, a Mercedes, in the short-term car park and select the bay nearest to the arrivals exit. He was then to stand in a prominent place at the arrivals gate and meet us with a trolley. Once the trolley was loaded, he was immediately to wheel it with all speed to the car while we marched smartly behind. The *gardien* was then to open the car doors, first the front passenger door for Tiger, next the back nearside door for me, before putting the luggage in the boot. As soon as he had stowed the trolley in the trolley bay, he was to drive to the exit, insert the parking ticket in the meter to raise the barrier, and we would be off. This routine was perhaps a little precise for most people's taste, but it was straightforward enough, or so one might imagine. The execution, however, was always fraught. Tiger made it so.

As soon as the automatic doors of the arrivals hall opened, he would immediately launch into a stream of invective against the *gardien*.

'Where is he? Where is he? *Where the fuck is he?* I don't believe it! Son-of-a-bitch! He's supposed to *be* here. I told him to wait at the front!'

Yet this tirade was gratuitous, for the *gardien* was always there, standing faithfully with the trolley, right at the front as directed. He was never once not there. Indeed he had probably been there for hours, just in case the plane arrived early. But Tiger didn't ever reappraise the situation or withdraw from this kind of attack, even when it was clear that it was without basis. At such times the world was evidently against him, and he had to deal with it in the best way he could. This involved anticipating disaster – and in these circumstances every conceivable hitch, however small, counted as disaster – and guarding against it. Thus:

'*Vous avez le trolley?*'

'*Oui, monsieur.*'

'*Il ne marche pas, le trolley?*'

'*Mais si, monsieur. Il marche bien.*'

'*Où est la voiture? La voiture est loin?*'

'*Non, monsieur. La voiture est tout près d'ici.*'

'*Vous avez le billet?*'

'*Oui, monsieur. Bien sûr.*'

'Il y a beaucoup de circulation?'
'Non, monsieur, pas beaucoup.'
'Il va pleuvoir?'
'Non, monsieur, il fait beau.'

This sort of exchange, endlessly configured and reconfig-ured, took place each time we arrived in France. Tiger always belligerent, fearing the worst, looking for trouble; the *gardien* unfailingly placatory, reassuring, a man of peace. It could have been a martial art. At such times, Tiger seemed vulnerable and I felt sorry for him. I wished he could have been less anxious. In between his fretful questions there were volleys of *'Allez! Allez!'* and *'Vite! Vite!'* which he discharged into the air with a slap on his thigh. As soon as we were seated in the car and the *gardien* was off parking the trolley, Tiger would exclaim in cadences reserved by others for calamity: 'What's he doing now? Oh, my God! Where has he gone? *He's mad!* I don't believe it!'

Was this genuine anxiety? Or was it a personality disorder? It seemed genuine, it sounded genuine, but its provenance was puzzling. The *gardien,* it was plain to see, was parking the trolley just a few metres away; moreover, he was parking the trolley as swiftly as any man had ever parked a trolley. It was never clear to me why we were in such a hurry, why this part of the proceedings had to be so stressful. Wasn't this meant to be a restful break from the mad scramble of London?

The need for haste characterised all journeys with Tiger. Only when he reached his destination did he begin to relax, and even then it was a curiously tense relaxation. Air travel was particularly challenging since all manner of things can go wrong. Bad weather, bomb scares, snow on the runway – the list is endless. Airports provide a serious test for a man who likes everything to go smoothly and speedily. Tiger knew that there was little he could do to prevent acts of God or acts of terrorism. He therefore did everything possible to expedite those matters that fell within his own control. His basic plan of action was to try to steal a march on his fellow passengers. The clear objective was to be first in the check-in queue, first through security control, first in the departure lounge. There he would pick the spot nearest to the boarding gate and stand at the ready like a sprinter in the blocks waiting for the starter's gun.

He always took charge of my passport as well as his own. At first I made a token protest – I was a grown woman, couldn't I be trusted with my own passport? But this sort of objection always made matters worse and I soon learned to fall in with what was required. Falling in with what was required became a governing principle in many different areas of our relationship. Sometimes, when I was feeling particularly trampled upon, I told myself I was adhering to one of Gandhi's main precepts: active resistance by means of non-resistance. It is always possible to retain some *amour-propre* if you put yourself in the same frame as Mahatma Gandhi. Resisting by not resisting, according to Gandhi, is an alchemical analogy. Far from being passive, it calls for active love and self-control. It's a challenging concept and I have sometimes wondered if it might be applied more widely. Believing by not believing? Seeing by not seeing? Feeling by not feeling? Fucking by not fucking? Could these too be alchemical analogies?

It sometimes happened that Tiger chose the wrong boarding gate, or perhaps it was changed at the last moment. On these occasions there would be a mad dash across the departure lounge, with loud artillery instructions rending the air: 'Quick! Quick! This way, beloved! Keep up! Follow me!' People would stop and stare, speculating about the nature of the emergency. Tiger did not subscribe to British etiquette governing queuing, and he made promiscuous use of elbows and shoulders to get ahead. Once through the gate there were valuable opportunities for overtaking during the headlong rush down the tunnel. Alas, there would be the inevitable jam at the entrance to the aeroplane and in the gangway as passengers found their seats and stowed their hand luggage. At these times Tiger hated his fellow man. He wore the black scowl of the misanthrope.

As soon as we disembarked there were even more things to worry about, the worst being the absence of a mobile phone signal. On Tiger's scale of personal adversity this counted as a catastrophe, and whenever it happened he was ready to kill the evil-doer back in London whose fault he decided it was. 'How could he be so *stupid*? I told him! He's a fucking idiot!' And right in the middle of the concourse, with people looking on, he would have a temper tantrum, stamping his feet, cursing, brandishing the mobile phone, shaking it, trying to whip it back into life. When he got excited he spat a lot, and a fine spray of globules glinted in the light. Like the old Soviet politburo, he could look threatening and ludicrous at the same time.

The best and easily the most relaxing part of the whole trip was the journey from the airport to the heart of the Dordogne. Nothing was required of me at this stage. I didn't need to keep up, I wasn't accused of anything, I didn't have to act out my bit part in the disaster movie. I could simply sit quietly in the back of the car for the next three hours while Tiger issued brisk instructions to the *gardien* on overtaking, driving speed, braking and the negotiation of corners. And soon we would be passing some of the best vineyards in the world. When I saw the gates bearing the names Château d'Yquem, Château Margaux, my heart would lift.

I came to love the Dordogne. The landscape I know best is the Scottish glens, the corries and rock-basin lochs carved out by glaciers thousands of years ago. I feel at home in the haunting bleakness of Glencoe, the rolling hills of the Southern Uplands, the rugged headlands of the east coast and the pink granite rocks rising out of a green Hebridean sea. There is a wild beauty about much of Scotland and, in the Western Isles in particular, a purity of light and colour, which, once glimpsed, will stay with you till you die. The Dordogne is different but, like Scotland, it is a land of contrasts.

From Bordeaux it starts off innocently enough along the wide estuary with its lush water meadows and rivers edged with poplars. Before long you start to recognise the names from wine labels. First is Saint Emilion, enclosed by medieval walls, sitting on top of a rounded hill. Beyond it the river twists and turns in the quiet, beautiful valleys. The richness of the landscape is set off by countless châteaux that hang, seemingly precariously, over the magnificent cliffs above the river. They are evidence of the region's turbulent past when the valleys ran with blood rather than wine.

You cannot travel through the Dordogne without getting a sense of pre-history as well as history. The limestone cliffs rise steeply, sometimes sheer, and you can see the horizontal grooves in the cliffs that formed rock shelters and became the homes of pre-historic man. Some of the overhanging rocks have been worn into fantastic shapes – spectacular mushroom-like growths and swellings. They seem to have been there forever and they look as if they will last forever. Henry Miller, who feared for the future of France during the ravages of the Second World War, thought that the Dordogne alone was imperishable. 'France may one day exist no more,' he wrote, 'but the Dordogne will live on, just as dreams live on and nourish the souls of men.'

Happily, there aren't many straight stretches of road, so you don't race along and miss everything the way you do on the M1. The road mostly weaves and winds with the river, altering the perspective with every turn, and checking the speed so that it's possible to notice fine details: enormous pink tomatoes on a market stall at the side of the road, old men standing on corners hitching their trousers, the shine on courgettes growing in the field. The pace was too slow for Tiger, of course, but even he couldn't straighten the bends in the road. Every so often there would be an unexpected hold-up, a farmer moving his cattle, a tractor crossing the road. At these times he would squeeze his temples and exclaim *'Mon Dieu! Qu'est-ce qui se passe?'* The *gardien* would dutifully explain what was plain for all to see.

The natural colour of the region is limestone, sometimes marble-white, sometimes wheat-yellow, but often dyed pink or amber by the ore in the rock. The countryside changes markedly with the seasons, becoming a kaleidoscope of shifting shapes and colours. In springtime, my favourite time, the hills look like busy weavers' looms, so quickly are they transformed by the different varieties of flowers. In autumn the colours are darker, purples and browns mainly, warm patchwork quilts covering the hillsides, repudiating the chill yet to come.

Autobiography is unreliable. A lot of what we remember is designed to shield us from painful truths. As is a lot of what we forget, or choose to forget. Divorce changes every aspect of life – that much I had already discovered. It requires radical adjustments in all the settled corners. You don't know what to keep, what to throw away. And sometimes, when you try to hold onto something to stop it slipping away, it slips away anyway. The substance, the detail – both of which once seemed so important – leak away into the dry sand, leaving just the faintest imprint.

By 1991, the year of my first visit to the Dordogne, six years had passed since the unhitching of my marriage. It's easy to underestimate the sheer bloody agony of separation and divorce, particularly since they are now so run-of-the-mill. To be married and then, suddenly, to be not married packs a violent punch. You move headlong from one reality to another. Being abandoned is not unlike being bereaved, and the shock can be just as great. Abandonment, however, comes without the fringe benefits of bereavement. There is mostly an absence of compassion and, though it is rare for sympathy to be completely withheld, it is quite usual to pick up in others the feeling that marital breakdown is not a blameless state, as widowhood is judged to be. Those who are left, so it seems, have colluded in their own downfall.

Widows and widowers are allowed to grieve, encouraged even, but the grief which attends marriage breakdown is often a silent secret thing. When a partner dies, the happy memories are sustaining, even if – perhaps especially if – they are touched up by a falsely bright light. Yet when a marriage falls apart, every happy memory is threatened, and the good times can be blackened overnight. There is nothing that cannot be re-interpreted. Divorce violates the present, but it also slithers backwards on its filthy tentacles and desecrates the past.

I did not recover quickly. It can take a long time to get the burning molten stuff out of the way. There ought to be a word for it – what people go through at this time. For the first few months I spent the days wishing for the nights to come, so that I could take off my brave face; and for many nights the misery of weeping and wakefulness made me long for daybreak and the release it would give. Lying in my great salt lake, I marvelled at the efficiency of tear-ducts. It is an exhausting business, just getting through, facing down unhappiness, trying to outwit it.

Meanwhile the children poured love all over me. And also over each other, some days seeming to fill all the available space with it. We kept busy – going down the track to the beach, gathering driftwood for fires, roasting potatoes in the embers, reading stories, making music together, hugging a lot, trying to come through. A lot of this time felt good and precious. In between editing and translating I tamed the garden, sawed fallen trees, chopped logs. The energy of grief is awesome. Weekends consisted in non-stop activity, or the simulation of it. This stage had its own value, its own rhythm. I existed only for the children – that was my sense of it. But of course, children are never truly an 'only': they are the best reason for existence, and being with them is the finest model we have of what it is to love. Every day, in large ways and small, they show us what it means.

You can't hurry grief. Even when the rawness heals, there

is still something heavy waiting in the wings, ready to engulf you if you let it. But slowly, gradually, something that could be called normal tiptoed back. And with it the faintest notion, once inadmissible, that something good would stagger out of the wreckage.

Men often assume that women who live on their own are desperate for sex. Women tend to get irritated by this assumption, and when the assumption is correct, as it usually is, they get even more irritated. And sex can look like love if you are confused about what love looks like. Men appeared from nowhere, like door-to-door salesmen, expecting rebuff but eager to display their wares anyway. Some were eager to the point of idiocy, and most bore the livery of solitary, unhappy lives. But evidently I had become hard to please. I knew – if I had not known before – it would take a long time before I was able to relax again, learn to let go again. I pencilled it in for some date in the distant future.

By the time the years had passed, however, an unlooked-for contentment had crept in and taken up residence. Being on my own no longer felt incomplete or wanting. I had adapted well. Life was good.

And then of course, just as I dropped my guard, it happened – bang! The oceanic moment, then the whelming and the vividness of – of what? Simply this: of coming to love again, and being loved in return. Put like that, this new love might be thought to be the same sort of thing I had known before. All I can say is that it did not feel the same, and it never has. Perhaps the intervening years had blocked the once familiar pathways, but there is no real way of telling. At any rate the world suddenly altered in the early part of 1991, and some months later, after the first madness had subsided, I sat in the back of a car travelling through the valley of the Dordogne and, looking up towards the distant peaks of the Massif Central, I thought of this new love back in Scotland and the mountains behind the mountains behind the mountains.

During the early nineties Tiger and I made several trips to the Dordogne together. Each visit lasted about two weeks. Tiger described them as working holidays, to himself and to others, but in fact the work proportion was often negligible. Sometimes there were proofs to correct or a book review to write, but it seemed that my chief *raison d'être* was to provide some company. He hated to be by himself. A routine was established during my first stay and adhered to rigidly on every subsequent trip. The routine governed eating, shopping at the market, watching cable television, afternoon swims, walks round the estate and feeding the dogs.

The last of these filled me with terror. Every second day, just before midday, the dogs were fed on raw meat. This was a high point for Tiger. The procedure was greatly ritualised, carried out with sacramental solemnity. First the three dogs would be shut in their kennels by the *gardien*, a preliminary to the feeding exercise. The kennels were situated about two hundred metres from the main house. They were the size of potting sheds and beautifully appointed with everything an *haut monde* dog could desire. The dogs knew the routine and would immediately work themselves up into a frenzy, throwing themselves against the kennel doors and barking their overbred heads off. The *gardien* would then fetch a basin of bloody meat from the back of his van, walk over to the paved patio where Tiger was waiting, and there he would ceremoniously hand over the basin as if it were the blessed Eucharist itself. Next, the dogs were put on stout leads, more like harnesses, and brought down from their kennels. I found it a terrifying sight: the *gardien* pulling one way, the dogs another, four sets of teeth being bared – the *gardien*'s as a result of straining every sinew to keep control, the dogs' collective choppers getting ready for the fresh meat on offer. But Tiger found it exhilarating. While the *gardien* kept a tight grip on the leash, Tiger would throw chunks of meat at each dog in turn, issuing commands in French – *'Asseyez-vous! Restez tranquilles!'* – making them wait their turn, showing them who was boss. He loved this feeding ceremony and he wanted me to love it too.

'Come, beloved! They are your friends! They love you! Give them some meat!'

But I never did. The very idea made my bowels turn over. I am enough of an Aristotelian to know that virtue resides in the middle way. A choice has to be made between absolute recklessness and absolute cowardice. The happy medium in this case was to stand in the relative safety of the doorway, half-paralysed with fear.

Tiger and I disagreed comprehensively on the subject of the guard dogs. As far as Tiger was concerned, his Dobermanns were noble, blue-blooded animals, standing out from less thorough breeds as aristocrats, dogs that could fittingly and effortlessly guard the House of Rothschild. They were not aggressive, merely powerful; they were not hostile, merely energetic; not threatening, just playful. Linguisticians call this 'semantic bleaching'. He also anthropomorphised like nobody's business: the dogs were sad or jealous or excited or upset, they wanted to play, they wanted to rest, they were missing their mother, they loved their master. He worshipped their bodies: their strong muzzles and wedge-shaped heads, their clearly articulated stifles, the unequivocal lines of their frames. When he looked at them he saw Olympian athletes – sprinters, hurdlers, long-jumpers. What I saw were tightly packed homicidal frames waiting to tear me limb from limb.

Normally I don't frighten easily. But for me these Dobermanns were in the same category as piranhas and great white sharks. It's easy to avoid piranhas and great white sharks. These serial killers, however, were living in our midst. They were the psychopaths next door, and they meant business. Tiger loved their qualities of strength and power; indeed he identified with them. But I identified with the dead goat that I watched being buried by the *gardien* on my first visit. I couldn't help noticing then that it was roughly my size. Tiger, who was still upset about the goat, could not bear to watch the interment. But Éclair, the killer, got off lightly. Tiger could not stay angry with him for long.

'*Tu es méchant!*' he said, wagging his finger at the impenitent.

It is 1994 and we are off to France once again. This time we are going there to write a novel. The publication of several non-fiction books has brought Tiger a sense of fulfilment, but there has been no lasting contentment. As the ancients knew and understood, pleasure is transient: it comes, it is savoured, and it goes. Descartes thought that the secret of happiness was to be satisfied with what you know you can have, and not to hanker after something you can't have. But Tiger differs from both the ancients and Descartes in his belief that almost anything is attainable provided you pay for it, and that by setting the sights high the chances of pleasure being permanent are correspondingly high.

And so, from one moment to the next, anything can happen. A moment ago a sixth volume of interviews was published, attended by a good deal of media interest, favourable reviews, and another round of newspaper profiles. In the *Daily Telegraph* Allan Massie described Tiger as 'masterly and sympathetic, the most self-effacing of interviewers and yet able to speak as an equal'. Robert Kee called him 'a magician interviewer of the highest order'. William Trevor wrote: 'Making real people real at second hand isn't as easy as it seems . . . it's the subtlety of interrogation that ensures these portraits emerge.' Tiger purred with pleasure. Everything was well in the world. The next moment we are writing a novel and the landscape has changed. *Sic transit gloria mundi.*

Tiger is convinced that the way ahead 'for us' lies in a different sort of publication. Interviews, newspaper articles, book reviews are all very well, but *the real test* is the novel. He lowers his voice at this point, enunciating each word slowly, a sure sign of scarcely being able to contain his excitement, elongating the word *real* to a disturbing length. He is captivated by the idea. This is not a whim. I know the difference between a whim and a serious proposition. This is a serious proposition. He will not be dissuaded. The tiger is not for turning. I feel the familiar panic pitching its tent somewhere in my lower abdomen.

'We need to evolve,' he says.

I do not demur.

How to write a novel? How to write someone else's novel? These two questions seem absolutely central. I wonder how I have arrived at this point without actually meaning to.

'What sort of novel are we thinking about?' I ask.

We are in the British Airways Executive Lounge at London Gatwick airport en route to France. The writing will be done in France. According to Tiger, France is the best place in the world to create a work of literature. Evidently we will have everything we need: the best food, the finest wine, a high-tech music system, a studio to work in, the fresh Dordogne air.

'We are thinking about a beautiful novel, very beautiful,' he says, and he looks somewhere into the middle distance, smiling rapturously, already transported by the sheer imagined beauty of it. 'And it will have a beautiful cover. We will make sure of that.' He taps out the last six words on the table.

'But what genre are we talking about? Are we thinking of a romantic novel? A thriller?' (These conversations are always conducted in the first person plural. The idiosyncratic use of pronouns is part of the charade and has become second nature.)

'It will be thrilling, oh yes. And also romantic. *Very* romantic. Oh, yes.'

'So, a love story then?'

'But of course! It *has* to be a love story. People associate me with love. I am *famous* for love. Isn't it?'

In certain circumstances, the plural pronoun would switch abruptly to the singular, from *we* to *I,* from *us* to *me.* There is always a compelling reason for the shift. In this instance, the snag is that people do not associate *me* with love. Unlike Tiger, I am not famous for love.

There is a long pause. The matter might have ended there, but for my need to establish the broad nature of the project. I have to ask some more. Tiger is almost certainly concentrating on the finished product, beautifully bound and wrapped in a seductive dust-jacket. My concern is how the finished product will be arrived at.

'What sort of love story do we have in mind?' I ask, as if we are discussing wallpaper or home furnishings and he has to pick one from a limited range. 'Is the love requited or unrequited?'

'Definitely requited. Oh yes, very requited.'

'And who are the characters?'

Even by our standards this is becoming an odd exchange.

'Sweetie,' he says, the tone long-suffering, humouring an imbecile. He takes hold of my hand in a kindness-to-dumb-animals sort of way. 'It *has* to be the love between a man and a woman. Do you think I could write about *poofters*? No, it has to be a man and a woman – a beautiful woman and very sexy. There will be lots of sex, but very distinguished. We will do the sex beautifully. Isn't it?'

'Long? Short?' I'm feeling desperate now.

He strokes his chin, weighing up the possibilities.

'Not too long, not too short.'

'And do we have a story line? Do we have any idea of what it is *about*?'

'Of course, beloved! I have thought of *everything*.' He squeals the last word in a spasm of exuberance. 'Let me tell you the idea. It is very simple. There is a man . . . he is like me some-

what . . . he is married . . . he falls in love with a woman . . .
there is a *huge* passion . . . and then . . . well, we will see what
happens after that, isn't it?'

There is another pause while I weigh things up. Then:

'Does he tell his wife? About the huge passion, I mean.'

'Darling, are you *mad?*' Tiger points a finger to his temple
and screws it from side to side. 'Why would he tell her? Why
would he hurt her?'

We had several more discussions just like that one. None went
beyond the man/woman/huge passion rudiments. At first I was
filled with a sense of the impossibility of proceeding on the
basis of such vague guidelines. But before long I realised that
vagueness is a blessing in its way. While 'Married man falls in
love with beautiful woman' is not exactly an original story line
or a detailed synopsis, it could easily be worse. For example,
it could be: 'Married woman falls in love with young army
captain in Moscow, has huge passion, cannot live with the consequences, throws herself under a train.' Or perhaps: 'Colonial
police officer in West Africa, married to a Roman Catholic,
falls in love with young widow, has huge passion, compounds
adultery with sacrilege, commits suicide.' You have to look on
the bright side. Much better to be given just the bare bones
to flesh out in any way that seems possible and plausible. Less
is more.

Tiger talked a lot about *passion* and *poetry* – the two main
elements that would underpin the book. He used the word
poetic sweepingly in the way others might say *beautiful* or *fine*.

To call something poetic was the highest accolade. It could apply to paintings, furniture, faces, conversations, encounters and many other things besides, notably sex. *Passion* on the other hand was a softening word for just one thing – sex. Over the years we had discussed sex many times, very often in the context of films we had seen, and he gave the impression that he favoured a kind of idealised romantic love with an overlay of crude fucking. I could sense danger ahead.

There is a great deal of nonsense talked about writing novels. The common assumption is that it is easy: we all have a novel in us, so they say. People talk carelessly about their intention to 'write it all down one day'. They encourage others with the same recklessness. They hear a funny/tragic/bizarre story in the pub one day and in no time at all they are saying that it would 'make a good novel'. As if the only way to give validity to a chunk of real life is to wrap it up in a novel. As if it were the simplest thing in the world. Where did this illusion spring from? It is a job to write a novel. And now it is my job.

Two days passed without a single word being written. I gave way to an assortment of displacement activities – sending faxes to my children, rescuing a trapped honey bee, filing my finger-nails – together with the modern equivalent of pencil sharp-ening: setting up the laptop, adjusting the chair, getting the ergonomics right. There was too much glare from the sun so the desk had to be moved. Perhaps an extra cushion would prevent backache? And iced tea would surely help things along nicely. But you can fool yourself only for so long. You can put things off only for so long. As it says in the Stone Garden in Kyoto: *You are here. This is now.* I stared at my blank computer screen and it stared back blankly.

How to proceed? Write what you know, they always say. But what did I know? Suddenly I knew nothing. In a bid to avert panic I decided to make a list of things in my favour. The list was not long but it was a start:

- I have written a lot already (just not a novel).
- I have read lots of novels.

For the first of these to count as an advantage you have to believe that all writing comes from the same place. I'm not sure that I do believe that. Writing prose is not writing fiction. The most I could hope for was that the experience of writing journalism, literary pieces, book reviews, and so on would act as some sort of training ground for writing a novel.

As for reading a lot, there is, sadly, no causal connection between the fact of having read fiction and the ability to write fiction. I know this at an instinctive level, and I think perhaps I have always known it; but this did not prevent me gathering together dozens of novels and taking them to France in my suitcase. It was an eclectic heap, selected from my shelves of paperbacks at home. I did this partly in the hope of discovering how to write a novel, and partly because I thought the systematic approach might compensate for lack of inspiration. The next two days were spent dipping into books by Penelope Fitzgerald, Anne Tyler, Carol Shields, Beryl Bainbridge, Alison Lurie, Anne Fine, Jennifer Johnstone. At the end of the second day I realised that I had been reading only women writers, surely a foolish exercise if I was to learn to write like a man. For the next two days, fighting off a slight feeling of frenzy, I read William Trevor, John Updike, Ian McEwan, Tim Parks, John Banville.

Spending days on end re-reading my favourite authors would normally be my idea of supreme happiness. But if you approach it as a technical exercise, it can remove most of the pleasure. I selected chapters at random, sometimes reading them several times, unpicking the prose, analysing the method, looking for clues as to how something was done – the way in which suspense, or perhaps interior monologue, was created, how one perspective suddenly turned into another without the seams showing. Gradually I became aware of different techniques and stylistic devices. When you are reading for pleasure and interest (the best way), you are aware of the good quality of the writing without necessarily noticing how it is being achieved. It's enough that it is there, and you are grateful for it. If the writer is skilled, the nuts and bolts don't show. How is the passing of time conveyed, for example? How to get to the flashback, how to jump forward in time? Is it merely to do with verb tenses? Or is there something more ingenious at work?

What I discovered was that, when time changes are handled well, you scarcely notice them; as a reader, you are perfectly happy to move through days and weeks and years in either direction provided your author has a safe pair of hands. The devices are subtle: the judicious use of a pluperfect tense, for instance, or the foreshortening of a character's history. The same applies to point of view: the narrator – even when the story is told in the first-person – has various tricks up his sleeve to allow the reader to know what the other characters are thinking and feeling. And the handling of dialogue was a revelation. Critics are fond of saying, 'the dialogue doesn't work', but when it works well it is, paradoxically, a kind of dialogue that people *believe* is spoken, or feel comfortable with; not what actually is spoken, which would not work at all. Often the very best dialogue is not in the least authentic. In real life, dialogue does not follow a logical sequence. People do not always listen to each other, nor do they always answer each other.

Of course, this systematic approach was doomed from the start. Utterly futile, in fact. In spite of all the unpicking and unpacking, or possibly because of it, it became clear that a novel is much more than the sum of its parts. It is a kind of commitment of oneself – an investment of something very personal. It is the writer's own energy, emotion and thoughts, in spite of the fact that these are conveyed by means of made-up characters. It is not mathematics; it cannot simply be reduced to different elements or separate equations. In all good novels there is something that transcends the constituent parts and resonates with the reader. This something is not quantifiable or discoverable or learnable. At least not in six weeks – Tiger's proposed timetable.

1994 was not confined to being The Year of the Novel. It was a busy year in other respects. On the personal front there were two deaths and a marriage – in that order.

Love has many elements, but scarcely any forms the basis for marriage. And marriage is precarious – my new partner and I both knew that – so it was never mentioned. Both of us had been left, that is to say that we had not done the leaving, and this single fact seemed to fix the way the light fell on the picture. It made us more wary perhaps, though it also bound us more closely. Three years after we met, however, the subject of marriage came up, like a crocus pushing through snow, when we were talking about Dante's circles of hell – at least that was what I was talking about, in particular the circle which is reserved for those who are wilfully sad. Without warning, he said: would I marry him, please? A long pause. Then, of course I would. Let's not wait, he said. This conversation took place in June 1994, three weeks after the death of his mother.

Falling in love gets such a bad name among mature adults: it's so twee, so outmoded, so mushily-slushily embarrassing. Women are counselled against it – it makes them dependent, passive, dewy-eyed. And strong men lose control – never a good thing. Yet we still do it. Even if we are suspicious of it, or marked by the pain of having once lost it. Falling in love just will not go away.

People who are not in love, or who have 'got over' love, condescend to those in the grip of love, or those who have just lost it. They say, oh, you'll get over it, or they welcome you, knowingly, back to the real world; but they have forgotten that love gives the illusion of a better world, a more beautiful one, a place where idealism doesn't seem inexorably doomed. Being *out* of love is the real misfortune. Being in love is perhaps not to be in the real world, but it is *ipso facto* more agreeable in a hundred different ways.

How had I managed for so long without it?

Meanwhile, in an overheated nursing home, my father was waiting for death. Four years before, diminished and demented, he had been booked in for life. At first he had to share a room with Mr Dixon, who sat in a chair with a wooden tray fastened in front. Mr Dixon stared ahead, unspeaking, apparently quite unaware of my father's presence, or anyone else's. But *his* presence was strangely unnerving, at least to me, and I felt obliged to talk to him, not to ignore him. Whenever I visited, usually with my children, there was always something loud on television. But my father and Mr Dixon had fixed expressions, suggesting they neither watched nor listened. Sometimes their chairs were at the wrong angle to the screen, and they both sat gazing past it. 'Do you mind if I switch off the television, Mr Dixon?' I sometimes asked. He never answered, but out of a kind of awkward politeness I pretended that he had, and that he didn't mind. I found it impossible to behave as if he weren't there. 'Would you like a chocolate, Mr Dixon? What's that you said? Oh, you wouldn't? Well, I'll leave it on your table in case you change your mind.' The children would sit wide-eyed during my inept ventriloquism, looking from me to Mr Dixon, trying not to laugh, so it seemed. And sometimes when they played together at home, this silent, staring presence was a character in their make-believe world. 'Shall I pull down your trousers, Mr Dixon?' I heard them say. 'Shall I put ribbons in your hair? It's really nice that you don't mind.'

One day when we visited the nursing home, Mr Dixon had gone. His chair was empty and his bed had been stripped. My father seemed indifferent. I told myself it was better this way. Much worse if he had missed him, longed for his company. Mr Dixon never reappeared, but for many years afterwards he was kept alive by my children who consulted him – an imaginary spirit at our table – on a variety of matters on which they were keen to supply the answers as well as the questions. 'What time do I have to go to bed, Mr Dixon? Oh, ten o'clock. That's good. Thank you very much.'

In the early months, before his strength seeped away, my father would occasionally escape from the nursing home in St Andrews. He would wander through the town, stopping to take in the sights – St Salvator's church, the medieval quad-rangles of the university, St Rule's Tower, still standing after forty generations had lived and died. Not being in a hurry, and looking slightly bemused, he blended well with the tourists. Sometimes it took a whole day to catch him.

But now he stayed in his room and made no bid for freedom. He seemed sad, vacant, his eyes looking out and in at the same time. Very occasionally his face would light up, and for a moment it could seem as if all was well and there had been some terrible mistake. These moments in their own way were more agonising than the others. But mostly he sat perfectly still in his armchair, staring ahead, doing his best to die. Sitting beside him, I could feel myself growing up. This is part of life, I told myself. This is what happens. Your parents die – they show you how to do it.

Two weeks before I was due to be married, they telephoned me from the nursing home and told me he was slipping away. I sat by his bedside all day, listening to his breathing. I talked to him, telling him the things that mattered, things I had never been able to tell him when he was not dying. Nurses popped in and out, jauntily, breezily. Did I want a cup of tea? Perhaps I would care to give my father a shave? It would make him look nice, they said – smarten him up, give me something to do. I rubbed in the shaving soap, tenderly, doubtfully, and drew the razor down his cheek. But it felt too awkward, too poignant. I couldn't do it. I said my goodbyes and left.

Next day they telephoned again and told me he was much better. When I went into his room he was sitting up in bed eating porridge. Evidently it was hard to die. He had come back to life, albeit a poor rendition of life.

He died a few days later, barely a week before my new marriage was to take place. The funeral was squeezed in a day or two ahead of the wedding. It was the right way round, we told ourselves.

~

Back in France I needed a beginning, a middle and an end. I needed them badly. I also needed at least two characters in order for the story to function at even a basic level – the main character, who was to be 'our hero', and the woman with whom he was to fall in love. The man, according to Tiger, was married, so perhaps his wife would also play a part in the story? Which made a total of three. Three characters don't sound terribly daunting – not as daunting as, say, four – but three characters can be quite daunting enough, especially when none has yet taken shape.

From one or two remarks Tiger had made I had a hunch that he already identified with the main character in the book. This was an interesting existential association given that not a word had yet been written. Confirmation came from an unexpected source, an interview with Tiger that appeared in the *Scotsman* newspaper around that time.

. . . His whole demeanour suggests passion constrained. He cannot sit still for long. He talks quickly, almost imploringly, and the words tumble over each other. 'You have to keep pushing at the boundaries in life,' he declares, 'or you don't exist anymore.' So, just as one tried to pin him down about his interviews and why he has done so many, he announces they are already in the past. From now on he is going to be a novelist. This is what is fresh. This is what is now. 'It is not going to be a beeg novel . . . It will be more a philosophical and a literary book. It's about my love of women and what would happen – what the consequences would be of such a love if . . . well, anyway, it's about a man who loves two women.'

'*My* love of women.' There, I knew it. A dead give-away. If it was a slip, it was surely a telling slip. There was now little doubt in my mind that Tiger saw himself as the protagonist. In some ways this simplified things – at least there was an abundance of source material to work from. But I soon realised that the fictional version of Tiger would have to be based on his own self-image. He could not be, like the most interesting characters in fiction, seriously flawed. No, our hero would have to be sensitive, compassionate, successful in business, of strong moral fibre, devout, impassioned and wise. He would probably also be something of a self-styled philosopher and he would have to have a great capacity for love.

And so, to work. I sketched out a plan in which the main character would be a wealthy businessman whose ordered life would be turned upside down by an extra-marital affair. This would arrive like a bolt from the blue and would coincide with a crisis in his life – the death of his beloved mother. I tried this out on Tiger. He pulled a face. Something wasn't right. It wasn't immediately clear what it was.

'Darleeng, PLEEEase, do we have to have the death?' He spoke imploringly, drawing out each word.

'You don't like the death?'

'I don't like the death.'

'Well,' I said, caught a little off-guard, 'I do think we need to have some sort of crisis, and a funeral is always quite a good focal point in a novel.' Then, gaining in confidence, 'Also, the emotional upheaval associated with bereavement would be a neat way of allowing the affair to take place. It would make it more understandable in a way.' Now the *coup de grâce*: 'I mean, we don't want to make him an uncaring bastard who cheats on his wife, do we?'

The mention of an uncaring bastard would surely be enough to win him round, but instead he pulled another face. I wasn't sure what was bothering him. He stroked his lower jaw and made a prolonged moaning noise, the sort you might make when someone is sticking a needle in your arm. Eventually he said:

'It's no good. We have to find another crisis. You see, my mother is still alive and, well, I don't want to upset her.'

This was endearing in its way, but not endearing enough to jettison the planned death. By now I had convinced myself I needed this death. Bereavement was something I thought I could 'do'; it was part of recent experience and I wasn't going to give it up that easily. We seemed to be nearing the edge of the unsayable, but I decided to say it anyway.

Gently but firmly, I suggested that it was important that the life of the main character was not matched in every single aspect with his own, indeed, it was essential that it wasn't; that the proposed book should be, in essence, a work of imagination; that it would be a pity if the critics dismissed it simply as a replica of his own life rather than a serious literary endeavour; and that it could quite properly reflect his own concerns while at the same time retaining its own artistic integrity. After which, he generously agreed – albeit somewhat ungraciously – to the death of his mother.

We had many conversations just like this one and we became used to our respective roles. Mine was to persuade; his – so I decided – was to be persuaded. I shamelessly used whatever devious means I could to coax and convince – anything to make the task ahead more workable in my own terms. I was cruel, and over the next month or two he endured a great deal. The main objective for me was not to win the argument but to gain enough concessions to be able to deliver the book. Although it would nominally be his book, and to that extent he would have to be happy with it, it was impossible to lose sight of the fact that the actual writing would be done by me.

Despite all the difficulties, we seemed, surprisingly, to have a mutuality of purpose. Tiger wanted the book to be done well, and I wanted to do it well. Ever since childhood I had been a watcher and a listener, taking it all in but not sharing with anyone, at least not in a structured way. Up till now I had thought that all the watching and listening had perhaps been wasted. Now I found I was putting it to use, making it work for its living. My reservations about the feasibility of writing someone else's novel never entirely disappeared, but in the weeks that followed I tried hard to set them aside. There is a brilliant observation in Mary McCarthy's *The Groves of Academe* to the effect that, if you have the duty of washing the dishes, renounce the duty – this leaves you existentially free to wash the dishes.

~

You don't know what will happen until you start writing. Only then do you discover things that previously you knew nothing about. There is a level at which you know what you are doing, it is a conscious process: you decide what to put in this chapter, what to leave for the next. But at another level, there seem to be deep forces at work that take you in unexpected directions. How much does the unconscious have to do with writing? Writers have spoken eloquently about this for generations. And in some sense it does seem reasonable to regard a novel as an accident of the unconscious, not in the sense of mishap, but in the sense of various buried strands colliding. The fact that I was writing as someone else – with a mask on, as it were – inevitably added yet another layer of complexity. I did and did not feel responsible for the words on the page, I did and did not feel that they belonged to me; I did and did not feel that I could defend them in my heart.

For the next week or so, however, I found myself doing a good imitation of a man writing a novel. I tried to free up the flow by telling myself that it was just another job that had to be done, that none of this mattered, that I was free to write anything that came into my head. I decided to call the main character Carlo – I had once known an Italian student named Carlo – and make him a successful advertising executive living in London. The novel would begin with Carlo's return to his

142

native Italy to attend his mother's funeral. The reason for giving him dual nationality was twofold: it fitted very generally with Tiger's own background, and it would act as a metaphor for further conflict and dichotomy. The trip to Italy was surely a stroke of genius: it would allow for our hero's journey in all senses – physical, mental, spiritual and emotional. It would also enable the affair to take place in the hot and steamy Mediterranean climate and, finally, it would conveniently provide the backdrop of Catholicism – Tiger's professed faith – which would in turn introduce the familiar tensions between faith and reason and passion. Carlo could be a latter-day Graham Greene character, tortured by Catholic guilt and spiritual *angst*. Catholicism provides such rich opportunities for this sort of exploration compared with other religions, even other Christian denominations. Who could imagine being interested in Methodist guilt, for example? I warmed to my theme. So far so good.

Except that I was kidding myself, whistling in the dark. Within a few pages, a central difficulty emerged and it never completely went away. The difficulty was, loosely speaking, the question of sincerity. While I don't for a moment imagine that all novelists have to write a personal story, or one in which they are intimately involved, I like to believe – even if I am wrong – that the author is sincere, and that the reader can sense if he (or she) is not. Words matter, the novel matters. That has been, and remains, my passionate belief. Writers are judged by the distinctive way in which words and the effect of these words on the reader combine. As a reader you somehow just know when every word is meant, even if the work is not a first-person narrative. Writing a novel is an intuitive thing and, while you can choose to write – or indeed ghost-write – an academic book or a work of non-fiction by doing the required research, it is probably true to say that in the case of a novel the subject matter invariably chooses you. I think you have to live with the idea for a novel, be obsessed by it even, before you are able to write it. Of course you might have just the vaguest of images as a starting point, or there might be an event that has lodged in the imagination. But unless you are committed, unless there is some element of compulsion attaching to it, the whole business can end up hollow at the centre.

Predictably, I agonised about the opening line. Again, it is a matter of confidence and belief. When you are searching your mind for that first sentence it is difficult not to be assailed by truths universally acknowledged and the similarity between all happy families. And easy to think that anything less brilliantly epigrammatic is small potatoes. The opening line also marks you. It can imprison you in a style and tone that are not easily shaken off. I pondered the possibilities, weighed and considered, wavered and faltered to the point of paralysis. Eventually, desperately, I wrote the first sentence:

Carlo surveys the land of his birth and contemplates death.

There! Done it. But would it do? It surely had a lot going for it – our hero is introduced in the first word, the present tense lends the journey a certain immediacy, and there is the neat juxtaposition of birth and death, a pointer to the weighty themes to come. It would do.

I tried to think myself into what I imagined Tiger's style might be, but the more I searched for his voice, the more I caught my own breaking through; the more I tried to realise his literary aspirations, the more my own seemed to intrude. The novel did not grow organically; it was force-fed and boosted with steroids. Set pieces and ruminations on the human condition were thrown about like salt. It became a stilted, studied thing. I was consumed by doubt. The characters were not 'real'; they were mouthpieces for various ideas, which shoved them around and kicked them to the ground. André Gide wrote something to the effect that the true novelist listens to his characters and watches how they behave, whereas the bad novelist simply constructs them and controls them. Without a doubt, I was constructing and controlling.

The more I struggled to be free, the more I felt constrained by Tiger's expectations. Muriel Spark believes that writers sin against God because they create characters who cannot bring about their own salvation. How I longed to create such a character, to sample this sinfulness. But our hero, it had become clear, was not quite ready to be the stuff of fiction. I knew even before he was fleshed out that he would have to be saved. It was the only permissible outcome.

The misgivings multiplied. It just wasn't working. I tried to make the writing light and airy, but the more I tried, the heavier it became. The harder I tried to handle it sensitively, the harder it would bite back. And in a moment of dreadful incaution, I hit on the structure of the novel: there would be fourteen chapters, each one a Station of the Cross, linking Carlo's painful journey with Christ's passion. One reviewer was later to describe this as 'an overweening conceit' and she was almost certainly right. With the curse of hindsight I can see it was a ghastly mistake (not least because it turned out that Tiger himself, though a cradle Catholic, was unfamiliar with the Stations of the Cross), but at the time I thought I could show off my knowledge of Catholicism. And in any case, I was desperate.

~

My parents gave me an interest in Roman Catholicism – exactly the opposite of what they intended to do. Religion, like bad grammar, is generally a habit picked up in childhood. But religious intolerance is a volatile substance which can have unexpected results.

It would be a mistake to imagine that sectarianism is confined to Northern Ireland or the west of Scotland. It is alive and well in the Kingdom of Fife. Nowadays the official line is ecumenical, but during my childhood religious bigotry was a legitimate occupation. Catholics – Papes we called them – were the enemy, and they had to be defeated before they took us over.

'They breed like rabbits,' my father said.

'They spread like wildfire,' my mother warned.

It was one of the few subjects on which they were completely in agreement.

On my way to school I had to pass St Patrick's, the primary school for Catholic children. The teachers were mostly nuns who lived in the convent next to the school. The school looked like any other school but the convent was hidden from the world behind a high beech hedge. In the wintertime I sometimes peered through the gaps in the hedge and saw dark figures swishing about in their robes. They looked so much more interesting than our teachers.

I made a friend called Mary McNamara, on whose mother's face my own mother professed to be able to see the map of Ireland. Though I looked hard, I was never able to find it. My mother said that Mary kicked with the left foot, which meant I wasn't allowed to be friends with her. The ban was strengthened by the fact that she lived in the scheme. But we usually left for school at the same time and would walk as far as St Patrick's together. We soon discovered that our birthdays were just two days apart – hers was on 4 February, mine on 2 February. Mary told me I was really lucky to have that day as a birthday and she wished she could swap with me. When I asked why, she said that the second of February was Candlemas Day, the Feast of the Purification of Our Lady. They always had time off school that day for a special Mass when they consecrated all the candles that would be needed in the church for the whole year. Consecration was evidently something the priest did with holy water and incense.

'Who's Our Lady?' I asked my parents when I got home. They looked completely horrified, so I explained, chirpily, that my birthday was apparently on the same day as Our Lady was purified.

'I'll Our Lady you!' thundered my father. 'We'll have no Our Lady in this house!'

'Sorry,' I said.

'If there's any more Our Lady, you'll find out what sorry is!' he said.

There were often fights between the Papes and Prods (anyone who was not a Pape was a Prod), but when Mary was with me I was never picked on. Once, when she was off school with chickenpox, a boy from St Patrick's grabbed my schoolbag and threw it over the high hedge that surrounded the convent. When I went home without my bag and explained what had happened, my mother reacted with predictable fury. She immediately went to what we called the Special Drawer and took out a new pair of nylon stockings with seams up the back. This could mean only one thing – she was going to see the Mother Superior. As she pulled on her nylons, she nursed her ire. She would show her, give her what's for, put her gas on a peep. By the time she left the house the veins stood proud on her forehead. She wore her Sunday coat and her second-best feathered hat – essential accoutrements for a visit to the convent.

'I'll Mother Superior her!' was her parting shot.

My mother and I went to church every Sunday. My father had stopped going to church before I was born. Apparently he had failed to get the contract for rebuilding the manse wall and had vowed never to go back. It was the principle of the thing, he said. I often longed for a principle like my father's so that I could stay at home and help him in the garden. In church we had our own pew with our name displayed in a small brass fitting at the end. Occasionally someone would sit in our pew by mistake. There was plenty of room, but according to my mother that was hardly the point. She would look daggers at the offending party and say in a loud highfalutin voice, 'Excuse me, this is a private pew.' She appeared to relish the plosive sounds of *private pew*. At such times I wanted to die.

I hated almost everything about having to go to church – my too tight coat with the astrakhan collar, the joyless atmosphere once we got there, the endless drone of the pulpit voice. At the beginning of the sermon my mother would surreptitiously pass me a pandrop which had to last the whole way through – on this point she was emphatic. I didn't ever dare bite the pandrop; in fact I tried not to suck it for fear it would disappear too quickly and upset my mother. Instead I would push it to a place of safety under my tongue and then open my mouth a fraction in the hope that the dry church air would preserve it. This was more difficult than it sounds. Sometimes, even when I concentrated hard, my mouth would fill with warm spit and the pandrop would dissolve before the sermon ended.

Mary McNamara was to take her First Communion.

'What's that?' I asked.

'It's when you get to wear a white dress in church,' she said. 'Mine has a lace bodice, puffed sleeves and pearl sequins.'

It sounded wonderful. I asked if I could see it but we both knew I wasn't allowed to visit her house. Mary said that maybe I could come to the rehearsal after school the next day. She would speak to the priest. I asked her if she was remembering I wasn't a Catholic.

'No, but you're a Christian, so that's all right.'

'I'm not a Christian,' I corrected her, 'I'm a Protestant.'

I knew it was risking a lot to enter St Patrick's Church, but it was a place of such out-of-bounds mysteriousness that I judged it worth the risk. Awe and trepidation were mixed together in roughly equal measures. There was a lot to take in – statues everywhere, angels on the ceiling, a huge wooden cross, and the smell of warm wax. I stood at the back waiting for my eyes to adjust to the gloom. The only light came from a few dozen candles flickering at the front. These would be the candles that had been sprinkled on my birthday, I supposed. The priest stood at the altar dressed in a long purple robe with gold round the edges. There were several nuns sitting halfway up the church. One or two of them turned round when they heard me come in and gave me a smile. After a few minutes, Mary and her friends entered by a side door. Just as she'd promised, they all wore pure white dresses complete with veils held on by rings of flowers. I suppose there must have been boys too, but I don't remember them. I had eyes only for Mary and the other girls. They walked towards the priest, a slow procession of miniature brides, their hands pressed together as in prayer. Mary had said it would not be the real thing, only a rehearsal, but I thought I had never seen anything so beautiful in my whole life. They all knew exactly what to do, when to bob up and down, when to kneel, when to make the sign of the cross. There was a lot going on in this church, much more than in our boring private pew.

I was late getting home. I had prepared a lie, but my mother was no fool. When I confessed, she was truly appalled – much worse than I had feared.

'Wait till your father gets home,' was all she said.

That meant only one thing: the belt. The belt was made of thick leather with the end slit in two for maximum effectiveness. It was used in schools throughout Scotland to deal with every classroom crime imaginable. The belt was made in my home town, Lochgelly, in a dark little room at the back of John Dick's ironmongery. I often went with my father to the ironmongery to have our garden tools sharpened. John Dick didn't look like the sort of person who would spend his life shaping bits of leather to punish children. He was a neat, amiable man

150

in brown overalls, and at weekends he visited his sister Bella who lived near us. She had a touch of facial palsy and a husband called Agnew. John Dick didn't have any children of his own, but in my mind this hardly excused what he did for a living.

For minor lapses my father belted us on our outstretched hands. If it was a more serious offence we were belted on the backs of our legs. It seemed there was no offence more serious than visiting the chapel – our name for the Catholic Church.

The days in the Dordogne settled into a rhythm. Every third day or so Tiger paid a visit to the *antiquaire* in one or other of the surrounding villages. His reputation for spending money had spread throughout the Dordogne valley, and those in the antique trade always looked delighted when they saw the Mercedes draw up outside. Tiger knew what he wanted and invariably went straight to the point.

'*Vous avez des femmes nues?*'

It was more the sort of question that might be asked at the massage parlour, or so I thought the first time I heard it, but it was clear that the shop owners were quite used to this opening bat and more than happy to oblige.

'*Bien sûr, monsieur!*' All French gestures seem to be a varia-tion of the shrug. Even when Frenchmen are enthusing and affirming, their shoulders go up and down.

'*Complètement nues?*' Tiger would ask, for nakedness was not to be compromised.

'*Bien sûr, monsieur!*' Another expansive, how-could-you-doubt-me shrug.

'Entièrement nues?'

'Bien sûr, monsieur! Nues comme les nunus!' – naked as nudists. Shoulders, arms and hands would swing and sway at the prospect of a sale. In practice each *antiquaire* almost always had something *extraordinaire* to show Tiger – a painting or perhaps a sculpted figure, something special that had been kept 'just for him'.

'Exprès pour vous, monsieur!'

Once in an antiques shop near Sarlat there was a wonderful happening that I felt privileged to witness. As soon as the *antiquaire* saw Tiger enter the premises his face lit up. Without waiting for the usual *femmes nues* enquiry, he took a key and unlocked the top drawer of his desk. He removed a large box which he handled with great care, confiding in a whisper to Tiger that what he was about to see was something truly *exceptionnel*. And it was.

The box contained a collection of original daguerreotypes – the results of an early photographic technique using silvered plates and mercury vapour – taken in the pleasure houses of Paris in the last years of the nineteenth century.[*] The women in the photographs, unlike modern pin-ups and models, were well filled-out, and seemingly happily so. They were arranged in a variety of tempting poses and looked distinctly huggable and inviting. Although they seemed perfectly at ease with their bodies, a slight shyness came through in some of the pictures, perhaps because they were not used to being photographed rather than because of any doubts about their profession. Tiger pored over the plates, savouring every one, soughing the occasional *formidable* and *magnifique*. After a while, he closed the box and said:

[*] Part of the collection was later published as *La Belle Époque*, Quartet Books, 1999.

'*Combien?*'

He had the look of a man who had searched for, and just found, the centre of human happiness.

The mornings were mostly taken up with visits to the market to buy the food for lunch. The kitchen was Tiger's domain. He loved cooking and prepared the most wonderful meals – fresh haricot beans in garlic oil and lemon juice, shiitake mushrooms in a herb marinade, salads straight from the garden. And sometimes we ate soft-boiled eggs freshly laid by the hens on the estate. 'Did you ever taste anything so beautiful?' he would ask. He didn't only cook, but laid the table and served the wine like an experienced *maître d'*. Afterwards he would clear up, washing and wiping till everything sparkled. He never allowed me to help, and he became agitated if ever I offered. As with other areas of his life he was fastidious in his attention to detail. Nothing was left to chance. As we ate, he kept up a running commentary on the food, its preparation, the health benefits it would confer, the character of the wine, the quality of the grape, and so on. At these times Tiger seemed deeply content.

In the early afternoons I would make my way to the studio with my laptop. The studio was some way from the main house, along a private track at the foot of the hillside, in the direction of the swimming pool and the original property. I thought of it as a kind of sanctuary, with its wraparound stillness, broken only by birdsong and the chirp of crickets. It consisted of a small kitchen and bathroom off a large open-plan room with a tiled floor and windows on three sides. The French doors opened to the south, but there was plenty of shade from the trees nearby. The light from the windows was also pleasantly dappled because of the wisteria and jasmine climbing up the outside walls. The creepers extended to the aviary next door, forming a canopy over the mesh construction that was home to dozens of exotic birds – parakeets, canaries, weavers, love-birds and finches. *Tous les oiseaux du monde*, said the *gardien* when he came to feed them.

~

To be a writer you have to have something to say. But what did I have to say? Nothing at all. And even if I had things to say, would I know how to say them? Then did I *feel* anything, I asked myself? Not enough to write about it. And so, in the absence of feeling, I decided that it would have to be an exercise in technique.

Slowly, painfully, the book took shape.

Almost the one thing I didn't mind was that it was to be a love story. After all, what else is there? It's only half a life without love. And a novel would be nothing without it. The prospect of writing about love was even faintly appealing. It is one of those eternal themes that can be endlessly reworked. But every silver lining has a cloud: as I had feared it might, love was coming perilously close to denoting sex.

Tiger was obsessively concerned with its place in the novel. Each day when I returned from the studio he would ask, 'Have we done the fucky-fucky yet?' I counselled against it, as anyone in my place would have done, suggesting that discretion was the better part of ardour. But he pooh-poohed and said that a novel by him would be *unimaginable* without sex.

'Beloved, we *need* the jig-jig! Don't you *see*?'

He laughed and clapped his hands, willing me to share his enthusiasm. But I didn't want to see.

I held out for a long time, pointing out that countless authors had believed they could 'do' sex in a novel and had ended up falling into a terrible black hole. I reminded him of the *Literary Review's* Bad Sex Prize, awarded annually by Auberon Waugh, a friend of Tiger's and a man who had made it his mission to discourage the tasteless and perfunctory use of sexual description in the modern novel. Surely he agreed with Bron? I argued that sex in the novel was nearly always bad sex, and that it was best avoided. I said that not even fine writers could manage it without sounding ridiculous or absurd or embarrassing. I argued that Jerry Hall – a woman he admired – was wrong when she claimed that bad sex writing was like bad sex, in that both were better than nothing. They were not better than nothing, I said. Nothing was better by far.

'You are talking like a *nun!*' he squealed. 'What's got into you? Trust me, beloved, we will do the sex beautifully! It will be very distinguished.'

Distinguished was one of Tiger's words. It covered a multitude of sins. It was becoming clear that sex was an argument I was not going to win. My reservations, however, were not based on squeamishness or prudishness. It was a matter of aesthetics. I sincerely believe that descriptions of lovemaking are high-risk for any writer. A lifetime's reading has convinced me that very few writers can manage them. Why should this be? Perhaps it's because the sexual act itself has little to do with words. And when it is put into words the inherent absurdity of trying to capture it is laid bare, in all senses.

The literary treatment of sex is beset with vexed questions.

First there is the problem of getting the characters to take their clothes off – buttons and zips and hooks can be so awkward, and you couldn't ever allow a man to keep his socks on. Then there are the body parts which either have to be named (very unwise) or else replaced with dubious symbolism. And what about the verbs, the doing words? How can you choose to make people *enter, writhe, thrash, smoulder, grind, merge, thrust* – and still hope to salvage a smidgen of self-respect? Not easily. If you doubt me, try it. The sound effects are even worse – *squealing, screaming, the shriek of coitus*. (In the event I opted for *sobbing,* which caused the man in my life to raise an eyebrow and quickly became a matter of regret.) No, the English language does not lend itself to realistic descriptions of sex. We are too used to irony. The alternative is to use metaphors, but metaphors are just asking for more trouble – all that edge of volcano and burning fire stuff. Some people claim that sex sounds better in French, and I'm inclined to agree, but that may be because just about everything sounds better in French.

What to do? What to *do?* Then, a sudden flash of brilliance: I *knew* what to do. Tiger had an abhorrence of bodily fluids – a mark of his Levantine origins, or so people believed. Whatever the reason, the abhorrence was comprehensive. His loathing of people who coughed or sniffed or spluttered was legendary – he once threatened to sack someone for blowing her nose, describing her conduct as 'totally unacceptable'. On the streets of London he walked in constant fear of being exposed to hawking and spitting. He did not like it when the office staff used the toilet facilities. And he could not cope with menstruation, not even with the general concept. A frantic look came over him if ever women mentioned their monthly cycles. Perhaps – and this was the stroke of genius – bodily fluids might come to the rescue in this situation. Provided that the sex scenes could be made sufficiently liquid, Tiger might decide to abandon them altogether. *Nil desperandum*. Bodily fluids would be my deliverance. I set about my purpose with a devil-may-care recklessness.

Strong and gentle as the waves, he swells and moves towards her like the sea to the shore. He dips and dives, eagerly but hesitantly, still fearing rebuff, until that moment of absolute clarification, when her ardour too is confirmed beyond doubt. Her lissom limbs quiver and enfold him into the sticky deliciousness of her sex.

Of course, one thing led to another, and it was hard not to get carried away. Tiger, far from feeling squeamish, seemed relieved that at last the lovers had got down to the business. I pressed on, telling myself it was a means to an end. He would soon change his mind.

He probes at her soft folds, innocent and beautiful beyond imagination. Everything is liquid and loosened. Droplets of moisture sit on her copper fleece like morning dew on a resplendent frond. In the moment before they connect and surrender he sees his soul's desire reflected in her dark bright eyes. In a spasm of ecstasy he slips and slides and sinks into the silken gulf. Fire within fire. The beat inside her rises and quickens, impelling them both to the edge of the world. A honeyed fusion of bodies and spirits, a melody of sweet abandonment, and the whole hillside begins to sing in chorus as he sobs his ejaculation.

Oh, Jesus. Every new splash or splosh was a fresh hell. But still Tiger held out. There was no capitulation. In fact he was exultant. He opened a bottle of Château Margaux and we drank to sex. 'Bravo!' he said, his highest accolade. This wasn't working out as planned. I would try one more act of sabotage. I had to make certain this time. Go for broke.

He traces the contours of her soft body with the tip of his finger. He slides over her moist skin, through the sweet damp valley between her breasts, around the slight swell of her stomach, pausing for a brief moment in the dip of her navel. Then down, down, down, across the symmetry of her loins.

They play with each other like wet seal pups, their bodies making succulent, slipping sounds. With his tongue he caresses her and spins a silver spider's web from the threads of her wetness. The pathway to heaven pouts like the calyx of a flower turned to the sun, the inner petals drenched in nectar. Her beautiful mound rises and falls as she rubs herself against his chin.

As she trembles and gasps and comes, he feels a surge of happiness and an infusion of supreme power. Her juices trickle down like a cluster of stars from the firmament. He can do anything now. He is God in one of his incarnations, spreading love and joy. Her amber thighs rear on either side like the waters parted for Moses. He rises and enters her.

At least four things happened as a result of all this incontinence. Tiger was overjoyed; he raised my salary; the *Sunday Times* described the novel as 'a strong contender' for the *Literary Review's* Bad Sex Prize; and my teenaged children were mortified.

~

The novel was launched in the spring of 1995. It was a glittering occasion with all the usual suspects, beautiful creatures plucked from London's fashionable set. Tiger had a well-deserved reputation for throwing the best parties in town. Lots of glamour and glitz and permanent tans. People asked if I knew Tiger and if I had read his novel. Afterwards I returned to Scotland and waited for the patter of tiny reviews. On the whole, the critics were kind; there was scarcely any venom, and derision was reserved for the sex scenes. According to the *TLS* reviewer, 'It is only in these scenes that the author comes close to losing control of his spare, precise prose.' The *Sunday Telegraph* reviewer wrote, 'I prefer to forget those brief, explicit embarrassments,' while another review was entitled simply: *'Less Sex Please.'*

By and large, people see what they expect to see. The reviewer in the *Telegraph* decided:

> This book is recognisably the product of a European Catholic sensibility, more a meditative treatise than a novel.

The reviewer from the *Oldie* agreed:

> Themes of love, death, sex and time are dealt with here in a fashion that is essentially the product of a Mediterranean Catholic mind, the same climate that shaped the stance of Lorca and Pasolini.

And this was the editor of the *Catholic Herald:*

> The love story provides a sensual leitmotif to the novel's
> cerebral and spiritual preoccupation with Everyman's
> burden: our ability to make sense of an existence which
> places our infinite spirit in a finite world . . . perhaps it
> should come as no surprise that the author, whose book
> of interviews with women was hailed for its perceptive
> portraits, should depict Petra as an articulate, passionate
> life force who overshadows the rather less interesting
> Carlo. Petra emerges as the focus of the novel, and it is
> her self-sacrifice that provides its most eloquent passage.

The reviewer in question cannot have known the trouble
she would cause by writing that phrase 'the rather less interesting Carlo'. Tiger was in a huff for days. He had a soft spot
for her – she was on his party list and he believed they both
occupied the same Catholic intellectual plane – but he was
hurt and offended that she had found Petra more interesting.

'How could she write such rubbish!' he said. 'Petra is *nothing*
compared to Carlo!'

Relieved that he didn't seem to suspect sleight of hand on
my part, I said what I could by way of comfort: that he shouldn't
take any notice, that reviewers had to work to deadlines and
were sometimes hasty or careless in their judgements, and that
in any case she had intended her remark as a compliment, a
tribute to his sensitive portrayal of the female character.

'So she is not attacking me?' he asked, looking for reassurance.

'No, not at all,' I said, happy to give it.

'But we should write to her, tell her she got it wrong, isn't it?'

'No,' I said, 'I think that would be a mistake.'

In truth I was puzzled by her review. Petra had been cobbled together in a great hurry. She was never 'real', not even to me. She is an academic, a woman of prodigious sexual appetite, and hardly the sort of person you would bump into in church – which is where Carlo meets her. In the novel's religious setting she is a subversive force, created largely out of a sense of mischief and cussedness, an agent for my own irreverent views. She is certainly not good *Catholic Herald* material. For example:

> She [Petra] herself has always thought of sexual congress as the most innocent of activities. She likes to think that God, whom she worships, might also regard it in this light. It pleases her to imagine that it is only a question of time and God's judgement before the link between divine love and sexual love is revealed. But it is a sophisticated notion and God has to wait until his people are ready to receive it.

The next excerpt discharges yet more bodily fluids and strikes me now as an act of delinquency, an experiment to see how far I could go and still get it past the censor.

> . . . Although she loves her Church she deplores the tortuous attitudes to sex which have dominated its teaching since earliest times . . . One of the consequences for the faithful is that at many points throughout history, salvation has depended on chastity, and damnation has been

inextricably linked with female licentiousness . . . It is not that Petra feels especially persecuted as a woman. She knows perfectly well that men have also been subject to the moral guardianship of the church. The fundamental view throughout the ages that sexual relations are somehow 'unclean' has affected men no less than women. In the course of her studies of celibacy, for example, Petra has waded through many volumes of moral theology devoted to the problem of what are delicately called 'nocturnal emissions'. The theology is based on the so-called pollution theory, whereby any priest who experienced such an emission in his sleep would not be in a state of purity to celebrate the Eucharist the following day. (It was later decreed that an emission would not be morally polluting provided the priest did not wake up and enjoy it.) This issue seems to have caused much the same amount of highly charged – and, Petra thinks, largely hysterical – debate as the more recent furore in England over women priests.

Although she is well aware of the multiplicity of theological arguments against the ordination of women priests, she cannot help thinking that the main objection rests on another taboo: menstruation. . . . Petra knows from private discussions with many of the Catholic clergy that the thought of receiving the sacrament from a menstruating woman would be more than their sensibilities could bear. Of course it suits the purpose of those opposed to women priests to appeal to scripture and the undeniable fact that God was made incarnate only as man. But actually it is the idea of a priest with a period which is unthinkable.

And so on. And so on. Looking back now, these passages seem to be the outpourings of a smarty-pants, an act of defiance, mischievous in their purpose. They really had no place in Tiger's novel. I was wholly aware of his irrational dread of what is delicately referred to as 'the time of the month'. He surrounded himself with young, beautiful well-connected women, but he simply could not cope if any of them complained of period pains or mentioned pre-menstrual tension. He regarded even the most oblique reference to anything of that sort as an outrage, a personal affront. 'Please! Please!' he would cry out, if ever the conversation seemed to be going in the direction of monthly discharges, and the 'please' was always expelled with a great whoosh – PAH-LEEZE – like a whale spouting. Once, to his extreme horror, he discovered a tampon floating in the lavatory bowl of his own private emperor's bathroom. The premises were protected, inside and out, by closed circuit cameras. Over several days, and with the patience and thoroughness of a forensic scientist, he examined each frame of the security videotape, looking for the culprit. While he searched, he told me earnestly that, until the offender was found, everyone was under suspicion.

'What, the men too?' I said, hoping to lighten what had turned into a very sombre investigation. But he just glowered. In these matters there was no room for levity.

I was therefore completely alive to the possible repercussions of linking Catholicism with emissions of one kind or another. But at the time it brightened up the task in hand, reflecting at the same time my own weariness with the fiddle-faddle of institutionalised religion.

Part Six
Retour à la Belle France

In the summer of 1995, just a few months after the publication of Tiger's first novel, we were back in France once again. By now the routine was quite familiar – going to markets, feeding the dogs, swimming in the pool, dining out at the best restaurants, visiting the *antiquaire* to acquire ever more splendid *objets* for the house and yet more paintings of an explicit nature.

And writing.

This time there was a particular sense of *déjà vu* because we were there to begin another novel. It was difficult to feel cheerful about the prospect. Indeed I could scarcely bear the idea of going through the whole process again. But Tiger had other ideas. We had had one of those 'repetitive strain' conversations in which Tiger did a lot of repetition and I took the strain.

'If we do just one, nobody will bloody believe us,' he said.

'What do you mean exactly?' (I often asked this.)

'What do I *mean*?'

'Well, what is it that nobody will believe?'

'What *is* it that nobody will believe?'

'Yes, what *is* it?'

'What *is* it? I'll tell you *exactly* what it is. I'll tell you *exactly* what nobody will believe. Nobody will ever believe we can *do* another one. Isn't it?'

'Well, is that really so important?'

'Is it important? Is it *important*? Darling, what's the matter with you? What's got into you?'

'Well, *is* it important? What people think, I mean.'

'I don't believe I'm hearing this! Of course it's important. They won't take us seriously! Don't you *see*? They will think the first one was a fluke!'

One difficulty for me during these exchanges was in determining how much to cavil. Was it worth saying that no novel – not even a ghosted one – was a 'fluke'? Probably not. Experience had taught me that if I went too far in raising objections, it could rebound very badly, good sense notwithstanding. It could mean huffs and pique, or even a spell in the wilderness. But the danger of not voicing misgivings was just as great.

In fact something quite subtle was at work during these conversations. Tiger, while affecting a boyish ingenuousness, was actually endowed with a Machiavellian shrewdness. He could flatter, disparage, coax and intimidate, interchangeably and with consummate artistry. He would do almost anything to get his own way. I had witnessed many performances over the years, sometimes from the wings, at other times from the front stalls, more often than not sharing the stage with him and fluffing my lines. At times it seemed ungenerous not to succumb to his childlike excitement, which came over as a kind of innocent hopefulness endlessly generated and regenerated. However, I knew it was driven by something that was not at all innocent. The more formidable his proposal and the

less appealing to me, the more fervently he tried to pros-
elytise. It would be so easy, a joy to do, I would soon be able
to see that for myself, and besides we would make *pots* of
money and, best of all, we would have *such fun*.

Fun ranked high in Tiger's scheme of things. And during
these dialogues he played his part well. He was the enthusiast,
the fanatic, the zealot, the mad inventor, the prime mover, the
armchair philosopher. I played the killjoy, the doubter, the wet
blanket, the party-pooper. I didn't enjoy my part much but,
over the years, we had settled into our respective roles, and we
stuck to them steadfastly.

'You don't want to? You don't *want* to? But darling, *why*
don't you want to?'

'It's just, well, a second novel will be quite a lot of hard work.'

'Beloved,' – the voice is lowered to impart a confidence –
'let me tell you something. *Life* is hard work. Bloody hell, we
all have to work hard. Otherwise we get *nowhere*. Isn't it?'

'Yes, that's true, but . . .'

'But what? What is this "but"? There is no "but". We can
do anything we put our minds to. We are *amazing* together!'

'All I mean is . . .'

'You still have a problem? Tell me your problem, my darling.
I will solve your problem. That's what I'm here for.'

And so on. And so on. The pattern of these exchanges was
invariably the same. In no time at all they degenerated into
low farce with a diminishing ratio of reason to emotion.

I set about the second novel with a joyless heart. This only
made things worse because Tiger loathed low spirits in others.
It was *joie de vivre* he loved – he often said so – and he could

not bear even the slightest lack of enthusiasm for something he favoured. Whenever he detected reluctance on my part he would put on his evangelist hat and set about converting me. Before too long it would usually strike me that the idea I was rejecting was preferable to the process of indoctrination, so I would generally cave in.

With this new novel he had explained that I could have *carte blanche* – 'You can do *whatever* you like,' he had said, and he clapped his hands together like a pair of cymbals, sealing his lavishness. He then sat back in his chair and smiled benignly. His expression was one of utter benefaction. It was not possible for a man to be more reasonable.

But it wasn't true. It turned out there was a requirement, though to hear him you might easily have imagined it was nothing at all. He was talking it down so much – 'It's just a small idea, that's all, it's not anything *big*' – and as he continued it got so very small that I imagined it as a tiny dot on an old television screen, disappearing into the void. Alas, this scarcely-a-requirement-at-all, this small thing-let, this little idea-let, slowly began to take on monstrous dimensions. As before, there were to be two women and a man. The man, so Tiger explained, was to be the lover of both women, and each woman would be aware of the other and quite relaxed about the sharing arrangement. So far so good. The women were to be cousins who had been born on the same day – 'Under the same star sign, so they're more like sisters,' said Tiger. Sounds quite manageable so far, I thought. There followed a lot of eager talk about how very close sisters can be, how twins can feel each other's pain, how they seem almost to inhabit each other's bodies. 'It's like they're one person, not two,' he said.

'Yes . . .' I said, beginning to wonder where all this was leading, looking out for the catch. I was not prepared for what came next.

'So,' he said, clasping and unclasping his large soft hands, working up to the *pièce de résistance*, 'when the one girl gets *orgamsi* the other gets *orgamsi* also!'

'How do you mean exactly?' I asked. I felt sure I had missed something. I took a few moments to consider the possibilities before venturing, 'Are we talking about simultaneous orgasm?'

'Precisely!' he purred in a go-to-the-top-of-the-class way. 'Simultaneous *orgamsi*. You've got it! Bravo!'

But I knew I hadn't got it. Not really anyway. As far as I was aware, simultaneous orgasm happened – if it happened at all – between the two principal players, as it were. It was not something that could be dispensed at will to a third party, not even a close cousin. Such a phenomenon would in any case have to be called a *telekinetic* orgasm. Strictly speaking, that is. This was no time to be finicky, however. I had to know more, I had to discover what was in Tiger's head. Besides, my mind was already racing ahead to the alarming business of having to convert this far-fetchery into plausible fiction.

'And how do you see that working exactly?' I asked, matter-of-factly. We might have been discussing a new business plan or profit-sharing scheme. 'Is the man stimulating both of them in such a way that they climax at the same time?'

Wrong question. Tiger smote his brow with the palm of his hand. It was his God-protect-me-from-imbeciles gesture.

'Daaarleeeng, you don't understand!' He was right. I didn't. I had led a sheltered life. 'The women are not *together*! They are *miles* apart!' He was shouting now. He always shouted when stupid people failed to grasp the essential point. At these times there was a huge expenditure of spit. A salvo of saliva.

'I'm afraid,' I said – and for once perhaps I was a little afraid – 'you're going to have to spell it out. I don't quite get it.'

He rose from his desk and started pacing up and down, his body language a narrative in itself. He enfolded himself in his own arms and rocked slightly from side to side, the way a man might move about a padded cell, trying to control the violent turmoil within. He fixed me with a look that said, how could you be so dim? The explanation when it came was bad-tempered and delivered *de haut en bas*. The gist of it was that the two women would be so closely harmonised, so much in tune with one another that, even if they were separated physically, even by oceans and by continents, they would be capable of experiencing the heights of pleasure at the same time. As he spoke he became more and more animated, his tiger eyes shining brightly in his head, his whole body in motion, semaphoric, balletic. And since I had been so obtuse, he did not mince matters. The speaking got plainer and plainer. To remove any lingering doubt he spelled it out.

'Look, it's simple! If one woman is in London, say, and the other is in New York, when he is fucking the one in London, the one in New York feels it in her fanny also!'

A number of conflicting thoughts went splat in my head.

'Now do you understand?' he said, regaining his composure.

'I understand,' I said.

Spinoza said that he had sought all his life to be able to under-stand – he had striven not to laugh, not to weep, and not to curse, *sed intelligere* – but *to understand*. Understanding is everything.

～

Writing is a lonely business; or, rather, it is a business done alone. In this sense writing imitates life. Although we may spend much of our time with other people, essentially we live our lives alone. It may seem as if we are sharing our lives all the time – with commuters on the train, shoppers in super-markets or, more intimately, with marriage partners, close friends, lovers. But these connections are as nothing compared with the lifelong communion we have with ourselves. What we tell others is only a tiny distillation of what we tell ourselves; and what we know of others is only what they choose to tell us, or what we have gleaned from the surfaces – the look in the eyes, the body posture, the sweat on the brow. Solitude is often seen as a dismal, cheerless state, yet there is surely great point and purpose in it. Indeed aloneness seems to contain a happy paradox: it is when we are alone that we best understand how we are hitched to the world, how we are connected to others. Our sense of self is manifestly shaped by others: our mothers, to begin with, then our immediate family and friends, also by random encounters and chance bondings. But that sense of self which is linked to our awareness of others resides, curiously, at the heart of being alone. Much of what is important in life takes place inside us.

Tiger did not share my liking for solitude. I often tried explaining that in order to write I needed to be alone. There is a separate world inside your head, I told him, and that's the place you have to try to occupy when you write. You can leave it behind and do other things, I said, but it is the place you have to return to each time. But he just looked at me as if I were insane. Sometimes when I asked for some time alone, he appeared to regard it as a personal affront. And even when I thought I had managed to get through to him, there would always come a point when he switched and started to view it as a business negotiation. 'OK, let's compromise. Go now, and at quarter to three,' – he checked all three watches as he spoke – 'I shall pass by the studio and we shall go together to the pool.'

He obviously regarded solitude as an unnatural state, quite menacing in its way. He regularly talked about how he hated to be alone, either in the office or at home or during normal leisure activities like watching television. He often mentioned that he was incapable of eating alone, something I knew from experience to be completely true. I have never been able to face food early in the day – my constitution seems to pucker at the mere sight unless I have been up and about for a couple of hours – but each morning in France, very much against my own inclination, I did battle with breakfast so that Tiger would not have to eat alone. Put like that, it seems quite mad, and indeed it was. The idea that a rational grown woman could allow herself to be coerced into eating a meal for which she had no appetite is patently absurd. But such was my anxiety surrounding breakfast that I sometimes set my alarm clock a full two hours beforehand in the hope that I would be in a state of increased readiness for food. This was preferable to the slow burn of ill humour that would have resulted from my opting out. A bad miff could last indefinitely.

Tiger was ravenous in the morning. The first meal of the day was a serious business and he was unfailingly eager to get on with it. If I happened to arrive at the table even a minute or two late, he would glower at me as if I had been off murdering children. I preferred to shower and dress beforehand, but for Tiger eating took precedence over his toilet. He would appear in a voluminous sleeping garment, a staggering creation in silk and blinding brocade that gave him the appearance of an opulent sheikh. It was always unwise to say anything beyond the normal courtesies before he had taken a certain quantity of food inside him. The first stages of breakfast appeared to be something he had to get through rather than enjoy, but he got through with a trencherman's appetite and seized the food as if plundering and pillaging. He would then relax a little and declare, each day in fresh astonishment, 'I am *so* hungry this morning! I don't know why I am so hungry.' Otherwise it was mostly a silent affair punctuated only by his exhortations to do what my mind and gut recoiled from.

'Eat! Eat! Beloved, why don't you *eat*?'

It was not enough simply to *be* there, and to supply companionship. Eating was the thing. Mercifully breakfast was not remotely a Full English, not even a Part English, but consisted of copious amounts of *fromage frais* drizzled with olive oil into which we dipped *pain de seigle*, delicious French rye bread. There were also olives and figs and various specialities of the region. Tiger pressed food on me constantly – his own *amour-propre* appeared to depend on it – and I became practised in the art of accepting as little as possible without seeming to lean too much in the direction of declining; than which there was nothing more likely to cause offence.

Though Tiger's conduct in this regard was challenging, it sometimes helped me to see it as an aspect of his sweeping generosity, albeit one that could drive the recipient quite mad. Generosity is one of the six transcending virtues of Buddhism, and it is through generosity that the true dialectics of compassion are revealed. I had recently learned this from the man in my life – in his youth he had spent some months in a Buddhist monastery in Japan. According to Buddhist teaching, so he said, it does not count as generosity if there is any expectation of return, or if something is given out of guilt, or shame, or pride. By these criteria Tiger passed the Buddhist test with honours. Moreover, the so-called Perfection of Giving is evidently best expressed without there being any conscious concept of giving; it should resemble a natural reflex – this according to the founder of Western Buddhism, a man who took the name of Sangharakshita, though he had been born plain old Dennis Lingwood in South London. Again, Tiger could scarcely be faulted in this respect. His giving did seem to be something of a reflex action, involuntary, compulsory even. Perhaps, so I reflected, Tiger was on the path to Buddhahood, and I was in the presence of a transcendent spirit? This theory went so far and no further, however, because another Buddhist condition is that the giver should be joyful when he gives; whereas Tiger was petulant and thrusting, at least over breakfast.

At other times too his urge to share could feel like an assault on one's independence and free will, almost an act of aggression, and yet this was obviously so far from his intention that it would have been brutal to suggest it. But his generosity was emphatically not like other people's; it had an existential significance and seemed to answer an urgent need in him, extending far beyond the normal human desire to share. It came over as an extreme thing, wild and unfettered, capable of sprouting extra body parts and strange accretions till it became a gargantuan creature, both wonderful and terrible, and in danger of toppling over.

Women sometimes collided with this creature and felt oppressed by it. Yet occasionally I was moved by it. Over breakfast, for example, he even shared with me his own special supply of vitamins and other pills, counting them out into two equal rows, his tongue held tight in his teeth as he concentrated, being let loose only when he cited the essential constituents of each item, their respective efficacy and cost. He doled out tablets for the smooth working of joints ('so you can walk better'), vitamins for oral health ('they cost a *fortune* but they stop your gums bleeding'), zinc to maintain a healthy skin ('this is *amazing* – it will prevent the pimples'), and a mud brown pill of truly alarming dimensions – 'a secret concoction' available only from Harley Street. The one he saved for last was 'the best that money can buy'. It was a long capsule containing powder the colour of tapioca and intended specifically for what Tiger called his 'prostrate', a factor that did nothing to lessen his largesse. 'You can have one too,' he said. I was touched by this.

Shopping at the market was another opportunity for unbounded lavishness. He strolled up and down the food stalls, hands behind his back, like a king inspecting the troops, stopping occasionally to sample an olive or a morsel of cheese. He loved the abundance of produce, the freshness of the fruit and vegetables, the way the stalls were set out so colourfully. But he was a sentimental man, and if ever he saw rabbits hanging by their ears, with tears of blood stuck to their mouths, he would say, 'It's awful what they do. *Les pauvres!* It shouldn't be allowed.' The *gardienne*, Monique, who always drove us to the market, stayed a couple of paces behind him, ready to receive whatever he bought into her basket. He asked for two kilos of everything, one for *la grande maison* and one for Monique and her family. This he did without expectation of gratitude or reciprocation, though it probably had the effect of securing her devotedness. On the day before our departure from France there was always a very grand spree. During the preceding week or two Tiger had earmarked certain items – mould-ripened cheese, jars of ash-covered *chèvre* suspended in oil, *Périgord* honey, truffle vinegar and other delicacies – for purchase on the last market day. On these days the *gardienne* brought with her a large shopping trolley for the great splurge.

Back at the house it took the whole afternoon to wrap everything and get it packed for the flight home. There was sometimes so much stuff that an extra suitcase had to be bought to contain it all. The Wrapping was an extended ritual and I was required to be in attendance throughout, though only as a spectator. In the manner of solemn preparation for a sacred act, Tiger began by setting out everything on the large kitchen table – scissors, adhesive tape, tissue paper, bubble wrap, newspaper, tin foil and string. Then, as if he might be engaged in the salvation of his own soul, he proceeded to package and parcel, swathe and swaddle. Jars of olives and *harissa* were mummified in newspaper and brown tape, while rounds of cheese were encased first in wax paper, then in foil, and finally in newspaper and plastic bags. During this lengthy process he seemed to be in the grip of some mysterious energy that had arrived from nowhere and taken charge of his mind and body. He had a look of intense concentration and he sucked in air noisily. As he worked away, he provided a detailed commentary on the proceedings, describing each and every stage – first we do this, now we do that, then we take the newspaper, now we need the Sellotape – and so on. Things had to be done in a particular way and in a precise order. The commentary seemed to be for his own benefit, and it took the form of a set piece, something learned by heart and recited by rote. He was completely absorbed, and yet he looked up frequently to check that I was watching and paying attention. If ever I tried to move away or do something else to relieve the tedium, he would shriek, 'No! No! *Sit!* Don't move!'

I sat alone in the studio wondering what to do, how to begin. It was a blow to be required to write another novel, especially so soon after the first. If I was going to be able to deliver, by which I mean produce not just a satisfactory number of words, but a book which would sustain my own interest, one I could finish as well as start, I felt I had to change tack.

My first resolve was to try to write from the inside out. The first novel was written from the outside in, in the sense that it is overly schematic and as a result lacks what might be called narrative truthfulness. It is sacrificed to the ideas it contains – everything from a homily on the categorical imperative to a description of life inside a white ant colony. This is hardly a surprise, for the book was written, if not exactly to order, then certainly with the customer in mind. And the customer in this case was not the reader, but the *soi-disant* author. Contemplating this new venture I felt curiously depleted, emptied of the will to repeat the exercise. If I was to commit to another novel, I would have to move away from what I saw as the flat, two-dimensional, soulless canvas. It had to be something layered and fully imagined, something more from the heart.

Then again, whose heart? Can one write from another person's heart? I am not sure it can be done. You can get all kitted out, only there's nowhere to go. Personal experience, which includes the imagination and what feeds it, is essentially the base from which people write. And personal experience is highly specific, each take on the world unique. You cannot write another's experience, only your own. Of course you can try, but it will always be in some sense attenuated. Without a doubt there is something intrinsically contradictory about ghosting a novel. It is of course *possible* to fake fiction, but it is difficult to see how it can be meaningful or eloquent. You have to write from inside your own skin, otherwise there is too much of a psychological struggle. It's like trying to fake sincerity.

Writers often say that they know a lot about their book before they begin. An idea has come to them some time before – perhaps it is no more than a faint humming in the head – but it is then stored away for a lengthy gestation period. At this point the writer's internal processes start to work. The idea is fed and nurtured, perhaps jottings are taken or notes of conversations heard on the bus. For a long time, perhaps even a year or two, the writer is responsive to everything that resonates with the idea, receptive to the smallest observable bits of daily life, the tone of someone's voice, the way the light falls on a building.

It is a time, so it is said, of heightened sensitivity. This process allows the idea to grow and take on different features. Writers generally agree that this stage cannot be rushed or forced.

In the ghosting process there is no time to wait for the humming in the head. An idea has to be plucked from the air, and you have to run with it. The ghost is generally preoccupied with getting the job done, as I had been first time round. According to Martin Amis, a writer's life is all anxiety and ambition[*], and the two are scarcely distinguishable from one another. I believe the ghost-writer is similarly afflicted, perhaps to an even higher degree because the work is done under greater constraints. The ambition is not publicly realised, because all honours accrue to the credited author, but there is plenty of personal ambition involved in trying to do the job well. Anxiety follows naturally from ambition and becomes part of it.

Being intent on getting the job done makes you concentrate on the technical problems, but it leaves no room for the spirit of the thing. You report for duty each day and you hope that the target number of words will be written. You consider the architecture of the book, the dramatic structure, the characters, the voice. The trouble is that you don't believe the voice, and you don't quite trust the characters, and you certainly don't suffer with them. This time I wanted to change all that. I wanted the writing to be alive at the centre, not just a technical exercise. I wanted it to be something that sprang from my own energy. I had to write about something that moved me.

~

[*] Martin Amis, *Experience*, Jonathan Cape, 2000.

In 1987 I read Ian McEwan's *The Child in Time*, a chilling piece of fiction that starts with the disappearance of a young child, Kate, while on an ordinary shopping expedition to the supermarket with her father. The assumption is that the child has been snatched, but there are no clues, no leads, no ransom demand. No body is ever found. When I was reading *The Child in Time,* my own beloved Kate was just seven years old, and this no doubt led me to identify even more closely with the story. The book addresses larger political and social themes, but over time I forgot them. What held me, and continued to hold me, was the personal story of grief and anguish. I was struck by the way in which happy lives can be turned by a single moment in time into the bleakest of landscapes. Ian McEwan's spare luminous prose is perfectly honed to capture the essence of despair and the concomitant disintegration of ordinary lives. It is a consummate execution of sorrow, perhaps the cruellest sorrow of all. It seemed to me that the grief was almost too sharp to be borne. I was tormented by the book, and it went on haunting me for many years.

In those days I thought a lot about how life could be turned upside down without warning. Lives could be thrown into disarray by a single decision acted upon, a simple choice made, a mad moment. This is not to say that the choice is always wrong, or the decision irrational. Reasons can be found for anything after all. It is rather to say that the choosers or deciders are generally caught up in something that has altered their normal vision, and they forget for a brief time that actions beget consequences. They are fleetingly freed by dint of passion or misery or some other driver from the normal shackles of cause and effect. A friend snubbed, a promise broken, a secret told, a lover taken, a family abandoned – any one of these can leave a trail of wreckage, unintended, unimagined in the mind of the prime mover. I believe this is an empirical truth.

The empirical truth that really worried me, however, indeed possessed and obsessed me for years, was not the terrible things we do to one another, but the random bolt from the blue which nothing can prevent. At a day-to-day level, so I persuaded myself and still do, we may to some extent affect what happens. With the people we love and those we meet, we can choose to make things better or worse, make a point of being kind or not kind; we can even alter the pattern of our existence, or make small adjustments to the way we live. But against the big blasts, the hammer blows, the freak accidents, there's nothing to be done. Once you sign up for this way of thinking it is but a short step to imagining unspeakable things beneath the murk, something nasty lying in wait at the bottom of the pile, ready to pounce. It is also an observable fact that there are no fair shares where suffering is concerned. There is no master plan to allot a precise amount of pain to one person and then move on to another. The sheer prevalence and casual concentration of suffering are proof against such a notion. Alas, it's all utterly, stupefyingly random. Tempting to think otherwise perhaps, but ultimately self-deluding. This baseless anxiety of mine gorged on *The Child in Time* and reinforced itself. The snatching of a child – how could it be borne? How could one go on? How might one go about surviving a loss of that order? At that point, in 1987, during the immediate aftermath of my marriage breakdown, I felt stripped bare by events and had the instincts of a nervous animal protecting its young. It was difficult to dislodge a vague sense of calamities to come. I could drive myself mad with imagined tragedies. They arrived in my mind in no particular sequence, and no effort of will seemed strong enough to keep them at bay. It felt like continuing to throw up long after you believed you'd finished.

~

Eight years on, I sat in the cool blue light of the studio on a hillside in the Dordogne, and as I looked beyond the trees and back in time, the scent of that fear came wafting back. It had lost its sharpness, but I knew it was still fetid in the memory trenches. I decided to go back there and smell it. I would start Tiger's new novel with the disappearance of a child and see where it led. I opened the laptop on the desk and typed the first paragraph.

> The summer's afternoon when it happened was to be etched, as if by a splinter of glass, in the hearts of all those who were there. The memory was validated by pain and the sharp sounds that broke a perfect Sunday in two. It was like a pencil snapping, and its jagged edges stuck out, waiting to snag anyone who came near.

I had only the vaguest idea of where these opening sentences might lead. But already I had received a fax from the design manager at the publishers asking for background information so that the illustrator could get to work on the book cover. It was clear he had been told that the book was finished and that I was in the process of copy-editing it. Where and when is the book set, he asked, and what do the women look like? Did I agree that they should be naked on the jacket? And was it a lesbian relationship? Straight questions, yet I didn't know the answer to any of them. I hadn't the first idea of what the women looked like, nor yet whether they should be naked on the jacket. Replying to him was therefore quite a challenge. As was the blurb for the dust-cover which had to be written before even the first few pages were complete. The world of blurbs is of course renowned for imprecision and exaggerated claims, but the blurb that is written before the book is properly begun is a rare arsy-varsy sort of specimen. It is a neither-fish-nor-fowl piece, relying heavily on generalities. Thus:

> This second novel is substantial and ambitious, subtle and intricate, with a strong moral dimension. The author shows great compassion for his characters, and by examining a critical point in their lives, he illuminates their qualities and frailties. It is a novel of melancholy with gentle comic touches, and although dealing with loss and sorrow, it also shows survival and the triumph of the human spirit.

It was, you might say, a blanket blurb. Though it was true that I didn't know at that stage what shape the book would take, I already had a feeling that the ending would be optimistic and humane. There was a desire to wander over the territory of loss, but despair would not prevail. This was a good thing, for I could now happily tick off *triumph of the human spirit* from the blurb list. And all would surely be well, provided I could mix together *frailties* and *qualities* and bake them in a moderate oven of *compassion*. This was only the beginning, and already a mild craziness was taking hold.

I spent the next few days trying to shape the narrative in my own mind, trying to ground it in something real. Of course it would be an account of something that *hadn't* happened, at least not to me, but the underlying drift would be that loss is generic, universal. The story would be a means of confronting the beast, looking at fear, and thereby taming it. The initial event, sudden and unforeseen, would trigger an immediate outpouring of grief, and this would be the catalyst for a range of hitherto dormant emotions. It would not be a detective story or a police investigation into the child's disappearance; rather it would be a study in bereavement, the tragic event acting as a means for probing fragile family relationships. I imagined two families, related by blood and marriage, coming to terms with the loss of one of the children. The shock and its aftermath would produce a sort of anarchy in which the normal constraints on family relations would give way. Perhaps this framework would allow for rather unorthodox entanglements – at the back of my mind I had the idea that the emotional chaos following the event would somehow accommodate Tiger's requirement. Beyond these initial thoughts about the book, I knew very little.

There was a near liturgical observance of the pattern of the days in the Dordogne. Each morning there was a market in one of the neighbouring towns, and we went to them all. On Mondays it took place in Les Éyzies, a town famous for its pre-historic caves, and on Tuesdays it was in the nearby village of Le Bugue, situated on the river Vézère near its confluence with the Dordogne. The market there has been held on a Tuesday by royal decree for nearly seven centuries. On Thursdays it was market day in the *bastide* town of Domme and on Fridays in Le Buisson. Each Wednesday and Saturday we went to Sarlat, the largest centre in the vicinity. Sarlat is an almost wholly unspoilt medieval and renaissance town with an abundance of culture, elegance and charm. It has the grandeur and simplicity of the Old Town of Edinburgh whose architecture the French copied and improved upon. The centre is a wonderful maze of narrow streets and wynds and split-levels. In the town square there is a statue of La Boétie, the sixteenth-century anti-royalist, idealist and beloved friend of Montaigne, the Dordogne's most famous literary son. Tiger loved to hear the story of how Montaigne was drawn to La Boétie from their very first meeting and continued to love him as a brother till his untimely death. His spiritual affinity with La Boétie famously defied analysis and when asked to explain his love Montaigne could only answer: *'Parce que c'était moi, parce que c'était lui.'* – 'Because it was me, because it was him.' Tiger's eyes moistened at these words.

I came to love the French open-air markets, and in particular the market people – those who sell the produce, grow it, bake it, bottle it, cure it. Their passion for what they do is unmistakeable. It is a place of sensual pleasures – the ancient sounds of people trading with one another, greeting each other, the rich aromas of fruit and flowers, garlic and Gauloises – all played out under a gentian blue sky. Everything strokes the senses and warms the spirit. The marketplace is also full of interesting characters – men in berets, hands in pockets, jackets buttoned up, assuming a *je pense donc je suis* attitude. And somehow French women know how to be sexy at any age, even women with baskets of hens or strings of onions. I loved just standing around, taking it all in. But it wasn't ever possible to linger for long. Tiger liked me to keep up, and he became ill-tempered if I didn't. If I strayed even a few yards or stayed in one place too long he would upbraid me under the guise of concern for my safety. 'I got so *worried*,' he would say, clutching his skull as if to stop it exploding with the worry of it all. 'Don't wander off like that.' I was never convinced by this. What actually bothered him was the slightest show of independence.

There was very little flexibility in Tiger's timetable, and virtually no room for spontaneity. Even a stroll in the grounds – 'taking the air' he called it – was planned ahead and allotted a time-limit in advance, making it impossible to relax. The days seemed to be divided up according to an externally determined set of rules. They were measured out in quarter hour spans in such a way that the next event was always anticipated and never allowed simply to happen. He kept up a running commentary on how the day would progress – we will do this, then we will do that, and afterwards we will drink some tea, and so on. Nothing was allowed just to happen by itself. Thus when we were eating lunch he would always announce the arrangements for dinner, or when we were at the market in the morning the shopping would be brought to an abrupt halt for no obvious reason, and we would have to sprint to the car as if fleeing from gunfire. The *gardienne* and I would exchange looks of sisterly sympathy as he clapped his hands and called to us *'Allez! Allez!'* As soon as we were in the car he would calculate our arrival time back at the house to the nearest two minutes. He consulted his three watches with grievous frequency and not at all in the reserved way of the British, who tend to glance at the time with a discreet flick of the wrist. Tiger's arm movements were exaggerated and unequivocal, like those of a policeman directing the traffic. And he would invariably announce his findings, often in a kind of what-on-earth-happened puzzlement. Thus: 'Let me see, what is the time now? OH, MY GOODNESS! It's seven minutes past eleven. I don't believe it!' I never got used to this element of his behaviour, and I never found a good way of coping. *What exactly is it you don't believe?* – I wanted to scream. *That three whole minutes have passed since you were last surprised?* He was also obsessed with punctuality – punctuality in his lexicon meaning being early rather than on time. He himself was never ever late, and he regarded lateness in others, or just-on-timeness indeed, as iniquitous.

What was it about, this unsettledness? Why was he fixated on time-keeping? Why was he afraid of things just taking their own course? Was it an attempt to beat time at its own game, show it who was boss? Once over dinner I tried to get him to talk about it. I told him that during philosophy tutorials at university we used to discuss the different theories of time, which have puzzled philosophers since the fifth century BC. He showed polite interest at first, so I explained that Zeno held that the appearance of temporal change was illusory, while Aristotle took the so-called 'dynamic' view of time, arguing that the future lacked the reality of the past or the present. Tiger did not appear to subscribe to the Aristotelian view. 'Me, I can't wait for the future,' he said. 'I am not the same like Aristotle. Oh, no! I *love* the future.'

And he did. Indeed he managed to project onto the future a reality that was absent in the present or the past, at least for him. He was never completely in the place that other people inhabit, but always halfway elsewhere, with only one foot on the ground, the other dangling fretfully in the air, trying to feel its way towards the next ten minutes. From the outside, it seemed an unenviable, tortured state. There was no time to pause and look, no time to tune into the deeper rhythm of things, no focus to set him firmly in the world or nourish the soul. There was a gap between him and the moment, so that the present was already part of the past and the future hadn't yet begun. It could have been one of Dante's circles of hell.

On another occasion, just for something to say, I touched on the logical feasibility of time travel. I mentioned the familiar thought experiment where the time-traveller goes back in time in order to murder his grandparents and thus prevent his own birth. At this Tiger became curiously uneasy. He found this sort of discussion sinister and threatening, and he immediately changed the subject. He felt himself on much safer ground planning the next half hour and checking the time obsessively. Inside his restlessness I wanted to believe there was a serenity trying to get free and bring itself into being. One day perhaps he would discover the joy of dawdling, of allowing the day to take its own course. Meanwhile there was an institutional regularity about the way of life in the Dordogne, and it could not be challenged without incurring a significant risk of miff or tiff.

~

Writing is hard and uses up a lot of energy. I think it is nearly always hard, though it is possible to forget in between times how hard it is. When a chapter has been worked and reworked into a finished piece, it is easy to lose sight of how it came to be that way and how long it took. Some afternoons I went to the studio and nothing happened at all. I would stare into space or look through the windows, letting my mind drift, hoping an idea would take hold, persuading myself that this is what real writers did. At other times I concentrated on removing tiny insects and bits of dead skin from the spaces in between the keys of the computer keyboard. There are moments of terrible bleakness with the creative process, when you question what you are doing and why you are doing it. Ghosting, which is just a job after all, ought to offer some protection. But for some reason it doesn't.

Some progress had been made, however, and the nuts and bolts of the new novel were already in place. The setting, the main characters, and the voice had all been decided, though there was a whiff of compromise about all three. I had started out in the first person, hoping to achieve the immediacy and conviction that can come with a first-person perspective. But it felt too personal, too intimate, and I soon abandoned it for the third person. I had also thought of setting the story in Scotland, but that too would have been too subjective, and besides, Tiger would have hated it. Although he claimed to love Scotland, it was purely an abstract love, for he regarded it as a curious foreign land, quite inscrutable, and much more 'abroad' than further-flung places. So instead I chose a sleepy Oxfordshire village in middle-class England. This is not my territory at all, but it allowed me to make one of the characters an academic at Oxford University (my daughter was there at that time and I had come to know it a little), and also to set a dramatic scene in the Ashmolean Museum (where I had first seen paintings by Pasternak). I drew up a list of main characters: the two married couples, their children, the vicar next door and his long-suffering wife. I had also decided that the academic would have an ex-wife – she would be the mother of one of the children and confined in a psychiatric hospital near Oxford.

Nabokov says somewhere that any writer who claims that his characters are running away from him and assuming their own identity is simply failing to keep them in order. From memory, I think Nabokov was quite bad-tempered about this. He believed that, since characters are the creation of the writer, they should be made to do exactly as they are told. Well, yes and no. In one sense this is obviously the case: characters can be plucked from the air and made to fit any description. They can be given a twitch, a limp, a divorce, thick ankles, a dark secret – anything at all. Lives can be invented that never existed, and never will exist – all this is possible. But in the end, even if the characters are 'invented', they are usually not wholly contrived. They turn out to be strange composites of people you have known, who behave in ways you have observed, saying things you have heard or thought about. And the strange thing – the thing that Nabokov doubted – is that they *can* start behaving in ways that surprise you. But the real surprise is that they do something you hadn't planned for them, not that they do something completely out of character. In fact what they do is usually absolutely right for them.

According to the American writer Paul Auster,* it is when

---

* Interview with Mark Irwin in *The Art of Hunger*, Penguin Books, 1997.

the characters in his books are most confined that they seem to be most free, and when they are free to wander, they are most lost and confused. This appears to be a baffling remark, yet it is more or less what I found to be true. For example, the vicar in the story has an obvious part to play in comforting the bereaved parents, but instead of being tied down to the predictable role of bumbling, well-meaning clergyman offering the strength of faith as proof against despair, he is allowed to wander freely and ends up lurching between extremes and having a crisis himself. I suspect he fails to convince, partly because of the Paul Auster paradox: the character seems to be set free from the obvious, but he finishes up trapped in another kind of stereotype – the vicar who has lost his faith. By contrast, I intended the vicar's wife to be 'confined', bound by the limitations of her role. She would be a peripheral character, someone just for decoration, giving tea to distressed parishioners, feeling oppressed, and so on. But out of these initial restrictions, she developed into a much more interesting character than her husband. A dull marriage had altered the balance of her mind, and her life was lived at depths of concealment, marked by shame and guilt and disappointment. She ended up playing a pivotal part in the narrative.

In the afternoons when the weather was fine we went to the swimming pool. It was a sizeable pool and beautifully maintained by the *gardien*, who used brushes and a long pole with a large ladle on the end to keep it free of leaves and insects. Sometimes as we drew near he would be scooping out a solitary fly or giving the tiles a final polish. But as soon as he saw us he would scurry off, for he knew that the poolside was designated a place of absolute privacy. The etiquette there was complete nakedness – *comme les animaux* – as Tiger put it, and it was a requirement – so he said – that applied to all his house-guests, without exception. It was a matter he often raised on the short walk to the pool, and invariably he invoked the health-giving properties of fresh air on bare skin or the freedom bestowed on the spirit once clothes had been discarded – as if the case for what he called 'being *au naturel*' had to be made anew each time. 'Skin is *amazing*,' he would say, sinking into a rhapsody. 'There's nothing like skin. It's so soft, it breathes, it is *alive*. Why on earth do we cover it up?' Why indeed, I would say, for it was easier just to agree, and in any case nakedness was no big deal. At other times he would ask, rhetorically, in the manner of Falstaff's disquisition on honour, 'What is the point of clothes? Do the beasts of the jungle wear clothes? Do the birds of the air?' His answer was brisk and decisive: 'No, of course they don't. Bloody hell, when you think about it, it's the strangest thing on earth to wear clothes!' Like a Bach fugue his subject could be cut up, inverted, quickened, slowed to half its speed, given a change of key, or several, but it always remained recognisably the same first subject, stated in all its clarity at the beginning.

What must we have looked like, the pair of us, as we lay side by side on the sunbeds by the pool? I often thought we must have made an absurd picture. Scottish pallor next to Levantine swarth – not to mention my blond mop, his dark walnut whip topknot, and our various assorted dangly bits and bobs. Of course, Tiger was quite unable to lie still. And his nudity was in fact not absolutely total, for he kept on his watches, checking them constantly and counting down the minutes and seconds till the next event, the designated time for launching himself in the pool. 'In fifteen minutes I will go in the water . . . in ten minutes I will go in the water . . . in eight minutes . . .' In between he talked about how relaxing it was, how peaceful, how calm. 'Don't you feel relaxed?' he asked every few moments. 'Aren't you calm?'

In truth I was far from calm on the days when Éclair, the killer Dobermann, was on the prowl. The security system was devised in such a way that the three dogs were shuffled round the various parts of the estate. This meant that there were always two guarding the main house and one guarding the smaller property and pool area. The theory was that, by moving them around, no dog would spend too much time on its own and all of them would enjoy a bit of variety. I dreaded the times when Éclair was on duty and I felt especially vulnerable in the scud. Tiger was aware of my fear and exploited it mercilessly. 'I wonder which of my babies is here today,' he would say, starting out innocently enough. And then with a devilish touch: 'Maybe it's Éclair. It's funny, you know, I haven't seen him yet. Have you seen him? I wonder where he can be – maybe I should call him.' He would discharge the short stiff laugh of the tormentor before calling out, '*Éclair, mon bébé! Où es-tu? Viens ici! Joue avec moi!*'

Can dogs smell fear? I have no idea, but it seems likely that they can. After all, we know that our nervous systems respond to stress with certain physiological changes such as increased heart rate and sweat gland activity. So although fear is an emotion, it almost certainly has a smell. As Éclair approached, I would note the quickening of my heart and a dampening on my skin. Sometimes there was cause for even greater alarm; for if dogs can smell fear, they can almost certainly smell a woman who is menstruating, as inevitably I was some of the time (not a subject that could easily be raised with Tiger). I had once heard a radio programme about grizzly bear attacks on women in Canadian national parks. The speculation was that women may be more prone to savage attacks because of odours associated with menstrual periods, and although the evidence was inconclusive the advice to women was not to camp in bear country during their periods. It may be argued that being under canvas in bear country and lying on a sunbed in dog territory are not remotely the same thing. But for me there was no conceptual distinction between being mauled by a grizzly and mauled by a Dobermann.

At these times of greatest dread it was always a relief to get into the pool and swim. I have always been at home in the water. Swimming is sensual and self-renewing. Water washes away pain. It holds you in a gentle embrace and allows you to let go. The rhythms of swimming feel natural; air in, air out, arms forward, arms back, legs together, up and kick, swishing cleanly like a kelpie. I feel I can keep going for hours without tiring. The body movements of swimming are efficient yet graceful, and they are woven into the fabric of the species more than any other form of propulsion. Walking and running are relatively recent activities, but man has known how to swim since before he was fully human. The water supports you and allows you to trust, to breathe deeply, to be confident and care-free. Swimming cultivates the imagination, the fluent motion relaxing the body and allowing the mind to roam free. There is rapture to be had in water.

Even so, no one who observed Tiger in the pool would ever have believed in an aquatic theory of evolution. Tiger was unable to swim and afraid to learn; yet, determined to do something of the same order, he went through a ritual that was much more elaborate and strenuous than even the most vigorous swimming. As I did lengths up and down the pool, he stood waist-deep at one corner and behaved like a man in the throes of a delirium. He performed a series of hectic exertions of his own devising, counting from one to a hundred for each separate activity, all the while panting and blowing like a birthing mother. The exercises involved desperate movements – slapping the water with the flat of his hands, or doing frantic futile kicks as he clung to the side of the pool – and they continued for a heartbreaking length of time. Because he didn't like getting splashed, he kept his eyes closed and his face screwed up during the entire frenzy. It could have been a form of theatre designed to disturb the spectator, or a morality play concerned with the forces of evil and man's Fall and Redemption.

When you come to write, things creep out of the back of your mind as well as the front. I suppose we carry our history around with us. The characters in the new novel were beginning to ride my hobby-horses and, though they struck out on their own from time to time, they had a curious way of returning to the familiar pathways of my own preoccupations: Russian literature, the puzzle of memory, the absence of God, the nature of truth. Show your workings, the teacher at school would tell us as we grappled with multiplication and long division. And now I was showing the workings of this novel, with the result that a gap was opening up between the thing begun and the unfolding story. Here is an example of what I mean. It occurs in the passage where the grief-stricken mother wanders through Oxford with no clear sense of purpose:

She felt it was important to be near people, to observe the details of ordinary living. In time she thought they would make her well again. Sometimes she found herself gazing at people, observing their pleasure second-hand, and feeling detached from it at the same time, like tapping into someone else's memory. Her daughter had asked her once if it was possible to have someone else's memories. No, she said, memory is an individual, subjective thing. Afterwards she had worried about her answer. She knew from her studies that memory can be distorted in various ways, not least by our knowledge and expectation of the world. We can also inherit memories and build our own out of the rubble of other people's.

Since the summer she had thought a lot about memory, and how much she had underestimated its importance. It was possible that a person's very existence could be measured in terms of the extent to which he entered the memory of others. It was her memory of Oliver, for example, and nothing else, which made him part of the present and gave him a place in the future. In Doctor Zhivago there is a passage where Yury tries to give comfort to Anna, who believes she is dying. He tells her that throughout her years on earth her identity has been firmly established in the minds and hearts of others:

You in others are yourself, your soul. This is what you are. This is what your consciousness has breathed and lived on and enjoyed throughout your life — your soul, your immortality, your life in others. And what now? You have always been in others and you will remain in others. And what does it matter to you if later on it is called your memory? It will still be you.[*]

As a student Kate had read these lines again and again, thinking them the most beautiful version of immortality she had come across, although no one close to her had yet died. Or disappeared.

There is a lot of cross-border trading going on here, between the details of the fiction and the story of a life — the life of the ghost in this case. The passage about memory, for example, can be taken at face value within the fictional context of a mother thinking about her missing child; at another level it was a veiled way of alluding to one of the bizarre aspects of my job — that of inventing episodes in Tiger's life and thereby 'giving' him memories that he couldn't possibly have. This was something that troubled me from time to time and applied particularly to his childhood, which I sometimes wrote about in newspaper articles, embellishing and enriching it in ways that pleased (and sometimes moved) him but had only a tenuous connection with biographical truth. Occasionally his child-hood was impossibly, even ludicrously, romanticised — water being drawn from the well where the Virgin Mary had drunk,

[*] *Doctor Zhivago* by Boris Pasternak, Collins & Harvill, 1958. Translated by Max Hayward and Manya Harari.

soil being tilled, and a wise old grandmother at whose feet the young boy heard tales of derring-do about the Ottoman empire. Once I had to check an atlas to establish if it really was possible to see the hills of Galilee, as I had described, from the spot of some invented childhood scene. At times it felt deceitful, but that didn't stop me. I'm no longer sure why I did this, although it seemed to be what was wanted at the time, and I think the absurdity of it all appealed to me. I also remember feeling a sense of power and being strangely excited by it.

And now the same sort of thing, only in reverse, was happening with the ghosting process. I was raiding my own knowledge and experience of the world rather than the author's. Although the novel is set in and around Oxford, for example, I deliberately used local place names from the East Neuk of Fife where I lived – Lower Kenly, Upper Kenly, Kenly Green. For some reason this was exhilarating. And in creating the character of the academic, I poked fun at my ex-husband who had something of a reputation among his colleagues for self-importance and a sense of his own suffering in the world. This felt even more exhilarating.

> Julian loved himself every bit as much as his self-adulation required. He considered himself the most moral of men, not in any prudishly upright way, but in the manner of a man who has examined his position carefully and separated right from wrong. Like the anti-hero in Dostoevsky's Notes from the Underground, he believed there were two sets of people: normal people and those like himself of enhanced awareness. This conviction came about through extensive reading and thinking about literature, which he believed contained all the truth of the

world. The penalty for his enhanced sensitivity was increased suffering. In his own mind Julian suffered more than most men, far more than Edward, for example. He loved his brother dearly, but . . . he felt a certain remoteness from him. Those who do not grapple with art, he thought, cannot hope to make sense of life. Nor can they appreciate – except in the most superficial way – the struggle between good and evil, duty and desire, honour and pleasure. They may be spared some of the agony of existence, but they will never truly understand the world.

Julian's pain was not always obvious to others since so much of it took place beneath the surface. Those who were less finely tuned than himself often failed to appreciate it. But he did not mind, for the rewards were commensurate with the suffering itself. These included deeper insights, a profound moral sense, and an understanding of the nature of love. It was in this last area, love, that Julian felt his heightened sensibilities had exposed him to the greatest pain.

And so on. And so on. Of course I did not tell Tiger that this Julian character was a caricature of my ex. How could I? But also, how could I *not*? I persuaded myself that what he didn't know couldn't hurt him, but that has ever been a woeful cop-out. In truth I think I had begun to sign away my soul.

One of the more pressing difficulties with the book was that I did not feel confident about being able to fulfil Tiger's orgasmic stipulation, so to speak. I had hinted to him that there might be complications in the literary execution, but he continued to regard it as a *sine qua non* of the action. I had been proceeding on the assumption that Tiger's idea was a male sexual fantasy. Men love the idea of having a third person in on the act – or so women think. A little elementary research, however, led me to believe that it was not an absolutely standard male fantasy, yet I still thought it would be best to treat it as fantasy in the novel. I broached this line of reasoning as delicately as possible, but Tiger was having none of it.

'What nonsense!' he barked.

'But surely, it's the only way,' I said. 'Otherwise it won't be plausible.'

'How can it be plausible if he doesn't *do* it? It can only be plausible if he *does* do it. Why don't you see that? We have to make him *do* it.'

There was a lot at stake here. I had to hold my ground.

'If he just thinks about it,' I said, 'if it stays in his head, then it will be more convincing. People have all sorts of strange fantasies. The imagination is a weird place. I think we can make it work at that level.'

'But who are we going to convince if it's all in his head? It will only convince *him*! And what's the good in that? He has to *do* it! It has to *happen*! For people to believe it, it *has* to happen! Isn't it? What's the matter with you? What is this nonsense?'

His heart was clearly set on it. The book would be a travesty without it – *Hamlet* without the Prince. Much of his eagerness, I believed, could be put down to his identification with the protagonist. As had happened first time round, he was projecting himself into the principal role. What was surprising, indeed alarming, was that quite early on it had also become clear that the two women towards whom Tiger would be the conquering hero, at least within the covers of the book, were in fact real live women. One was an attractive, intelligent former employee based in London, and the other was her cousin living in New York – both, as it happened, born on the same day.

Each day after I had finished in the studio Tiger would ask for a progress report. 'Have we reached the *orgamsi* yet?' he would enquire with dispiriting regularity, although it is only fair to say that the question never seemed salacious or even coarse. It was more like a child asking that familiar question from the back seat of the car: 'Are we nearly there?' If I even hinted at possible difficulties, he became downcast for a moment or two before firing questions in rapid succession, all of them beginning with 'but' – his way of seeking reassurance.

–But they're not serious, these difficulties? –

–But we can solve them, no? –

–But we don't have to abandon the plan? –

–But we will finish soon, isn't it? –

It seemed a mercy simply to agree. The orgamsi, as he called it, was enthused about and relished at every opportunity. He took obvious pleasure in imagining how beautifully it might be done, delighting in what he supposed would be the reaction of readers. Anticipation was the sweetest pleasure for him. 'Just you wait,' he would say, a smile playing on his lips, 'just you wait till they read that bit.' As if it might happen all by itself if only I waited. I couldn't help thinking that the particular readers he had in mind were the two women on whom his flight of fancy was based. He even wanted to use their real names in the title of the novel – a completely mad idea, I said.

In the end the actual names were abandoned and replaced by aliases with a similar ring to them.

I had tried several different ways of trying to effect the – what shall I call it? – the reverie. The original idea was to have the two principal women (one the mother of the vanished child) as the close cousins, and I just crossed my fingers that a suitable character could be created to fill the stud role. It was not something I enjoyed thinking about. I also sweated over how the sexual congress might best be arranged, flirting briefly with a number of options:

1 passion and conflagration leading to ecstasy all round
2 copulation brutal and loveless but with unexpected benefits for the women concerned
3 variations on the above.

But I would journey only so far down a chosen route before encountering some grim problem that had me scurrying back up again. For example, would this 'outreach' climax be some sort of unintended consequence? Perhaps. Or would it be delivered with intent and joyfully received? Probably not. All things considered, it would presumably just *happen* to the third party, willy-nilly – or, in Tiger's phrase, nilly-willy – in which case it would surely happen at a time not of her choosing. And if it was unsolicited it could easily be inopportune, particularly if it had to travel across different time zones. It hardly bore thinking about. Yet I thought about it constantly. Psychologists have written learned papers on the impossibility of refraining from thinking about a pink elephant, or anything else, for any length of time. The intention to refrain from thinking about something evidently activates the very thought you are trying to avoid. This pink elephant phase lasted for several weeks.

Of course, illusions have to be rendered, but how do you stop yourself from pricking them? Here was another quibble. Tiger was obviously keen to break new ground, in the sense that our hero, and he alone, would be capable of producing this amazing synchronous effect on two women in different parts of the globe. But as I understood it, the joint cousinly climax had to be contingent upon the exceptional closeness of the women in question, so unless they were both virgins, not to mention unlucky in their experience of lovemaking, they must surely have climaxed concurrently before. With someone else. Someone other than our hero. And if not, why not? Thus the armature of contrivance kept breaking through, and I was continually hampered, not by a failure of nerve exactly, rather by humility before ordinary reality. An inbuilt crap detector is an awkward piece of equipment for any woman trying to carry out this kind of mandate for a man. Yet it had to be done, so I pressed on. The hero in John Banville's *Shroud* says: 'I cannot believe a word out of my own mouth', and I suppose I had arrived at a similar position.

In the circumstances it was not an easy matter to deliver quality orgasms to those taking part in the story. And so, a compromise was reached, though it had all the drawbacks of a trade-off and no obvious benefits, at least not for Tiger, whose high hopes were cruelly thwarted. The idea of the two families remained, but I simply could not effect the needful with grown-up, sexually mature, sane adults. So instead, and in a spirit of greater realism, the cousins – together with their fanciful frolics – were switched to the younger generation. This is how the ground was prepared:

It was as if their closeness had been preordained. By some extraordinary coincidence they had been born on the same day in late August, Tara greeting the world as a strong healthy screaming baby, her cousin slipping out vulnerably six weeks ahead of schedule and scarcely bigger than a bag of sugar . . . As the years went by, they became closer and closer. They shared secrets, made every conceivable kind of pact, took vows of confidentiality, became blood sisters in a solemn ceremony and crossed their hearts and hoped to die. They played language games and devised exclusive ways of communicating.

Establishing the bond early on allowed it to be infinitely strengthened by the disappearance of the young boy – the brother of one of the cousins. Ordinary life is suspended after the tragedy and the days seem to merge one into another. The adults are so busy coping with their own grief that the girls – by now fifteen years of age – are left to get on with life and their own feelings largely by themselves. They befriend the boy next door, only son of the vicar who is helping the bereaved parents, and gradually they retreat together into their own world, all three bound by a common neglect. They have a secret meeting place in the grounds of a disused farmhouse and it is here that their sexual awakening takes place.

> . . . And so united by a common hurt, the young people had begun to experiment. It was something that had developed gradually, as a natural offshoot of their pain, which became diffused and softened in the thrill of the new.

The line between innocence and knowledge is scarcely
a line at all; it is much more a meandering stream, flowing
sometimes this way, sometimes that, occasionally turning
back on itself before finding the way forward once more,
reduced to a trickle in places, at other points surging
ahead. It is not something fixed or predetermined, but
something that finds its own level and makes its own way.
This is not how they thought of it at the time, but it is
a truthful description of how things happened.

It is clear from these lines that the writer is struggling a
bit. It is not only the river that is meandering and turning
back on itself. The reader is being asked not so much to
suspend disbelief as to indulge the author. Moving from the
adult world to the realm of adolescent desire was definitely
a bit of a cop-out. But I felt that Tiger's dreams, albeit in a
modified form, might be fulfilled there. I thought that writing
about the freshness of first love would perhaps be less awkward
and would have fewer pitfalls. It might also allow for strange
elaborations. That, at least, was the theory. Here was the practice:

James lay now between the girls, propped up on his elbows,
looking from one to the other with complete adoration.
The sun and fresh air washed deliciously over their bodies.
He longed to possess them, to merge his body with theirs.
Gently, as he had done many times now, he ran his fingers
over Tara's coppery sheen of tightly curled hairs, springy
to his touch. She guided his hand between her legs, where
his practised movements brought a sudden slick wetness.

He pushed his fingers inside her. As he worked his hand in the rhythmic movements he knew Tara loved, he felt skilled and powerful. He traced the outline of her hard nipples with his tongue and drew them, first one, then the other into his mouth. He exulted in the pleasure he was giving; and also in the pleasure he was taking, for Claire all the while was rubbing her breasts against his back. Her arms were round his waist and she held his erection in one hand, stroking the tip of his penis with the other.

He had read about premature ejaculation in magazines, that it was not good, that it was something to be avoided, something you had to control. But if it was undesirable, no one seemed to think so, least of all himself. It did not put an end to their lovemaking; it merely prepared the way for more. The girls seemed to love it. It made them even more excited, and afterwards they kissed and stroked him with renewed passion till their bodies were a tangle of limbs and caresses. He almost wanted to write to the magazines and tell them they were wrong. But what was the point? All that mattered was here and now. There were no rules of conduct, no one had to prove anything. They just did what felt right; out of love, and out of a kind of unspoken disdain for their parents.

Tiger did not conceal his disappointment. It was absolute and comprehensive.

'But they're children!' he scoffed. 'Why are we writing a children's book?'

'It's not remotely a children's book,' I said, slightly horri-fied. 'It's an adult book with children – young adults – in it.'

'They are *children*!' he insisted. 'They haven't even done it before!'

'That's the beauty of it,' I said, glimpsing a straw that might be clutched, 'they're not yet set in their ways.'

'And they're doing it all together! They are not apart at all. We agreed they would be miles apart! We've made it into an *orgy!*'

So sudden, this prudery. So unexpected.

'Well, it's hardly an orgy,' I said, trying to placate. 'They are just feeling their way. It's a kind of innocence in fact. And anyway they love each other.'

This was desperate stuff.

Tiger was not to be appeased. He fumed and frothed. And scowled as he read the passage again. He moved his lips as he read and his breath made a susurrus, like bamboo in the breeze. Then came another objection, overlooked the first time.

'We don't even say that the girls have orgamsi *together*. At the same time. Why don't we *say* it? How can people under-stand if we don't say it? We have to *say* it.'

And so we said it. And this is how we said it:

> . . . She lay on her front on the bed, her face buried in
> a duck-feather pillow. James had entered her from behind,
> urgently and without much preparation, as he often did
> now, knowing how it made her wild . . . .While James
> lay on top of Tara, Claire knelt at the end of the bed,

straddling James's legs, moving rhythmically against his firm flesh. She clasped his buttocks and rocked him in and out of Tara. At these times she felt that she herself was making love to Tara, that James was an intermediary, a vehicle for her own passion. When she heard Tara's gasp, a long swishing sound, like skates stopping on ice, she knew absolutely that it was the moment of most intense feeling in her life so far. But then, a second or two later, at the height of her own ecstasy, that moment was replaced and transcended by another, even more intense. At these times she knew what it was to feel love, to ache with love, to want to die for love.

This was a terrible letdown for Tiger. It was not at all what he had dreamed of. The pinnacles reached were not transatlantic, and our hero, far from being a representation of the author, was a sixteen-year-old spotty youth. This marked only one of several disappointments with the novel.

By contrast, I felt a lot better once the tripartite orgasm, the three-piece suite, was out of the way. It had been oppressing me and I felt relieved to have dispatched it. Another reason to be glad was that the warm country air of the Dordogne valley had now been swapped for the cool salt air of St Andrews and I felt I could breathe more deeply and freely. It was always a bit of a relief to be home. I split huge logs on the chopping block and stacked them up in the garden. For the first few days it felt strange to handle money again or make simple decisions for myself. Ordinary domestic life seemed slightly exaggerated, larger than normal, as if seen through a lens. I didn't have to eat breakfast at 7am, and the man of the house did not force food on me. There was no strict timetable. I would walk around the house and garden, finding my footing again, touching familiar objects, bringing them back into my life.

But the peace didn't last for long. There was a book to be finished. I would have liked to polish paragraphs and weigh each word, but there was no time for that. The telephone started ringing at half past eight every morning and the questions were invariably the same.

'How are we doing? Are we nearly done yet?'

I hated this pressure. It was such a strain trying to hold the novel together. With this frenzied haste there was a danger of everything falling apart in my head. Now and then I begged for thinking time as well as writing time, and it would then be graciously suggested that of course I must take as much time as I needed – 'Bloody hell, we all have to think!' he said, every inch the man of reason. But all the while the publication date and the launch party were being arranged, and there would be more phone calls to tell me the details – 'Just so you know what's happening'.

As the chapters became ready they were faxed to London for approval. Or sometimes I delivered them in person. For the most part they got through on the nod. Occasionally, however, a complaint would be lodged and something would have to be changed. For example, towards the end of the book the vicar's wife, Diane, who has led a life of quiet desperation, finds herself in bed with Edward, father of the boy who has disappeared. This is how it is described:

It was such a long time since Diane had used certain parts
of her body that she had almost ceased to consider them
at all. She occasionally felt desire in the place that her
mother used to refer to as down there, but she had learned
over the years to channel it into sleep. As she turned over
in her mind what had occurred, trying to give an account
of it to herself – in order she supposed, to confer some
reality upon it – she could not readily name those areas
where she had just experienced such wonderful sensations.
The feelings were still intense, but the manner in which
they had been arrived at was already beginning to fade.

Tiger thought that the scene was not explicit enough and that
it was difficult to work out what was happening. 'And it's not
poetic,' he lamented. 'Sex should be *poetic*.' Ah, that elusive word
again. But the main problem was the description of Diane's body,
for it broke the sacred principle of idealised beauty. It fitted the
story to say that Diane had not looked after her body and that
she felt some shame in having neglected it. But Tiger could not
bear the idea of sagging breasts and a rounded belly, not even if
they were contextually apt. He hated anything displeasing or
unpleasant – obesity, illness, unsightliness of any variety. It was a
sort of corollary of Dostoevsky's belief *Beauty will save the world*
– the idea that the world might be destroyed by ugliness. It had
to be hidden away, not talked about; that way it ceased to exist.

More importantly, he believed that he had detected something wrong with the narrative. He seemed pleased by this.
'There is a mistake,' he said gleefully, and he gave a watery
smile like a pale sun after rain. He then rose to his full height

and started pacing up and down majestically. Now and then it struck me that there was something operatic in our dealings with one another. 'Oh yes,' he snorted, 'I have spotted a *big* mistake. Just you wait.' He asked me to sit down while he read the offending passage to me. 'Listen carefully,' he said, 'and we will see if you can spot it too.' This is what he read:

> Edward was a validation of something she had wanted to believe and had forgotten was possible: that there could exist between a man and a woman something beautiful and loving, unattended by expectations, needs, grasping selfishness. Set against all those people who sat at her kitchen table – people whose lives were disfigured by disappointment, misunderstandings, cruelty, injustice – this encounter seemed to have reached beyond ordinary experience. As a result, the significant thing she had forgotten was beginning to seep back into her memory. It was not yet fully delineated, but she thought she could detect in it the beginnings of a belief. It was the belief that love, even when it had gone from a marriage, could come to dwell there again.

He raised the volume in the last sentence, so that it was impossible not to grasp that the big mistake must be contained therein. When I looked blank, he read the last sentence again, booming out every word, adding after a pause for dramatic effect, 'Don't you *see*? Don't you *see*?' When I still didn't see, he recited with studied patience the list of characters from the novel, then he proceeded to verify their marriage partners, and only when we were in complete agreement about who was who and who was married to whom did he deliver the final judgement: 'Now listen! We say that she believes love could come back to the *marriage,* but we have put her in bed with *Edward*, we have not put her with her *husband*!' To remove any lingering doubt, he threw his hands in the air and exclaimed, '*Now* do you see? It doesn't make sense! How can we say love comes back to the marriage when she's fucking someone else?'

These moments were quite depressing, because they showed how far apart we were and how impossible it would be to get better connected. Such exchanges were hard to manage, not least because I truly wanted him to be happy with my work. In that respect my happiness was contingent upon his, and each new declaration of discontent was a blow to my spirits. At the same time this was evidence, if any were needed, that we occupied different ontological spheres. He was not interested in things psychological or the winding ways of the subconscious; in fact he was rather afraid of them. He was insensible to the notion that apparently ordinary, sensible people can often have quite ridiculous private lives.

As in life, so in books – he preferred the text to be straightforward and unambiguous. I was made intensely aware of this point on the occasion when he took a flight to Edinburgh in order to read Chapter Eight. He had told me of his plan the week before, so there was no question of the chapter not being finished. I picked him up at the airport and drove him to the Caledonian Hotel, where he had booked the finest suite overlooking the castle.

'Did you bring Chapter Eight?' he asked as soon as he had checked in.

'Of course,' I said.

'Then give it to me and I will put it somewhere safe. We don't want it to get lost.'

I had imagined he would want to read it straightaway, but no, he would settle into his suite, make some telephone calls, and at 6.40 precisely we would drink some champagne before having dinner at the Pompadour. Afterwards he would read the chapter – 'I will be relaxed then' – and in the morning we would discuss it – 'Come to the hotel at 8.20 a.m.'

Next day I knew the moment I saw him that all was not well. He was perfectly courteous, but at the same time there was a stiffness and formality in his approach that made me feel as if I had been called to the headmaster's study. We sat opposite each other at a desk and he placed the chapter between us. He licked his fingers and turned over the pages one by one, about twenty of them, making the same comment on each, repeated verbatim –'With this page I have no problem, with this page I have no problem'– and so on, until he reached the very last page by which time the tension was almost unbearable. 'But with *this* page, number one hundred and nineteen, I have a big problem. There is something missing. It doesn't make sense.' And as before he read it to me so that I too would see. The chapter in question deals with the deepening friendship between the young people and ends with a description of the two girl cousins asleep in bed together after a stressful day. The final paragraph reads as follows:

> In the confusing no man's land between deep sleep and consciousness Tara was faintly aware of a door opening and a shaft of light cutting through her bedroom. She moved in a kind of reflex action, and she felt the weight

and stickiness of Claire's limbs on her own body. The last thing she registered before drifting back into the depths was the click of the door closing.

By the time he reached the last sentence Tiger had worked himself up into what appeared to be a state of anger, banging out each word on the table. I could not imagine the point he was trying to make. I remained silent and uncomprehending. After a few moments he banged the table again.

'*Who* closed the door?' he suddenly demanded to know. 'We say there is the click of the door closing, but we don't say who closed the door!'

'No, we don't,' I agreed.

'But *why* don't we say it? We *have* to say it! Otherwise how can the readers know? I read it so many times – twenty, maybe forty times – and each time I asked myself, "*Who closed the fucking door?*" I got so irritated.'

This episode was something of a watershed for me. I suddenly felt weary. The tension between absurdity and normality was becoming too much. If you don't resist the madness, you become part of it. I had not resisted it, and now I was part of it. This was a crystalline moment and marked what I now think of as the beginning of the end. There was absolutely no point in trying to explain to Tiger the nature of dramatic suspense or the need to keep the reader in a state of curiosity. It was best left alone. There was such a thing as dignity, wasn't there?

~

I finished the book. It was, in the famous phrase, a learning experience. I travelled to London and handed it over, glad to be free of it. When I arrived back in St Andrews a few days later, a large package was waiting for me. The covering letter informed me that the author had delivered his typescript and it was now ready for editing. Could I kindly turn it round as quickly as possible?

Publication of the second novel coincided with the French edition of the first novel, and I persuaded myself that all that liquid romping really did sound better in French. Who would not agree that *il glisse sur sa peau humide* is more appealing than *he slides over her moist skin*? Or that *des gouttelettes perlent sur sa toison fauve* is a vast improvement on *droplets of moisture sit on her copper fleece*? Robert Frost thought that poetry got lost in translation, but perhaps poetry can also be found.

The party to launch the book was a bizarre event for me. People asked if I'd read the new novel, and what did I think of it. Sometimes I said, yes, and that it was very good, and sometimes I said, no, but I was looking forward to it. What I said didn't matter, I told myself. But later that same evening it did matter, because Tiger took me by the arm and introduced me to one of the guests, a well-known (but not to me) literary agent.

'This is my editor,' said Tiger to well-known agent.

'But she told me five minutes ago she hadn't read your book!' said well-known agent to author.

'Bloody hell, if she hasn't read it, I'm in trouble!' said Tiger.

Awkward laughter all round. Our alliance was a curious compound and we were held together by its strange elements.

The reviews of the new novel were mostly kind, though there was general agreement that the three-way extravaganza was a mistake. The *Daily Telegraph* reviewer was particularly clear-sighted. Having commended the author's 'mild, thoughtful tone' he gave the cousinly capers the thumbs-down:

> . . . they [the girls] embark on mutual sexual consolation, an unexpected occurrence that reads like an after-thought of which, once considered, the author could not bring himself to let go.

By far the most interesting and favourable review came from the novelist Alice Thomas Ellis. In the *Literary Review* she wrote:

> [the author] has an uncanny awareness of the atmosphere of loss, how it affects the bereaved and those on the periphery . . . he knows how people gather 'in small groups, like vultures sensing the presence of death. They discussed and told what they knew and what they did not know, and felt the particular dismay reserved for other people's misfortunes.' He knows that Kate moves in a 'sort of sepia fog' and he knows about the 'huge surge of happiness' that overwhelms her when she sees a child in a party of schoolchildren and mistakes him for her son. 'For the rest of her life that feeling did not come again, neither in its intensity nor in its immediacy.' This is heartbreaking.

Tiger was thrilled with this review and read it out to me on the telephone. I too was pleased, but I also felt something else – something akin to shame and compunction. For I knew from a newspaper article that, some twenty years earlier, Alice Thomas Ellis had lost her son, aged nineteen, in a freak accident. Suddenly, this fictional account of loss struck me as a trivial counterfeit. I had believed all my adult life that writing was important, that the novel mattered, that the reader should be able to trust the author. Now I had sullied that belief. Frederic Raphael once said in an interview, 'Novel writing is really a matter of coming to terms with your own squalor.' Whatever he meant by that, I agree with him.

At the end of her piece Alice Thomas Ellis wrote something intriguing, and if I ever meet her I shall ask her if perhaps she had rumbled the fact that things were not quite what they seemed.

> [the author] has a sensitivity and an insight into human
> nature unusual in a man, and he writes quite beautifully.
> This is not the first book he has written in which I find
> the character of the author, his invisible presence, as inter-
> esting as any of the people on the page.

The author accepted these words at face value and in due course they appeared in bold print on the cover of the paperback edition.

In the end I decided that this novel for me was not after all a complete sham. Of course it was contrived, but in the contrivance there emerged a certain shape to the world that was quite telling. The way things bubble beneath the surface is deeply mysterious, and if they occasionally boil up and spill over, something is set free. Indeed whenever I managed to loosen the shackles of the ghost, I quite enjoyed writing. There were even the beginnings of a belief that I may always have been a writer in my head. As a child I had a sense of strangeness, a sense of otherness that has never entirely left me. I was always trying to make sense of everything, in thrall to the power of language and, later, being thrilled with what it could do. But then you grow up, and for a long time you forget who you were.

What I discovered was that writing has a lot to do with unlocking secrets that are inside you. The familiar maxim 'write what you know' implies that you describe something that has happened to you, and in so doing you are examining the past and trying to make sense of it. We know this works, and it can work well. But in fact what I came to understand – and this was a startling revelation – is that in some sense you also write in advance of what you know, and that as you write you create the shapes and patterns that emerge later in your life. 'What you know' may in fact be what you know only at a subliminal level, and it might not be 'known' in the normal sense for a long time. This is not as arcane as it might sound. After all, the imagination is not some obscure element unrelated to living; indeed we imagine our lives even as we are living them. Imagination is rooted in memory and experience. And often what we imagine is what we are then impelled to live out. Through writing we are not so much creating a new pattern as uncovering one that is already in us. There is an interplay, only dimly understood, between the novels and the life. Writing is always personal. You reveal yourself to yourself. This may not become clear immediately, perhaps not for years afterwards. That second novel – I can see now – was about the letting go of pain. It also contained the genesis of a resolve: to pull out of this bizarre arrangement. To give up the ghost.

Part Seven
Beginning of the End

I had arrived in a place that felt dangerous. I had begun to think hypothetically, contingently, subjunctively. If only I didn't have to do this. Supposing I were simply to hand in my notice and leave. What if? What then? I wanted to write something different, something more open that didn't betray obvious signs of strain. Language creates us and defines us, but the stuff I was producing was a curious hybrid. I could never really trust it; it was too artificial, too much like a confidence trick. In odd melodramatic moments I thought of myself as a slave, toiling away, belonging to someone else, deprived of freedom.

Tiger was displaying a luminous sense of purpose and flitting from success to success. He promoted himself on a heroic scale, talking excitedly about all his projects, usually in the context of lavish displays of generosity, such as champagne lunches for journalists and newspaper editors. He loved these occasions and was an excellent host, working the room with his charm, his fine feathers fluttering, his coloured crest sparkling with purpose and poise. Even if the outcome was only a small paragraph in a diary column it was considered a triumph. There was now a steady trickle of commissions from serious newspapers, and the great and the good were queuing up to be interviewed. Amidst the everyday frivolity of life at the imperial court, a new gravitas was emerging.

Meanwhile I was losing the will to ghost. Outwardly I remained calm and got on with the work in hand, while inside I was building up a quiet fury at every new demand, every fresh enthusiasm. Psychologists call this emotional dissonance, pretending to feel one thing when you experience another – and it is bad for you, so they say. If you hide your negative emotions while displaying positive emotions, you can end up a bit of a wreck. This is one of the reasons why people who work in customer service centres suffer from early burnout – they have to be nice to people who scream and shout at them, and after only a short time they can't take it any more and start biting the carpet. Evidently there are two kinds of emotional dissonance: *residual*, when feelings from a previous event or conversation are carried over to the next; and *anticipatory*, when the prospect of the next event or conversation leads to an emotional schism. I'm sure I experienced both kinds.

The dishonesty was also beginning to weigh more heavily. My mouth was filled with half-lies and half-truths. At dinner parties people asked me, and what do you do? I'm an editor, I said, or sometimes, I'm a researcher. But this seldom put an end to the questions. (*And what do you research? What sort of editor?*) Eventually I began to take a perverse delight in saying that I was a housewife, even though by the mid-nineties this risked pity or scorn by the bucketful. There's no harm in dissembling, I told myself. But there is. If you can't say what you do, if you can't talk about your daily life, there is a penalty to pay. Curiously, despite all the lies I told, or perhaps because of them, a truth was uncovered: that you can't go on living that way without suffering a loss. Over time I became a martyr to social events where I might have to give an account of myself. I avoided questions, even from close friends, and was deliberately vague about my work. Secrets and lies are corrosive, I discovered, and when they begin to take over it is hard to get back to yourself. At times I felt I was living someone else's life, occupying someone else's head. And losing the way in my own.

Up till now I had tried to look upon the day-to-day pressures as living intensely, surely preferable to any number of dull existences. And the situation had contained enough weirdness to have a kind of wacky appeal. Tiger could be unconsciously hilarious, and mostly I had been able to see things through a comic prism, and if not comic, then ironic. Irony and absurdity, these two leaning towers, had exerted an enormous pull on me, though it was striking that they counted for nothing with Tiger. What had kept me interested was so very different from what kept him going. But all of that seemed to be changing. The absurdity was beginning to pall, and I was finding it hard to keep everything afloat – the pretence, the masquerade, the constant magnifying of an ego. It was sometimes exhausting. And having embarked on the writing of fiction with Tiger, it seemed that fiction now permeated everything. He could easily deny what was in front of his nose, and reality – whatever we mean by that – was cloaked in a layer that was not reality. Even something that had just occurred, something I had witnessed with my own eyes, could be transmogrified in an instant. The speed at which this could happen was truly remarkable. Innocent remarks were construed as vicious attacks, a glaring defeat presented as another dazzling success. One thing quickly became another, and it would be hard and then impossible to separate the new thing from the old.

Although I was gradually convincing myself that it was time to make a move, I was deeply alarmed at the thought of living without a salary. My children were beginning to be expensive – two were already at university and my youngest would be starting at art college the following year. In addition to my mortgage I was also still paying off the company loan that had helped me secure the family house. Part of me was appalled by my own pusillanimity and mixture of motives. At least Tiger was openly ambitious, unashamedly self-publicising. He believed in his own story enough to act on it, and ambition insulated him from the world. He had an absolute commitment to whatever was happening in his life at that moment, a complete confidence in what he was saying or doing. But my own position was more complex and ignoble: the ghost was actually getting above herself. I wanted to give up, but I didn't want to be without money; I felt aggrieved at being exploited but I think I also enjoyed a sense of having become the power behind the throne; I had imagined myself immune from delusions of grandeur, but no – a feeling of importance, the proximity to celebrity, my vital role in the construction of a rising scribbler – these things gave me a vicarious kick. A megalomaniac ghost – what a weird idea. Shades of Lady Muck in the Roller once again.

A job is just a job, declared my Now-Husband (N-H). He had taken to wearing odd socks in flashy colours, just like Tiger's. No, no! I protested. It's much more than a job – why, it's almost a vocation. It certainly wasn't a normal job that could be left in the normal way, I said. And what about references? I could hardly expect Tiger to write me one. Then write one yourself, said N-H, you write everything else, don't you? In any case I had probably unfitted myself for other employment. This, and much more besides, was what I rehearsed to myself and to the man at home. Tiger and I had become so much a tandem act, I told him, that it was now hard to imagine us functioning independently of each other. We were like two trapeze artists performing dangerous stunts in mid-air – he the flyer and I the catcher. How could I possibly give up? It would mean unmaking that which I had helped bring about, strangling the thing I had breathed life into.

And so I did nothing. Or rather, I continued to do what was expected of me, pretending to Tiger that I shared his enthusiasm, while complaining on the pillow at night about each new assignment. 'Give it up,' said the man on the other pillow. He was very patient, but even a patient man can feel he's had enough. Talking it over at home also helped me to see how weird the situation had become and convinced me that I had to take the necessary steps. More than once I resolved to say something to Tiger, but our exchanges were becoming ever more circumscribed. Only once did I raise the possibility that one day I might leave.

'But why?' he asked, sounding hurt. 'Don't you like it here? And what would you *do*? What on earth would you *do*? '

'Well,' I wavered, 'I thought I might try my hand at writing.'

'Writing? *Writing?* You think it's *easy* to write?'

At that point my nerve failed me and I drew back from conveying what was in my heart. Much easier to stick to the familiar pathways. It was to take another four years before the parting of the pathways. In the meantime I played to Tiger's expectations and got on with the job.

~

As luck would have it, just as I was hatching small doubts and raising them to be big strapping quandaries, Tiger was feeling particularly cock-a-hoop. In the summer of 1996, just before the second novel appeared, he gave an interview to Adam Nicolson in the *Sunday Telegraph* in which he said: 'I'm so excited. I've got so much to do. I've got four books coming out, I'm so optimistic, I'm looking forward so much to what is going to happen next.' I pretended to share this excitement, albeit a bit toned-down, but the fulfilment I had once experienced in the job seemed to have vanished. It had been there a minute ago, before I blinked and opened my eyes to the possibility of a different world, and though I sometimes searched for it still, or fancied that I felt it anew, it had actually gone.

No more novels, I had decided. But Tiger had different ideas. In a review of the first novel in the *Independent* Andrew Biswell had written:

> [the author] has written a book that is big despite its brevity ... he proves he is capable of writing an outstanding novel.

'You see,' said Tiger, 'he says we can write.' In my head I heard strange sounds, like circuits shorting. I could tell he had another novel coming upon him.

And indeed he had. It turned out that his imagination had been fired by the opening story in Julian Barnes' *A History of the World in 10½ Chapters*, in which there is an account of

Noah's Flood, told from the point of view of a woodworm.

'It's so clever, don't you think? Don't you agree?'

'Yes,' I said.

'It has given me an idea,' he said.

Which was to draw on another Old Testament story, namely the destruction of Sodom and Gomorrah.

'It will be amazing,' he said. 'Can you imagine? *Everyone* will want to read it.'

'What makes you so sure?'

'Because of Sodom and Gomorrah! Let me explain. With the Flood there's no sex, but with Sodom and Gomorrah we can put all the sex we like! And sex sells! Isn't it?'

He rose from his chair and launched into the now familiar ardour for a new project – how beautifully we would do it, how simple it would be to write, how the critics would love it, and so on. At these times he reminded me of a Harlem Globetrotter – fast, deft, agile, bouncing his enthusiasm around the room, potting a new shot every minute or two, yet taking the time between goals to impress and bewitch. As always it was a masterful performance. But my own spirits were diving. I had been in this place before and I just couldn't face another novel. Even so, I didn't refuse outright. Instead I said I would have to research the subject and think about it.

'But we shouldn't think for too long,' he said, 'or someone will pinch our idea.'

Mercifully, a different project soon beckoned: Tiger was to be a columnist on a tabloid newspaper. He was thrilled. The column was to appear once a week and would feature a woman in the news at the time, the particular slant to be left up to him. The fourth estate trusted him now. His massive volume on women had recently been reissued, and this had consolidated his reputation as an authority on the subject. 'It's like the bible,' he told a journalist in an interview. 'People look it up when they want to learn something.'

By this time he was working from new premises, a fine five-storey house in the heart of Soho, with spacious salons, a private bar in the basement and a studio flat at the top. He had poured love and money into its refurbishment, and it was now a source of great joy. The opulence of his new surroundings seemed to reflect his confidence in the future. The main room, which occupied the whole of one floor, was like a Cecil Beaton stage set: extravagant, resplendent and technically perfect. These qualities extended to the props and special effects – crystal chandeliers, elegant bookcases, photographs in silver frames, a sumptuous sofa, and of course the precious tiger skin. The colours of the paint and fabrics were bright and bold, softened only by the soft peach-pink flesh tones of the many female nudes that adorned the walls. The other *objets* also had a sultry, seductive quality, giving the room the air of an erotic theme-park. Visitors felt themselves transported to another time and place – the Moulin Rouge perhaps, or a seraglio at the Ottoman Court. Tiger was in his element. Since he himself was always a blaze of colour with mad rococo touches, he seemed to *belong* here. He wore a different suit every day, each with its own eye-popping silk lining and matching trimmings. Some days, in certain colours, he could be perfectly camouflaged in the room, like a lizard on a rock; other days, in different colours, he looked conspicuous and splendidly gift-wrapped.

In line with the surroundings, the emperor also seemed

bolder. This might have had something to do with his momentous decision to have a completely new hairdo. The substantial but delicate upsweep of many years had finally been removed, and he was now a skinhead to be reckoned with. He loved to feel the fresh air on his head, he said, and he took to stroking its new contours. 'Anyhow, why should I pretend I have hair when I have no hair?' Why indeed, we all said. 'It was a stupid idea!' he said, as if the thatch that had sat so precariously and required harnessing in the wind might have been a lapse of short duration. In fact the new look suited him, and everyone agreed it had been an excellent move.

Another decision was that there would be no supernumeraries in the new palace. Most of the staff would be in other buildings, but here, close to the throne, there would be only a small, select company of girls who would be chosen for 'the lightness of their shadow', a vital quality that had its origins in an Arab proverb. Someone whose shadow was light would have a certain reticence and, though she would be competent, she would be content to stay quietly in the background. Tiger's language was lit up by inscrutable sayings from the folklore of the Middle East in which the kissing content seemed curiously high: *Kiss the dog on the mouth until you get what you need out of him*; or *Kissing hands is fooling beards*. But it was lightness of shadow that he alluded to most. If ever he had to sack one of his lovelies, official grounds would be found for doing so, but the real reason would invariably be because her shadow was not light.

There were only three people to help run the new premises: a devoted young secretary who answered the telephone and kept Tiger's diary; a beautiful Girl Friday whose jobs included cleaning, polishing the silver, serving lunch, manicuring his nails and putting drops in his ears; and a society chef, a delightfully skittish young woman who prepared and cooked lunch to order each day. The dining-room was just as lavish as Tiger's private room: the walls were lobster-red and there was a huge antique mahogany table with matching chairs, and solid-silver place settings. Different guests arrived for lunch every day and all were given a conducted tour of the palace. No one left without a swag-bag containing signed copies of the latest books and occasionally, if the guest was particularly favoured, a silver heart in a black velvet pouch.

The arrangement for the weekly newspaper column was that Tiger would choose whichever woman was to be the subject, and we would then discuss the line to be taken. He would write down all his thoughts and fax them to me in Scotland whereupon they would be turned into what he liked to call 'beautiful prose'. Beautiful prose was a potent concept for Tiger, amounting to much more than the arrangement of words on a page. Beautiful prose was a transcendent thing, an indication of good character, a mark of decency, a moral register almost. Good and bad writing, like good and bad in the world, was a Manichean struggle between conflicting forces. And actually, though our touchstones were quite different and we weren't always in agreement about how this beauty might be captured, I felt something of the same, and still do.

The first column was to appear in the middle of January 1997, and so I travelled to London in the first week of the year to discuss the general approach to the new venture. As usual there was a sort of shopping-list of basic ingredients, the eggs and tinned tomatoes of the undertaking.

'It must be very distinguished,' said Tiger.

'Of course.'

'But we must never be boring,' – his voice was low in line with the warning – 'otherwise they will drop us immediately.'

'Do you want it to be polemical?'

'Polemical?'

'You know, controversial. Something that people will talk about over breakfast.'

'But of course! It *has* to be controversial. People expect it of me,' he said. 'But we must also be poetic. *Very* poetic.'

The newspaper in question was not exactly known for its lyricism, but I judged it wasn't worth putting a damper on things when they seemed to be going so well. For years Tiger had dreamed of having a regular slot in a newspaper and he was thrilled by the idea of a huge readership. I too was keen, mainly because I believed I could manage a column, and yet it would be demanding enough to keep the unthinkable – a third novel – at bay. And because Tiger knew so many famous women that there would be no shortage of material. 'We'll have such *fun*,' he said to me, 'and you'll make some money too.' This second point was certainly true: the newspaper would pay £500 for five hundred words, and I was to receive half of the total – a much better rate of pay than for anything else I had done.

Tiger made a confident start, dashing off page after page in a bold hand with lots of his trademark CAPITAL LETTERS, randomly dispersed to smack the reader in the eye. For the first few weeks, each time he phoned to tell me he had sent his piece by fax, he would say, 'It's so easy! You won't believe it, I wrote the whole thing in ten minutes!' In fact, I did believe it. But I also hated when he said something was easy since this usually meant that I would find it especially hard, a point that strained relations over the years. My role in this instance was to sort out the material, keeping as much as possible of the original, type it up and fax it back – straightforward enough in theory, but in practice something of a challenge. As a child I was always slightly in awe of language, and I suppose I have never really got over this feeling. But Tiger had a different starting point: language was there to be used, so what are we waiting for, where is the problem? Wittgenstein believed language has meaning because those who use it have agreed basic rules of syntax and signification, just as in a game of cards the players are agreed about the different suits and what is trump. I sometimes wondered what Wittgenstein would have made of our exchanges. In truth, Tiger had taken shelter in English and lived there for a long time, but it was not his natural home. In spite of this, his language was so powerfully engaged with its purpose that the style had an inimitable, inscrutable verbal genius all of its own. And yet his sentences were a riot of hangings and danglings, while the subject and predicate, being scarcely ever on speaking terms, always put up a fearful fight before being mediated into a suspension of hostilities.

Tiger also insisted on the requisite dash of philosophical depth or literary allusion. If ever these were absent, there would be a plaintive, melodramatic cry at the other end of the phone – 'Darleeng, where is the *literature*? What about the *philosophy*? You *promised*!' – as if he might burst into tears. Another required element was psychology, or rather its younger punchier sister, pop-psychology. The woman featured in the column was usually put on the couch, her character assessed, her faults or virtues or motives laid bare. 'We have to say what makes her tick' was how he put it. Which was interesting, since he, more than anyone I have known, preferred to stay fixed and immovable on the surface of himself. I once asked him what made *him* tick. '*Me? Tick?*' he said, as if I'd nabbed the wrong bloke, in immediate denial of the possibility that he ticked at all. He seemed afraid to probe, while still wanting to be thought of as a man who delved deep into his own soul. When it came to contradictions he could spin on a sixpence – his view of himself simply did not cohere. Perhaps this is true of most emperors.

I did quite a lot of spinning too. In the world in which I moved, there was a feeling that lying, pretending and dissembling were all just part of the repertoire. It was reality that was the danger – always loitering with intent, ready to pounce at any moment. If you weren't careful, if you didn't guard against it, everyone would soon be telling the truth, and then who knows where we'd all end up. No one said this, but you could feel it in the air.

I also thought a lot about the extent to which I deceived myself about what I was doing and why I was doing it. On the face of it, self-deception is an odd idea. At university my philosophy teachers even argued there was no such thing – according to them it amounted to no more than an interesting paradox. How could you set about misleading *yourself*, they scoffed. Surely you would know what you were up to, which would undermine the deception. And if you knew what you were doing, how was it possible to trick yourself into believing otherwise? But philosophers have always overestimated the rational side of human behaviour. Self-deception may have a paradoxical look about it, seeming to require that the same person must be both the deceiver and the deceived, but of course we all know what is meant and understood by it. And we're even quite lenient on it, precisely because it is thought to be an unconscious, irrational, minor-moral-flaw sort of transgression.

People are much tougher on deception – which is also odd, given the sheer ordinariness and ubiquity of it. Deception is part of everyday life – from the polite thank you for something we would much rather not have received, to the calculated lie to maintain a friendship. It is one of the ways we engage with the world, and we seem to have a special aptitude for it. We deceive one another to protect our emotional attachments, but we also cling emotionally to abstract ideas, like fame and power. Certainly, those who lie and deceive don't have any special identifying marks. It's not possible to tell from the outside – they look just like you and me. We all wear masks; it's just that some masks are worn so closely and tightly that they begin to consume the face behind them.

Something I learned as a ghost was that there is an interesting connection between deception and self-deception: lying to others plays a vital role in lying to yourself. Which is to say, you can more easily fool yourself if others are fooled too. On the other hand, it is not at all easy to lie to yourself while telling the truth to others. Especially to a new man in your life. Once N–H entered the picture, a definite limit was placed on my scope for self-deception.

~

After a month or two the columns settled down into a series of set pieces, almost formulaic in manner and matter. Judging the length became second nature – I could estimate 500 words standing on my head. Typically they were controversial and opinionated, packing a bit of a punch, and often containing elements of Tiger's own history and experience, such as details of an encounter with the woman in question. I paid attention to the form as well as the content, but the style was at times orotund, the tone defined by a kind of moral seriousness often expressed in a range of truisms. John Updike has spoken slightingly of 'the undercooked quality of prose written to order', but mine was generally overcooked, and sometimes it came out burnt and carbonised. I also inserted a semi-colon at every opportunity because it was Tiger's favourite punctuation – 'The semi-colon, such a beautiful thing. I love it!' And though absolutes were starting to look suspect in the country at large, absolutes nonetheless abounded. The pieces were larded with ominous phrases such as *the forces of darkness, the redemption of man*, *the sanctity of life*, and *the human condition,* and they tackled the much beloved big themes: love, God, betrayal, sex, innocence, art, humanity, and so on.

All of this was arrived at painfully, by trial and error, by learning what pleased Tiger most and upset him least. For me the aim was twofold: to try to achieve good presentable copy and to avoid incurring Tiger's displeasure. It took a while to get the hang of it, and the hang hung precariously between the two. If he liked what he saw, if he thought I had done a good job, I would immediately feel a surge of relief, something close to happiness in fact, now and then extending unbounded to a sense of cosmic joy. This visceral response, the extent to which my own emotional state depended on his, surprised me and worried me in equal measure. Why did I care so much? Why was his approval so important? Why did it matter? Why did I try so hard?

Occasionally, as soon as I picked up the phone, I knew I had got it right, for his reaction would be touchingly appreciative. 'I love it!' he would say. 'It is the best *ever*!' This often had to do with poignancy, the *lacrymae rerum* rating. If the finished piece brought a lump to the throat he was delighted. As usual he would read the text back to me – 'Are you listening? I will read it to you . . .' – and with the 'good' pieces, he would start back at the beginning again as soon as he reached the end. There was more to this than liking the sound of it; the act of reading it aloud turned it into his own creation.

Real happiness, however, was an allusion – usually given a thorough working over since it was unwise to assume any degree of conversance. Once, for example, in a piece on Elizabeth Taylor, I wrote about the phoenix building itself a funeral pyre, flapping its wings to fan the flames and burning itself to death, then rising from the ashes to start all over again. Each stage in the life cycle was carefully spelled out.

'Is it true?' Tiger asked as soon as he had received the fax.

'Is what true?'

'About the phoenix. I was so moved I nearly wept. But is it *true*?

'Well, mythologically speaking, it's true.'

'It's amazing! I love it!'

There was something endearing about this, in much the same way as when children ask after a bedtime story: Did they *really*? Is it *true*? And something that provoked similar feelings of fond protectiveness. Indeed Tiger could be heart-movingly open to new knowledge – the history of ideas, natural laws, classical references, biblical quotations, and so on. Provided there was no trace of condescension, and Occam's razor was applied to every explanation, he would embrace well-known facts as marvellous new discoveries, greeting them with a radiant, childlike wonder. Or occasionally, if my attempt to explain something didn't quite come off, he would listen politely in a state of baffled incomprehension, but with eyes displaying a kind of clever-buggers-these-Chinese look. I liked this side of him. It was guileless and open-hearted. But every so often I sneered inwardly at his ignorance of something or other. How could he not know *that!* – I gasped, looking down on him from my cruel smug perch on Mount Parnassus. I hate myself for that now. Tiger knew many things I didn't know. Besides, Orwell was probably right: ignorance is strength.

As often as not, however, Tiger didn't like what I'd done with the column, and this would lead to contentious phone calls often stretching over several hours as I tried to shape it to his satisfaction. And sometimes, even the beloved allusions could go terribly wrong. Once, for example, I began a piece with:

> They fuck you up, your mum and dad.
> They may not mean to, but they do.

'Are you *crazy?*' Tiger's phone calls were all mid-stream specimens – he didn't mess around with *hello, how are you* formalities. 'You want to get us sacked?'

'What's the problem?'

'Beloved, we can't say *fuck*! I don't believe you put it! No newspaper will let us say *fuck*!'

'Well, we can put three asterisks if you like.'

'Asterisks? No, I don't like asterisks. We have to find another word.'

'But it's a quote. From Larkin. It says so in the next line.'

'So you mean it's not something *we* say?'

'No, it's Philip Larkin. It's poetry.'

'Poetry?'

A pause. Poetry – this could change things.

'Yes, it's poetry.'

He thought for a moment. I held my breath. Would poetry prevail?

'No, we still can't do it. We have to find another word. Have you got pen and paper? Let's say, "they *screw* you up, your mum and dad". There, we've solved it.'

He was also sensitive to repetition in any shape or form, even if it was intended for stylistic effect, or when it was entirely innocuous as with repeated pronouns or common verbs. The first thing he did when I faxed the finished copy was to hunt down a repeated word and ring me up with his findings. 'There is *repetition*!' he would say, triumphantly, loftily. I found *three* "takes". We have to throw two of them.' And sometimes – this fascinated me – he would object to a particular word, not a word that was in any way improper or out of place; but a perfectly harmless, unoffending, plain, ordinary, innocent sort of word. For example, he hated the word *befell*, as in 'a tragedy befell the country'; such a word could spoil a whole day, never mind a tabloid text. By the same token, he would never allow *quantity*, though he couldn't quite say why. 'I just don't like it,' he said, pulling a bad-smell sort of face, though when pressed he said that it wasn't poetic. Which was true after all. As well as proscribed words he also had favourites, and I learned to scatter them like seed: *wisdom, mystique, serenity, exquisite, perilous, beguiling* and, most beloved of all, *vicissitudes*. 'Ah, vicissitudes – such a wonderful word . . . '

Once I used the word *humility*, as in 'I felt a deep sense of humility' – to explain how Tiger had felt in the presence of a woman he very much admired and who had borne a heavy cross. I was confident that he would love *humility*. But he didn't.

'Isn't it the same like *humiliation*?' he asked.

I thought: up to a linguistic point, Lord Copper. But what I said was:

'I think humility is the right word in this context. It's to do with feeling humble in comparison to her strength and courage.' He wasn't convinced.

'Humble . . . humble,' he said, trying it out for size, 'no, it's not good for me.'

And then, with the thoroughness of a lexicographer, he did an eyes-closed sift and search for the right word. When he found it, he said:

'I've got it! I've got it! *Foreboding*. Listen – "I felt a deep sense of foreboding." It's much better. Write it down.'

This is Lewis Carroll territory, I thought.

> 'When I use a word,' Humpty Dumpty said in a rather scornful tone, 'it means just what I choose it to mean – neither more or less.'

But I held out for humility. Foreboding never moved anyone to tears, I said, whereas humility could pack a powerful punch. Nothing else would do. When the piece appeared he received a letter from the woman's husband, the editor of a broadsheet newspaper, saying how moved he had been and confirming that 'we all feel humility in her presence'. Tiger, jubilant, rang me up and read me the letter.

'Aren't you pleased now we said *humility*?' he cooed.

Anyone who has written a weekly column will know that after a while it exerts a kind of tyranny. Although it appears just once a week, the other six days are also affected, each day slightly different from the next depending on its position relative to the deadline. Copy for Tiger's column was required on a Wednesday for publication on a Friday. On the Thursday the newspaper sent a proof to him by fax, and he then faxed it on to me. It is not easy to read – far less to proofread – a fax of a fax of newspaper print. The text is blurred, the punctuation unclear, the precious semi-colons obliterated. I asked Tiger to arrange for the newspaper to fax me the proof directly, but he wouldn't hear of it. Several typos slipped through the net in this way.

Fridays were the best days for both of us: it was the single day I didn't have to think about the column, and for Tiger the pleasure of it appearing in the newspaper was more than enough. He bought lots of copies: one for keeping in a leather-bound file and the others to give to guests invited to his new Soho palace. I came to love Fridays – their relative quietness and normality. But the other days assumed a pitiless momentum. In a previous existence I used to think that people probably dashed off columns over a cup of coffee. How could I ever have believed that? It could take over your whole life if you weren't careful.

Because of the column I wasn't allowed to have holidays. 'We don't want to lose our slot,' said Tiger, his voice taking on a low, death knell pitch. And because the pieces had to be topical, they couldn't be written in advance and banked. Sometimes I forgot I was a man and wrote something careless. I once described (in the first-person) how Tiger responded to a stressful situation by curling up on a sofa with a hot-water bottle and cucumber patches on his eyes. 'But that's ludicrous!' said N-H when he read it in the newspaper. 'That's what *you* do. No man would ever do that!' In desperation I made a decision: I would think about the column only on Mondays, Tuesdays and Wednesdays. That way there would be four remaining days – more than half the week in fact – in which to sort out my head and restore the balance necessary for A Happy Home Life.

But this worked only for a short time. As the months passed and the column became established, Tiger was content just to choose the subject and leave the rest to me, provided we went through the normal rituals of reading aloud, repetition checks, and so on at the end. Which would have been fine, except that he became pathologically anxious about the deadline being met. His anxiety levels could be calibrated by the number of phone calls he made to check on progress – 'How are we doing? Are we winning? Are we nearly there?' – until the daily tally was scarcely to be borne. He seemed determined that the column should occupy my frontal lobes at all times.

When I first started working for Tiger he had paid for a dedicated telephone line to be installed in my house. My children called this The Hotline – they knew from an early age never to pick it up – and the name had stuck. Its ring, though distinct, was perfectly ordinary, but it carried such undertones of urgency that the whole family reacted whenever it rang and there would be a chorus of '*Quick! It's The Hotline!*' If I was speaking on the other phone in the house, I used to hang up immediately whenever The Hotline rang. Tiger didn't like to be kept waiting, and in any case he just kept ringing till I answered. Friends at the other end of the phone sometimes got upset about this – what could possibly be so urgent and why couldn't I ring *him* back, they asked – and they chided me for being a complete pushover. One even wrote me a stiff letter on the subject, breaking off our friendship, saying my behaviour was offensive, that he and his wife felt badly treated and that they were sure other friends felt the same. But it's my job, I said pathetically, as if that explained everything. When I moved house in 1995 The Hotline came with me, and I had extensions fitted in the kitchen and the sitting room, as well as my work-space in the garden. N-H drew the line at our bedroom. 'We are not sleeping with The Hotline,' he said.

The Hotline was never so hot as during the years of the newspaper column. It started ringing at 8.30am and it continued shrilly throughout the day. One day I counted the calls, drawing a line of a stick man on the gallows each time the phone rang. At the end of the day there was a graveyard of forty-seven lines and five hanged men. Tiger was rhetorically committed to reasonableness – 'I don't want to disturb you,' he sometimes said when he rang in the evening or at weekends, but he seemed unable to help himself. In fact, I think he meant well and saw it as his way of helping *me*. Even on Fridays he was already thinking about the following week's column – we *must* find someone, *who* is in the spotlight? *Who* can we write about? This was all part of the teamwork. Sometimes he got fretful: My God, this is terrible, he would say, we're running out of women. On Saturdays he would scour the newspapers for a suitable subject, and if he failed to find one, he bought the early editions of Sunday newspapers, available in London on Saturday night, and intensified his search, phoning me at frequent intervals to discuss the options, occasionally edging towards hysteria. 'Time is running out. We *have* to find a woman.'

In the beginning, N-H complained very little, but I knew he was nursing a slow-burning resentment. 'It's too much,' he sometimes said, 'he's too big in your life.' And so The Hotline became a sort of barometer of domestic harmony. Its ring could stop a marital moment in its tracks, sending a sudden depth-charge through our Shangri-La. I had been so programmed over the years to respond immediately that I found it impossible to ignore and would leap across the room like some mad thing. 'Leave it! Just leave it!' N-H sometimes said, but there was no point. Tiger could outring any resolve of that sort.

Things came to a head one Saturday evening. We were hosting a dinner party for some visiting speakers to the university. Dinner parties in St Andrews can be nerve-racking occasions – getting the academic mix right, being prepared to talk about post-structuralism while serving linguini, making out that a small medieval town in the East Neuk of Fife is at the centre of the intellectual universe, trying to appear competent and nonchalant at the same time. On this occasion, however, things

240

were going well, and we were feeling rather pleased with the shape of the evening. Until The Hotline rang.

Whereupon N-H, who has a naturally accommodating vision of the world and a serene manner with his fellow man, quite forgot himself and leapt to his feet, shaking his fist, raging at a nameless adversary, and screaming blue murder in my direction: '*Kill that fucking phone, will you! Just tell him to fuck off and leave us in peace, for fuck's sake!*' As I grabbed the phone and left the room there were concerned looks, which seemed to say: It's just a phone ringing, isn't it? Does he always react like this when the phone rings? Why, only a moment ago, this gentle, quiet man was filling our glasses with Pinot Grigio, and now he is completely deranged. Perhaps the sea air does this to people after a while . . .

'This can't go on,' said N-H after everyone had gone home.

'No, it can't,' I said.

At some point in 1998 it became clear that money was in short supply. This was quite a shock since there had always seemed to be more than enough. Indeed those of us who had observed Tiger's extravagant lifestyle over many years had supposed that there was wealth without limit. But it appeared we were wrong. There had been times in the past when he had cried hard up, but no one ever believed him because his protestations were always at odds with what we saw – supreme spending and splurging. He was quite open about it and loved talking about his latest acquisitions. 'Wait till you see what I bought!' he would say as he showed off the latest painting or Oriental rug. 'And look at this piece of lapis – it's the biggest piece ever! It cost a *fortune!*' And so, although a certain mystery hung over his financial affairs, we assumed that the money would go on for ever. But it turned out that the debts had been growing for some time.

At first he was bullish. What were they so worried about? They'd get their money. There had been financial crises before, hadn't there? Just leave it to him – he would sort it. But somehow we knew this was more serious. The details were never fully disclosed; just vague references to cash flow problems and the need to recapitalise the company. To this end a financial backer was sought. This was the obvious way forward, Tiger said. He was in any case fed up with being a one-man band – what he needed was a financial partner, a kindred spirit. And so, letters, dozens of them, were sent off to potential investors, and though they read like investment opportunities I thought of them as just fancy begging letters. Perhaps Tiger knew this too, but nothing was ever said. As each envelope was sealed he said he had a good feeling about it – this one surely would bring a positive response, he just *knew* it. I felt sorry for him, but if ever I said so, he bridled. 'Never underestimate me,' he began, the grim warning before the tirade. 'People have made that mistake before and have lived to regret it. I enjoy a fight. I will not be beaten. If they think they can destroy me – just let them try. No one is a match for . . .' and at this point he would begin to talk about himself in the third person, as if he were sending another man into battle, hailing the man's reputation for fearlessness, praising his defiance, extolling his name – his own name – again and again. Arthur Scargill used to do this during the miners' strike.

('As long as Arthur Scargill's in charge, the miners will secure a victory. Make no mistake, Arthur Scargill's a fighter. There will be no defeat under Arthur Scargill . . . .')

I was spending much more time in London now. N-H's work took him there for quite long stretches and I wanted to be with him as much as possible. Tiger seemed pleased that I was able to be in London more, and he made the magnificent library in the new palace available for me as an office. A lot of letters had to be written and he liked having me on hand to do them. When I wasn't writing letters or doing research for the interviews I worked on the column and other journalistic bits and pieces. Because of his other worries Tiger said it was important for him to keep busy on the creative front. He accepted everything that was offered – the *New Statesman* diary, commissions from the *Observer*, the *Sunday Telegraph*, the *Jewish Chronicle*, the *Tablet* and so on. There were also regular approaches from the tabloids for 'rapid reaction' pieces: three hundred and fifty words by midday on some topical crisis, sensational divorce settlement or tragic event. And sometimes I did book reviews, though I wasn't allowed to write what I really thought. The thrust of the piece was determined by Tiger's connection with the author –

'We *have* to say we like it. We *can't* not say it's good.'

'What, even if it's not good?'

'Even if it's not good. Why make enemies?'

Perhaps this is not very different from the way a lot of reviewing works. And since there was often a thank you card from a grateful author, this was vindication enough.

'You see how she loved it? I told you, it's much better to write a nice review.'

Reading over the different articles now, I am able to recall my particular state of mind as the deadlines approached. Just from a single phrase it is possible to tell whether I felt confident or discouraged, rebellious or simply desperate. I can even detect the odd personal crisis. I can as good as hear the thud of my own heart.

The small spaces between the newspaper articles were filled with wild thoughts, all of them variations on the theme of breaking free. But how best to go about it? And could I afford it? I considered my mental state, my bank balance, my home life, my blood pressure – this last, bafflingly, being the lowest you could have without being in a semi-permanent faint. At home I judged it was best not to complain too much, and so I began to pretend that everything was fine, that things had improved. But they hadn't, and I had shamefully embarked on yet another level of pretence, this time with the man I loved. In fact, the largest area of my consciousness was still occupied by Tiger, and it included, ironically, the Tiger of my own invention, a protean chameleon-like creature who rhapsodised over the stuff he believed he had created, a man upon whom I had ghosted beliefs and opinions he didn't hold, feelings that he didn't feel. And it was the keenest irony that we were both ensnared by the same myth.

Some assignments were completely weird. At the beginning of 1998 Tiger gave lunch to an agent who represented a high-profile society girl. He worked his magic on her and by the end of lunch there was a deal on the table: Tiger would publish the society girl's story. When he told me about it, he was hardly able to contain his excitement and immediately plunged into his Harlem Globetrotter routine: this would be the biggest *coup* ever, she was such a babe, she was hip, she was cool, she was right at the heart of the British social scene, rubbing shoulders with aristocrats and rock stars alike. Bounce, bounce, bounce, and now – wait for it – the goal! This book was a once-in-a-lifetime chance: it would attract more publicity than all the other books put together, it was a sure-fire winner.

'And who will write it?' I asked as the ball dropped through the net.

'*We* will!' he said. 'It's so easy – let me tell you how we will do it. I am going to interview her; I have arranged to do three sessions of two hours. And there are *thousands* of newspaper cuttings. So with the tapes and the cuttings we have all we need to write the book. There's no problem!'

But there was a big problem. I didn't want to do it, and this time I told him so. I could not bring myself to be interested in this girl, I said – she represented everything that was trivial in the world, she was no more than a glamour girl flitting from party to party, a sugar mouse, a modeller of designer frocks, a freeloading lightweight, famous just for being famous, irredeemably superficial. Why was such a person exalted? And why did we have to add to the glorification?

'You are so highbrow,' Tiger said, spitting his contempt. This was a most terrible charge: being highbrow belonged on the same spectrum of iniquity as coughing or menstruating.

'And she's so dim,' I spat back.

'*Actually*' – he elongated the actually, as if he'd just unearthed the vital clue, the incriminating evidence – 'you're completely wrong. This girl is the smartest around. You could learn a thing or two from her.'

And so the interviews took place and the book was started.

It was a bizarre project with multiple layers of identity issues: I was impersonating Tiger who in turn was impersonating the society girl whose intimate first-person story he had contracted to tell and under whose name it would appear as an autobiography. It felt more than a little mad.

Most of the time my approach to the situation, and how to change it, was not in the least rational or methodical. I just became used to a feeling of mild desperation, which sometimes got better, sometimes worse, and I simply kept going, trying not to think about it too much or talk about it at home. Home was increasingly in London – far away from the fresh sea breezes of St Andrews and my little sanctuary in the garden. I was spinning in Tiger's orbit, navigated this way or that by the latest enthusiasm, each one laid aside after a while to make way for the next. Sometimes it seemed as if I scarcely lived in the world at all, except maybe at one or more removes. Leaving the Soho building one night after work I turned onto Regent Street where there was a man wearing a sandwich board that exhorted sinners to abandon sex and turn to God. He was walking ahead of me, though with difficulty, for the board was long and he himself quite short. The bottom edge clipped his heels with every step – a pitiful sight that brought tears to my eyes. Was *he* just doing a job, I wondered, or did he actually believe in what he was doing?

~

The ghost-writer is aptly named. Real ghosts, if we accept such a thing, are constrained to live in a world they no longer properly belong to. They are suspended in limbo, unable to move on. There is something disquieting about them: they are the spectres at the feast, they never seem to sleep, their presence disturbs. Writer ghosts are much the same. They upset those who are in the world, reminding them of things they would rather ignore. They spoil the party, they can appear at inconvenient moments, and their energy lingers for a long time.

When I was in St Andrews, hundreds of miles from London, I was an absent presence in Tiger's life, a ghostly creature he could summon at will. Did I even exist at all? Most people would have doubted it – just as with a 'real' ghost. After all, much of the evidence was purely anecdotal and therefore prone to construction and interpretation. In the early days, at a launch party for one of Tiger's books, I got talking to a magazine editor, a commanding force on London's literary gossip circuit, who said he had heard that Tiger was helped by 'some woman up in Scotland'; adding, surreally, that since no one had ever met her she probably didn't exist. The strangeness of this encounter appealed to me, and in any case I was still at the stage of finding it restful to hide behind someone else. It seemed to be a natural continuation of the translation work, and in fact I felt this for many years. Concealing your identity can actually be a strange sort of liberation; it can even be self-affirming, since eventually you work out who you really are by living who you are not.

In later years, when I was spending more and more time working in the London palace, I still remained a shadowy spirit. Famous people regularly turned up to lunch or to be interviewed. I would have loved to meet some of them – particularly those whose books I had read or whose biographies I had researched – but as soon as the doorbell rang I knew it was time for me to disappear. 'Make yourself rare!' Tiger would say.

~

For a while Tiger continued to perform breathtaking juggling acts with money, all the while firing off more scatter-shot letters. Surely one would hit the target? But time went on, and no outside investor came forward. The bank, keen to protect its own interests, applied more pressure. It was a gloomy time.

The Bank: gradually, these two little words came to symbolise all that was wrong with the world. They were shorthand for ruination and disaster, they fuelled resentment and a feeling of persecution, they were the reason for everything and nothing. They stopped books being published, they cancelled parties, they plagued every conversation and spoiled the fun. Phone calls with his girls, normally a wellspring of happiness, consisted of fractured, plaintive talk – 'Beloved, if only I could! I would love to. But, you know, *the Bank* . . .' Letters from the Bank arrived every week, and from time to time a middle-aged man with a briefcase and a double-breasted suit would visit in person. In the days and hours before his arrival a pall of darkness was draped over the building, but the minute he had gone the light would come flooding back. 'I charmed him,' Tiger always said. 'I had him eating out of my hand. He *loves me!*' And he would grin as if the past few months had been a stupid misunderstanding or a trick of the imagination. For a day or two he went on a spree, and his spirits lifted, shored up by bright hopes and whistles in the dark. But the stay of execution soon expired, and it was back to 'But, you know, *the Bank.*'

The gloom pitched its tent and looked as if it might stay a while. Gloom, being the colour of sludge, sat awkwardly in the glittering palace with its bright bordello colours. And like pollen, it rubbed off on anyone who came into contact with it. Tiger stopped inviting beautiful people to lunch. 'How can I entertain someone when I have *the Bank*?' was a recurring *cri de cœur*. At lunch he had to make do with the Girl Friday, his secretary, the cook and me. In spite of the lightness of our shadows, we were a grim second-rate bunch and a constant reminder of the sinking state of affairs. We didn't eat in the splendid dining-room but sat at a small table in the base-ment bar where, in keeping with the prevailing mood, there was no natural light. Mostly we tried to cheer him up, take his mind off things, but it didn't work. Everything was too effing terrible, too effing awful. Occasionally, just for the hell of it, we tried to outgloom him. It couldn't be done.

During this time, just to make matters worse, the columns came to an end. The editor at the newspaper had moved on and Tiger's slot was soon swept away by the new broom. 'Just imagine!' he said, banging his desk with brute force. He looked suddenly so strong and angry – any minute now he might tear up telephone directories. 'Getting rid of us! It's an outrage! What fools these people are!' And he rose to his full height before gliding goose-winged round the room, fulminating against the new editor who couldn't even kiss a donkey's saddle, he said, never mind the donkey.

Every so often, in a bid to lift his mood, he would splash out on something he didn't need. He would appear in the doorway of the library where I worked: 'Come! We shall walk together for five minutes,' and we would leave the building without delay and head for Bond Street. At times of great purpose like this, he moved like a speed-walker, his hip joints rotating in their sockets, his arms bent at the elbows to aid forward propulsion. People in the street stopped to stare. When we reached the shops he would quickly buy something he didn't need – a leather jacket maybe, or a fur hat. It was all over in an instant, the item grabbed randomly and purchased speedily, as if he couldn't wait to leave the shop and get it over with. 'Don't bother to wrap it,' he would say to the puzzled assistant, as he snatched the beautiful garment from careful hands preparing to tuck it into soft tissue. Such a mission had the feel of a desperate, almost furtive act, like a quick trip to a whorehouse, something to answer a need rather than fulfil a desire. Out on the street he would immediately tear up the receipt into tiny pieces before throwing them into a bin, and on the way back to the palace he would tell me that he had *dozens* of leather jackets. 'What do I want with another one?'

This appetite for *divertissement* grew stronger as the crisis deepened. It was usually something impulsive and gratifying, like oysters from Fortnum and Masons, or a dash to the latest fashionable restaurant to eat marinated kangaroo and talk about it afterwards. But there were regular indulgences too. Every Friday morning the chauffeur picked him up at 5.30 and drove him to Bermondsey Market in south London where he wandered from stall to stall in search of very particular arte-facts: phalluses carved out of ivory. In a short time he had built up quite a collection – dozens of sculpted male figures with huge penises. 'The sale of ivory is banned now,' he said merrily, 'so they are worth collecting.' The day I went with him he showed me how he worked the stalls, making eye contact in the half-dark with certain sellers who would then indicate if they had something interesting to show. One man in a cloth cap and fingerless gloves gave a nod. Tiger grabbed me by the arm – 'Look, he's got something for me!' – and we pushed through the crowd towards him. 'Let's hope it's a good one.' Evidently it was, and Tiger was content to pay a small fortune for an ivory twosome with outsize erections in a homoerotic tangle. Back in the car he said, 'I'm so happy now.' It seemed a precarious happiness, but it served the purpose of nudging the gloom sideways for a moment or two.

In a similar vein, and despite the crippling cash flow problems, he ordered on a whim the manufacture of thousands of key-rings made of solid silver. They had been specially designed in the shape of exaggerated male genitalia. 'It's a brilliant idea, don't you agree?' His eyes twinkled. He loved to provoke a reaction. 'The poofters will love it! I am sitting on a goldmine!' I said I couldn't possibly judge but hoped he was right. Part of his undoubted thrill was to show off his latest craze to people visiting the palace and judge them according to their reactions. Women who were exceptionally favoured might even receive one as a gift, though it became clear that the number of women to whom you might, even in a gesture of uncomplicated beneficence, give a silver phallus key-ring, is actually quite limited. I once witnessed someone failing the character test, a woman of wit and intelligence and deputy editor of a respected magazine. On being shown the key-ring and exhorted to hold it – 'Go on! Touch it! Feel it! It's solid silver!' – she could not hide her distaste and, with a curl of the lip, she uttered the fateful words: 'Oh dear.' Whereupon she was cast into outer darkness and never invited back. Indeed her name could never be mentioned without Tiger recollecting her reaction and cursing her anew:

'Do you remember? What she said about my silver penis? How did she get to be deputy editor with an attitude like that?'

Though it was hard not to admire his willingness to take risks and to back a hunch, the key-rings did not sell. Somewhere there is a silver penis mountain waiting for good homes.

Out of the blue, a saviour materialised – a *deus ex machina* who would avowedly deliver Tiger from his torment. This was a saviour so perfect that had he not existed it would have been necessary to invent him.

'Our problems are over,' said Tiger, eyes bright with relief.

'That's wonderful news,' I said.

It was October 1998 and we were on our way to the Frankfurt Book Fair. The *deus* in question turned out to be Greek, which I thought was incredibly apt, given that Greek dramatists were the first to think of dropping a god from a contraption above the stage to sort out the tragic drama beneath.

'How did you find him?' I asked.

'I didn't. He found *me*,' said Tiger. He was laughing now. Everything was going to be all right.

'So you don't actually know him?'

'Of course, I know him! We've known each other for thirty years!'

I wondered why hadn't I heard of him before. I had worked for Tiger for nearly twenty years, and The Greek – as we came to call him – had never been mentioned. Closer questioning revealed that they had met, *once*, thirty years ago. And no, Tiger didn't actually recall the meeting, though The Greek remembered it very well. Oh God, I thought, I don't like the sound of this. But Tiger was upbeat, and during the flight to Frankfurt I swear the angels sang. Evidently The Greek had important contacts in the Saudi royal family who were looking to invest in London. This was the break Tiger had been waiting for. The Sah-oo-deez, as he called them, regarded his empire as a golden opportunity, and they were keen, in fact *very* keen, to sink money into it.

'They are *so* excited.'

However, there followed many miserable months of false hopes and broken promises. The Greek seemed permanently to be sorting out the final details with different banks, documents were just about to be signed, and the money was always just on the point of being paid: it was coming on Monday for sure, by the end of the week without fail, and then without a shadow of a doubt the following week. It was an endless cycle and always, at the last minute, there would be some unexpected hitch that strained credibility. Tiger was told the Sah-oo-deez had fallen out among themselves, or that they had to return home for Ramadan, or a vital signature was required from a high-ranking family member and *just my luck, they can't fucking find him!* There were also trustees, shadowy figures in the background, who complicated things and according to Tiger were a law unto themselves. And so it went on, a form of Chinese water torture designed to drive the prisoner mad.

Being at someone else's mercy was not a role that suited Tiger – he was much too used to being in absolute control. But he seemed to have run out of options: he had given his word to the Bank, he had staked everything on the money coming through, and the future depended on it. As time went on and the Bank increased the pressure, he demonstrated that the human capacity to put a positive interpretation on something is infinite. Every new difficulty was explained away as an unfortunate happening, an unforeseen difficulty, just one of those things. Thus blind belief in The Greek was prolonged without a shred of evidence that he was *bona fide*. In a tragedy the tragic hero cannot see himself; no more can he save himself, and we cannot save him either.

At the outset of negotiations Tiger had purchased two state-of-the-art mobile phones: one for himself and one for The Greek, so that they could be in constant communication about the deal. He was pleased with this plan – his way of staying in control. With a dedicated mobile he would never miss a call and the line would never be engaged. 'I will know exactly where he is at any given time,' he said. Soon this private mobile became the focus of an obsession as well as the central visual metaphor for the grimness of that time. It tyrannised and enslaved him, but it was also a kind of lifeline: for it held out the promise of a solution to the crisis, and in so doing seemed to protect him from the unimaginable. His day was organised around it, and his careful routine altered to accommodate the critical calls that came on it. At the end of each call from The Greek he would extract a promise of a further call, pinning his tormentor down to a precise time, agreeing it, confirming it, then repeating it at the last one more time so that there could be no misunderstanding. During these conversations his voice was permanently raised. The time in between calls – usually no more than an hour or so – was taken up with compulsive checking of his watches and waiting for the mobile to ring. Meanwhile everything else assumed the proportions of a small catastrophe. *'Where is my mango?'* he would roar down the intercom to the cook in the basement. *'Why is it late?'* And after a swift mango delivery: *'I hate it with a spoon. I need a fork!'*

This was how he kept control. There must be no seepage points. Which meant that things that really did not matter started mattering a great deal. Threatening missives had to be written to Westminster City Council on the subject of bollards outside the palace, and indignant letters were fired off to newspaper editors who had failed to review his books. The water in the humidifier by his desk had to be kept at a certain level *at all times*. He accused imaginary enemies of imaginary crimes. He became ever more neurotic about punctuality and hygiene. He raged at the world and the unfairness of it. And the more things declined on the large scale, the more he wasted energy on the small. Each new dawn brought a fresh panic, a new layer of agitation – a light bulb blowing, the wrong size of envelope. One day he gravely summoned me to his room and charged me to conduct an investigation: 'Listen carefully, one of my girls has done a poo in the loo. Find out the culprit and report back to me.' When I protested, saying that I couldn't possibly do as he asked, he rose in a fury and bellowed: 'I will not tolerate it. The smell is appalling. How dare they behave like that!'

As the time of the next expected call from The Greek drew near, he would start the countdown – 'In ten minutes it will ring . . . in five minutes it will ring . . .' He had moved the mobile carefully to a position right in front of him on the desk, as if proximity might prompt it to action. And then he would stare at it, *come on, come on*, willing it to ring. 'Why don't you ring?' '*Why don't you ring, damn you?*' he would say, gorging on the pathetic fallacy. And then a few moments later, almost insouciantly, as if regaining the upper hand: 'Just wait,' – a knowing smile in my direction – 'you'll see. It will ring now. I know it will.' I always had a powerful urge to withdraw at this point and often tried to excuse myself, saying I had work to do, but he wouldn't hear of it. 'Wait! Wait!' he would say. 'Don't go! Just stay there!' I found it a dispiriting business, an exercise in futility, as we sat around endlessly, peering at a gismo and wanting something from it, like two lost souls out of *Waiting for Godot*. I was full of pity for him, while knowing how much he would hate it. I imagined him at night, sitting up through the small hours, staring at this wretched gadget while the rest of London slept. Couldn't *you* ring *him*? I asked more than once. But no, he couldn't. 'He's at the bank, you see,' or, 'He's meeting the trustees.' Sometimes when he could endure it no longer he did try ringing The Greek, both on the mobile and at home. But it was always the answering machine, which just made matters worse. Tiger hated answering machines.

There was a piercing hopelessness to all this, like the lost dream of a Chekhov play – the impossibility of getting to Moscow, or the destruction of the cherry orchard. The agony expanded to blot out everything else; it filled the air and it was impossible not to breathe it in and be infected by it. Those of us in the thick of it didn't trust The Greek an inch, and we said so. 'You're mad,' said Tiger. 'Why would he double-cross me?' We didn't know why, though we still believed he must be a confidence trickster. But if ever one of us suggested that he have The Greek investigated or have his story checked independently, he flew into a temper and did simian leaps around the room, shouting down the doubter. The strain was beginning to show. How would it all end? we asked ourselves. Sometimes, when fatigue set in, he would remove his beautiful shoes and stretch out on the sofa in his room. Once or twice, unaware that he was resting, I went into the room and saw him lying on the sofa, eyes closed, the mobile propped up at his feet like the tag on the toe in a morgue.

During this time Tiger continued to interview interesting people – Raymond Briggs, Lord Callaghan, Ken Livingstone, Victoria Glendinning, Richard Holloway, Rabbi Lionel Blue, and many others. John Colvin had described him as 'the John Aubrey *de nos jours*', with the result that those he approached hardly ever turned him down. To some extent the interviews took his mind off things, but his heart wasn't really in them any more. They took him away from the mobile for two hours, which was more than he could comfortably bear. Occasionally the shape of an interview was ruined on account of vital questions not being asked. He was a swimmer tiring in the water, giving up with the shore in sight. Afterwards, when we talked about it, he would say that he had been forced to cut it short because he had been expecting a call from The Greek.

'But surely he would have rung you back.'

'I couldn't risk it. Things are at a crucial stage.'

Things were perpetually at a crucial stage, it seemed. I had never met The Greek, but I greatly resented him and his power to disrupt everything, even the interviews. I was also deeply suspicious of him. Tiger knew this and it was a source of tension between us. This tension came to a head in a most unlikely place: in the beautiful Ettrick valley, just outside Selkirk in the Scottish Borders. Tiger had come to Scotland to interview Sir David Steel, the Presiding Officer of the new Scottish Parliament. I had picked him up at Edinburgh airport and was driving him to Aikwood Tower, David Steel's home, a distance of forty-seven miles from Edinburgh. The journey was tense. 'Are the miles longer in Scotland?' Tiger asked in between fraught calls with The Greek on his mobile. 'No,' I said, 'it just seems that way.'

On arrival at Aikwood Tower, a magnificent sixteenth-century keep, David Steel came out to meet us and invited me to sit in the kitchen while the interview took place in the drawing-room. 'No,' said Tiger, 'she's my driver. She *must* stay in the car.' Most of the time Tiger had beautiful manners, but everything came under threat in the present crisis. In fact I had been instructed to listen out for the mobile while he was *hors de combat* with the Presiding Officer. Something was going to happen today, he was sure of it. The Greek had said so.

'But you've told him you're tied up for the next couple of hours. He won't ring you till afterwards.'

'He might. I can't risk it.'

Two hours later, Tiger returned to the car.

'Did he call?'

'No, he didn't.'

'You're sure?'

'I'm sure.'

I asked him how the interview had gone, but he didn't answer – he was already dialling The Greek's number. Alas, there was no signal. 'Oh my God!' he said, in an instant panic. This was the worst disaster ever. To be completely out of touch at such a critical time! How could he have been so stupid as to risk coming to Scotland, where you couldn't even get a fucking mobile to work! At which point it occurred to me to check *my* mobile phone. I had a signal. When I passed my phone to Tiger, despair turned to joy. 'Bravo! Bravo!' he crooned, 'you've saved the day!' I wasn't convinced. And sure enough, despair soon returned. The Greek's mobile was off and his home phone was switched to the answering machine. 'Damn! Damn! He must be at the Bank still.'

Then the strangest thing happened. A few moments later, as I was driving down the private track leading to the main road, my mobile rang. I didn't recognise the voice, but the voice was angry and demanded to know who I was and how I had got hold of his number. I thought at first it was a crank and hung up. But it rang again straightaway, and it was the same angry man asking why I had telephoned him. His accent was hard to place. But of course! It must be The Greek. I handed Tiger the phone. Things were very nearly resolved, he told Tiger. In fact he was extremely hopeful – he had just stepped out of the bank in the City for a moment to make the call, and now he was going back inside.

Which was a lie. He wasn't at the bank at all. For according to the display on my mobile he had telephoned from his home number, which meant that he was at home, not at the bank as he claimed. He must have checked the number of the incoming call, not recognised it – hence his call to me a few moments later. 'This proves he's lying,' I said to Tiger. But he didn't want to know. 'Why are you attacking me?' he said, as he always did when someone put a different view. I told him it wasn't an attack – I just couldn't bear to watch him go through this and I wanted him to look at the evidence and think carefully about what was happening. But it made no difference. 'There must be some other explanation,' he said, 'you don't know what you're talking about.' He had reached that point where the victim colludes with his tormentor, filling in the unexplained gaps, making up stories to fit the picture; and when inspiration runs out, repairing to the last refuge of the wishful thinker. When I continued to press the point, he lost his temper. 'Enough!' he screamed. After that he didn't talk to me for nearly two months and would communicate only through a member of the Old Guard. We had begun to move against one another. The finely balanced symbiosis was under siege.

Question: At what point does something stop being the thing you think it is? Answer: Not before you are ready to admit it to yourself. When does a chair stop being a chair? When the back breaks off? When the legs give way? But look, there's no problem, why do we need legs? – the seat is still intact, and anyway we can sit on the floor. At what point do you accept that someone is dying? When the diagnosis of terminal illness is given? When the medication loses effect? When the vital organs start failing? When the eyes close, the breathing stops? You probably know at each stage, yet it is possible to go on denying, in contradiction of the evidence, right till the end and even beyond.

And so it was with the money. By this stage Tiger was such a hapless puppet that The Greek did not even have to be very good at his game. In retrospect it was clear almost from the start that there was no deal, that there never would be a deal, that there was in fact no money. But the clearer it became that The Greek was a fabulist, the more fervently did Tiger believe in him.

'It's all true.'

'How do you know?'

'Because he said so.'

'But how do you know he's telling the truth?'

'He has no reason to lie.'

Tiger had to talk to me again when he was invited to contribute to a new erotic magazine. It styled itself as a literary magazine for sensualists and libertines, and according to the *Financial Times* it favoured 'a literary approach to libido'. I saw it more as a nonpareil of thinking man's smut. But there was clearly a certain cachet to appearing in this publication, and for a short time Tiger's spirits soared.

'This is amazing,' he said, 'all the literati write for it. It's a real honour.'

The first article was on knickers, not a subject that excites many women, but I made an attempt at a vicarious thrill. If you are a woman, writing as a man in a dirty magazine is a risky business, full of pitfalls. But after a paragraph or two on the etymological history of knickers, with small detours by way of drawers, bloomers and combinations, I settled down to the thesis that the reason knickers give rise to erotic fantasies is because of the mystery that attaches to them.

At one level, the introduction of the gusset between the legs might seem to have closed off an erotic dimension. But it only seems that way to those without the capacity to dream. The imagination is far more easily flamed by ambiguity than precision, by the understated than by the loudly declared, by the half-dark and candlelight, rather than the full glare of electric beams. Knickers are about concealment and contradiction; they are the last barrier, and also the gateway to paradise.

Churning out this stuff made me feel slightly queasy, dressed in the wrong skin. 'But it's erotic!' said Tiger, as if I had missed the point entirely. It struck me that a woman writing as a woman on the subject of knickers would have taken quite a different approach, perhaps offering a thoughtful analysis of the sort of knickers that men tend to give as presents, the kind that are often scratchy and apt to pinch in the wrong places. But a woman writing the thoughts of a man – to wit a man inflamed by knickers – is restricted by a number of factors, not least imagination. This was no time to quibble, however: anything that relieved the gloom was probably a good thing.

I was certainly not prepared for the postbag that followed. From all over England men wrote letters in response to the article, one fondly reminiscing about drawers *sans entre-jambes,* another pointing out that many men, like himself, preferred to wear ladies' knickers rather than what he called men's undies. Worst of all, a man from Surrey wrote to say that Tiger had been talking 'nonsense' when he claimed that the mothers of men now middle-aged had their undergarments open at the crotch. He gave the impression of being quite overwrought:

> At no time that I can remember did our mothers join in the disgusting activity of allowing air to waft around their private parts.

This man's views were obviously sincerely held, and he cannot have known the repercussions that would follow his charge of 'nonsense'.

'This is very serious,' Tiger said to me, very seriously. 'We mustn't make mistakes. We have to do our research properly.'

'Yes, but I'm not sure we did make a mistake.'

'Can we prove him wrong?'

'Well, yes, I think so.'

'And me right?'

'Yes, I suppose so.'

'Then do it. We must defend ourselves, otherwise we will be a laughing-stock. I will ring the editor.'

After a quick trip to the V & A, and consultation with aged friends prepared to talk to me about their underwear of yester-year, the following letter was written:

> Apropos your correspondent's comments – in brief, what happened was this: in the old days there were no knickers at all. This should not occasion shock and horror, since modesty was adequately served by layers of petticoats. But natural functions were possible only because access was relatively unimpeded (aside from the underskirts). By

the end of the nineteenth century, women were becoming more emancipated in their habits and dress. All the same, long skirts (hobbled or bustled) persisted, and 'open drawers' were a matter of practical convenience. No doubt they were sometimes taken advantage of by young men in a hurry, but that is another matter.

The drawers, later known as knickers, consisted of two full leg sections and were fastened at the front waist. There are examples in the V & A Museum's collection which include a pair in black satin with lots of lace and frills to trim the legs and, by contrast, a rather more prosaic pair of drawers (dating from 1909) in yellow flannel, buttoned at the back and open – very open indeed – at the crotch. In some parts of the country crotchless knickers were known as 'free traders'.

The first directoire knickers, often referred to as 'passion killers', began to appear around 1910 but they did not replace the crotchless variety until they became necessary because of the rapid abbreviation of the skirt, from mid-calf in 1939 to knee-length in 1941.

Yours faithfully,

The next article, at my suggestion, was on female ejaculation. I was up to my old tricks, trying to sabotage the assignment by the squelch of bodily fluids again. Tiger was doubtful, but not doubtful enough to abandon writing for the erotic magazine.

'You mean women can squirt the same like men?'

'Oh yes, sometimes they can even out-squirt them.'

And I told him of one American study in which a woman

had managed a huge projectile gush, ten feet out. He decided it was best to leave it to me.

'Just make sure of our facts this time.'

At least I was on more familiar territory, I thought, though I tried hard to slant the article from the point of view of a man feeling threatened, even emasculated, by the thought that women now seemed capable of almost everything. Alas, the readers' response was even more alarming than with the knickers. It transpired that men up and down the land – though curiously concentrated on the coast, notably in Southampton and Clacton-on-Sea – were being swept away by hot tidal waves from their women.

'Amazing,' said Tiger, 'who would have believed it?'

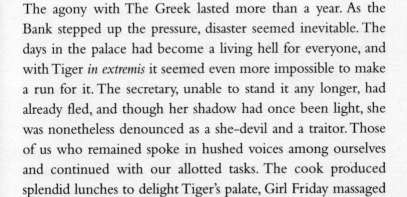

The agony with The Greek lasted more than a year. As the Bank stepped up the pressure, disaster seemed inevitable. The days in the palace had become a living hell for everyone, and with Tiger *in extremis* it seemed even more impossible to make a run for it. The secretary, unable to stand it any longer, had already fled, and though her shadow had once been light, she was nonetheless denounced as a she-devil and a traitor. Those of us who remained spoke in hushed voices among ourselves and continued with our allotted tasks. The cook produced splendid lunches to delight Tiger's palate, Girl Friday massaged his head and pushed back his cuticles, and I got on with writing the next line.

The journey to Frankfurt in 1999 was unusually grim. Right up to the last moment the trip was in doubt – 'How can I go when I have this crisis?' he kept saying, though the situation had gone on for too long to be called a crisis. Only the requirement to be seen at the Book Fair made it happen: 'We have to be seen, otherwise we're dead.' He was wearing a burgundy shahtoosh – a delicate wool scarf made from the hair of the wild Tibetan antelope, a critically endangered species. 'Feel it! It's much softer than pashmina. The antelope hair is so much nicer than the goat hair, so much nicer. A whole shahtoosh can fit through the ring on your finger!' At the airport I handed over my passport meekly and followed him through the boarding-gate and down the tunnel to the aeroplane. Sometimes you don't need to see a man's face to know how he is feeling. You can tell from the way he walks, you can even tell from the back of his head.

Everything proceeded smoothly from bad to worse. The atmosphere was baleful. To survive the journey, I tried to concentrate on lines of poetry and pieces of music, hoping to drive out malign forces in the shape of mobiles and Greeks and banks. Once we landed in Germany, I absorbed the language around me, listening in on conversations, reading newspapers over people's shoulders. German was much safer than English.

We arrived at the hotel in the late afternoon, the same luxury hotel in Kaiser Friedrich Platz. 'We must continue to live well,' said Tiger, heading for the presidential suite. 'We must never compromise our standards.' He told me to be ready to go down for dinner in one hour and fifty minutes. I lay on the bed and let my head empty. Blissful to be alone.

~

Five minutes early, in good time for dinner, I knock at the room of the presidential suite and wait for the usual 'Come!' Nothing happens. Perhaps he is in his bathroom, I think, so I wait outside for a decent interval, long enough to allow for a chain-pull and hand-washing. But as I wait I hear a terrible sound – not the sound of a flushing loo or hands being washed, but the sound of a man sobbing. Slowly, tentatively, I open the door and see him sitting at the leather-topped desk, head in hands. I approach the desk hesitantly, saying his name so that I don't startle him, but because of the sobbing he doesn't hear me, so I say it louder, and he looks up, his vision blurred by his sad salt tears. There are few images from art or from life that can still evoke universal pity and compassion: one is that of a man weeping. Especially a man like Tiger who is not given to weeping, or who is afraid to weep, or perhaps has forgotten how to weep. I go round to his side of the desk and put my arm on his shoulder. He is making quiet, choking noises. I ask what's happened, what's the matter, what's wrong, the way helpless people do when they want to help but know they can't. And in any case, there's no need to ask, for I *know* what's wrong. The Bank – that's what's wrong. There is no other possibility. They have pulled the plug. It's all over. Tiger hands me a sheet of shiny fax paper – confirmation from the Bank. Liquidation. Ruination. End of Empire.

But it's not from the Bank. It's from the *gardien* in the Dordogne and this is what he has written:

J'ai de mauvaises nouvelles. Éclair est mort. Je l'ai amené au vétéri-
naire, mais y avait plus d'espoir. J'espère que ça vous fera du bien de
savoir qu'il n'a pas souffert longtemps. Il s'est endormi bien vite, et
pour la dernière fois, dans mes bras.

    Cordialement

        Michel

~

This moment lives with me still. The tight mask had slipped
and I felt I had glimpsed another man hidden inside the man
I had known all these years. A vulnerable man, broken by the
death of a dog.

Once it was over, however, it was as if it had never happened.
This place, the place where he had wept, was at such depths
of concealment that he could not remain there for long.

The End

There is no normal perspective in this story. It is not a rounded picture. For me, it is a way of gaining a little purchase on some things that happened long ago and not so long ago. If it were a painting, we would think the composition lopsided, asymmetrical, in some way foreshortened. The size, the relative positions, and the point where the earth meets the sky – all these would be distorted. In a sense, it is more like a child's drawing where the most important part, the clue to the workings of the child's mind, is out of proportion to the rest of the picture.

Everyone tells stories. And all story-tellers are liars – not to be trusted. They have an excessive need to make sense of experience, and so things get twisted and shaped to suit. It need not be deliberate, but it's as well to admit that it happens. We fumble about in the fog, and patterns come to us eerily like distant foghorns over water. We put forward versions of ourselves. And versions of others.

What is known about any man is finite, but what is not known is infinite. Others who worked for Tiger might say, no, this is not the man I know. Or perhaps, yes, this is the man, but only in some measure, not the whole man. What they would probably all confirm is that he lived as people rarely do nowadays, dangerously and passionately. His obsessive personality could cause fury and despair in those around him, but his faults were all tangled up with virtues. And a warm heart more than made up for the failings. In an age of big business publishing characterised by remoteness and detachment, he was heroically original and human.

The Greek turned out to be a charlatan, not so much a crook as a terrible fantasist. 'Can you *believe* it!' Tiger squealed, as though it were a shock. But the main feeling seemed to be one of relief that it was finally over. Accountants moved in, but there was no dramatic Fall of Empire, no moonlight flit. They did their job and spoke calmly of temporary liquidity issues. Everything was going to be fine. And like a phoenix – a phoenix come true – Tiger rose from the ashes, wearing his brightest colours and finest jewels. Before long there was talk of the next book. 'I have an idea – we could do a big book on God.' It was definitely time to leave now.

When Tiger realised I was serious he announced his retirement from the literary world. The last thing to be written was a valediction. It was styled, in Donne's beautiful line, a valediction forbidding mourning. Poetic to the end.

Three months later, I left the palace bearing the gift of a Mont Blanc pen. 'We made a great team, you and I,' he said as we hugged each other goodbye. In Regent Street I caught a No 12 bus and tears fell all the way to Waterloo.

Things would never be different again.

Acknowledgements

The author and publishers acknowledge the following sources of quotations reproduced in this book on the pages listed.

p. 97: Germaine Greer, 'The Sultan of Soho and his harem', *The Observer Magazine*, 11 October 1987.

pp. 105–6 (Enoch Powell): Naim Attallah, *Of A Certain Age*, Quartet Books, 1992, p. 235, reproduced by kind permission of the author.

p. 106 (Mary Soames, Diana Mosley): Naim Attallah, *Asking Questions*, Quartet Books, 1996, pp. 451–2, 278, reproduced by kind permission of the author.

p. 107 (Francis Stuart): Naim Attallah, *In Conversation With Naim Attallah*, Quartet Books, 1998, p. 315, reproduced by kind permission of the author.

p. 120: Henry Miller, *The Colossus of Maroussi*, Penguin, 1950.

p. 139: Gillian Glover, 'Cat who got the cream', *The Scotsman*, 18 November 1994.

pp. 144, 157, 158, 161–2: Naim Attallah, *A Timeless Passion*, Quartet Books, 1995, pp. 1, 75, 75–6, 98, 30, 82–5, reproduced by kind permission of the author.

p. 159: Carole Mansur, 'Murder, metaphor and mystery', *The Daily Telegraph, 1995*.

p.160: Ulick O'Connor, 'Less sex please', *The Oldie*, June 1995.

p.160: Cristina Odone, 'A lusty Beatrice leads her Dante', *The Catholic Herald*, 9 June 1995.

pp. 181, 182,195–6, 197–8, 202–3, 203–4, 204–5, 206–7, 208, 209–10, 212: Naim Attallah, *Tara and Claire*, Quartet Books, 1996, p. 1, flyleaf, pp. 175–7, 131–2, 47,106, 115–16, 148–9, 166–7, 167–8, 120, reproduced by kind permission of the author.

p. 214: Nicola McAllister, *The Daily Telegraph*, Saturday Review, 23 November 1996.

pp. 215, 216: Alice Thomas Ellis, 'A sensitivity unusual in a man', *The Literary Review*, October 1996.

p. 223: Adam Nicolson, 'All that twinkles', *The Sunday Telegraph Magazine*, 9 June 1996.

p. 223: Andrew Biswell, *The Independent*, 22 July 1995.

p. 234: Philip Larkin, 'This be the verse', *High Windows*, Faber and Faber, 1974.

p. 262: Naim Attallah, 'Knickers in a twist', *The Erotic Review*, Nov–Dec 1998.

pp. 263, 263–4: Letters, *The Erotic Review*, March 1999.

273